D0773402

Vanishing LOBO

The Mexican Wolf and the Southwest

JAMES C. BURBANK

JOHNSON BOOKS • BOULDER

© 1990 by James C. Burbank
ISBN 1-55566-071-1

Cover design by Molly Gough
Cover illustration by Elizabeth Cook

Library of Congress Cataloging-in-Publication Data
Burbank, James C.
    Vanishing lobo: the Mexican wolf and the Southwest /
James C. Burbank.
    p.   cm.
    Includes bibliographical references and index.
    ISBN 1-55566-071-1
    1. Mexican wolf—Southwest, New. 2. Mexican wolf—Southwest,
New—Folklore. 3. Endangered species—Southwest, New. I. Title.
QL737.C22B84   1990
599.74'442—dc20   90-45714
                                                        CIP

Printed in the United States of America by
Johnson Publishing Company
1880 South 57th Court
Boulder, Colorado 80301

Man is not at home in the universe, despite all the efforts of philosophers and metaphysicians to provide a soothing syrup. Thought is still a narcotic. The deepest question is why. And it is a forbidden one. The very asking is in the nature of cosmic sabotage.

—Henry Miller

Contents

Introduction   xi

Chapter 1
First Encounter   1

Chapter 2
Brother Wolf   13

Chapter 3
Great Beast God of the East   25

Chapter 4
Wolf Way, Skinwalkers, and Shape Changers   41

Chapter 5
Lobo Misterioso   54

Chapter 6
And God Gave Man Dominion   70

Chapter 7
Too Stupid to Survive   97

Chapter 8
Beloved Wolf   111

Chapter 9
When Wolves Run Free   128

Chapter 10
The Green Fire Dying in her Eyes   144

Chapter 11
Eco Rage: Howling at the Empty Moon   161

Chapter 12
The Moon Howls and the Wolves are Silent   176

Wolf Readings   185

Index   201

Foreword

The wolf is at the heart of the problem for restoring any semblance of the original wilderness. This is not standard ecology, it is not saving a stand of timber to save an owl. The wolf is dangerous and a direct threat wherever it is found, not because it will cut off your electricity or slash your tires or mug you on the subway, but because it brings with it a vocabulary and diction filled with frightening signals. The human imagination has invested the wolf with a powerful presence, bringing to mind images of the pack, the chase, the hunt, blood, exuberance, unleashed passion. The wolf represents great hunger, relentless appetite.

These are troublesome and disturbing characteristics. Although we know there are human beings with lupine drives, "civilization" has always hated the wolf because it has used the wolf as a measure of its presumed superior arrangements. The wolf has been used to signify the human outcast—the lone wolf—and the human rapacity represented by the changeling—the werewolf—which is the direct descent into savagery. Then there is the finality of being "thrown to the wolves," a term of utter abandonment. Humankind has traversed the millenia by keeping the wolf from our doors.

Having eradicated the wolf during the middle ages, the European, accompanied by domesticated sheep and cattle, confronted a fresh population of wolves in the New World. The new arrivals encountered a native human population that had hunted with the wolf and included the wolf in its clan affiliations for several thousand years. The wolf's diet needed no improvement. But the killing off of its native prey and the introduction of line-bred ungulates changed the sources of food available to the wolf, which, as in the Old World, brought it into direct competition with human economic interests. The arrival of sheep and cattle has always been used as the excuse to get rid of everything that didn't conform to the traffic in cut meat.

When Jim Burbank describes the wolf as the "psychological symbol of spiritual wilderness and the dark chaos of emotion," he takes us back to the medieval conception of the wolf, in which the creature was dismissed as vermin. In the West, this designation evolved into the Varmint, and thus became the catchall word for any predator with four legs or two. But it is not so easy to dismiss a species that has occupied the territory far longer than licensed hunters. Wolves can smell, see, and track, and they don't need four-wheel drive to get there. Wolves have had their noses in the wind for twenty thousand years, and they've got a right to be here. Anyone who is concerned with the radical decline in the environmental and spiritual health of the world should ponder this story of the wolf.

Ed Dorn
Professor of English
University of Colorado

Introduction

Just before I completed this book, I had a dream in which I saw a shaman with long raven hair. His task was to crawl on his belly out onto an ice floe. As he cautiously did so, he approached an area of open slush. It was seemingly impossible for him to be supported in this manner, but his companions surrounded him and, through their mutual support he was able to move out onto the open water where he spoke to the creatures of the sea.

Writing this book has been a journey similar to my dream. I have moved out over the treacherous ice floes, and I have received much valuable support and encouragement from friends and associates in the process.

In considering the material presented herein I have made many a leap of faith to interpret meanings I have discovered in my search for the Mexican wolf. Any shortcomings or errors are my own.

I wish to thank Michael McNierney, former editor with Johnson Books for placing his confidence in me. Without his active and enthusiastic encouragement this book would not have come to be. I also wish to thank Rebecca Herr, Mr. McNierney's successor, for so ably taking on this project and shepherding it through to its successful conclusion. Early chapter drafts were reviewed and critiqued by two demanding and extremely helpful readers—Sharon Niederman and Janet Voorhees provided honest, thorough, and indispensable help in doing so.

I wish to thank Mark Watson and Susan "Wolf" Larsen DVM of the Mexican Wolf Coalition for providing me support, patience, and information delivered at times on the spur of the moment and with great openness.

Denny Gentry of the New Mexico Cattle Grower's Association gave me an understanding for the ranchers in the Southwest and provided me with ready assistance. Thanks are also due to Alfonso Ortiz, who exercised patience and understanding during our meetings. His good humor and keen intelligence I deeply appreciated.

Ron and Janet McFarland of the American Endangered Species Foundation near Golden, Colorado, opened their home and their wolf pen to me from which I learned much. Kent Newton of the Rio Grande Zoo provided me with warm humor and insight into Mexican wolf behavior.

Thanks are due also to Dan Moore who proved helpful in providing information on the wolf lawsuit. Also many thanks and blessings to Walt Kennedy and Daniela Kuper for opening their house to me during my trips to Boulder to visit with my publishers.

For all those acknowledged here and for those many friends who aided, comforted, and supported me during this writing, I offer profound thanks.

Writing is a great and dangerous journey. It is not so much the arrival that proves important but the adventure of going that enriches one's life. To all those who have assisted me and to those good readers who share the journey of discovery this book is dedicated.

CHAPTER ONE

First Encounter

Everyone knows that
wolves howl and dogs bark.
Yet even the wisest cannot
tell what moves these
animals to call or explain
why wolves howl and
dogs bark when they do.
— after Chuang Tzu

My fascination with the Mexican wolf began one December morning when I was taking a walk with my friend Ray at the Rio Grande Nature Center in Albuquerque, New Mexico. The Nature Center park stretches along the Rio Grande breaks for a few miles, and trails and paths lead through salt cedar, Russian olive, and cottonwood forests, called the *bosques* by New Mexicans.

We enjoyed the simple pleasure of following our path to an open area by a stand of trees near the river bank where some beavers had recently been active. Fresh wood chips littered the ground covered by dead cottonwood leaves. I was examining tree stumps gnawed and gouged by these beavers when a sudden loud splash attracted my attention.

"Hey, what was that?" I asked.

"Probably a panther," Ray grinned. A chubby little muskrat paddled for all he was worth to reach a hollow where tree roots and soil had been washed away by successive seasons of river erosion. We watched the muskrat disappear in his burrow beneath the bank.

After a few minutes of river gazing, we decided to head back. Ray was due at his wood shop, where he worked making custom furniture, and I had an article waiting for me to complete on my desk at home. During our return trip Ray mentioned that panthers had once been more or less common in the high desert country of New Mexico. I lamented the disappearance of panthers from New Mexico's wilderness. Ray commented that the eradication of so many creatures was a symptom of our times.

We had just arrived at the visitor's center from our stroll when we decided to stop for a drink of water. There pinned to a bulletin board by the water fountain was an article from the local paper that drew my attention.

The story told how the Chairman of the New Mexico Game Commission, Gerald Maestas, during a January 1988 "ABC World News Tonight" interview, said that the Mexican wolf was "too stupid to survive." The article described recent unsuccessful efforts to reintroduce the wolf into New Mexico's wilderness following a silent campaign during the latter part of the nineteenth century and throughout the twentieth century to drive the animal into extinction.

Controversy Emerges

As a journalist, I found the comment fascinating. Days later I kept turning it over in my mind. Why would a man charged with the responsibility of supervising the state's wildlife be either so insensitive or careless about public opinion to say such a thing on national television? After all, America was waking up to "animal issues." Right here in isolated New Mexico we had been sensitized to animal rights activism.

Bob Barker, emcee of the Miss U.S.A. Pageant held in Albuquerque a year ago, dismayed local officials and amused the public when he refused to appear if contestants wore fur coats. Barker's animal rights boycott had given the local papers a week of banner headlines.

I also thought about remarks made by James Watt in January 1983, concerning Native Americans and reservations as an example of failed socialism, which raised a hornet's nest of controversy before he resigned as Secretary of the Interior during the first Reagan Administration. Watt had seemed genuinely mystified by strong reaction in the press to his insensitivity. Garrey Carruthers, New Mexico's current governor, served as Assistant Secretary of the Interior under Watt. Carruthers had appointed Maestas to the Game Commission.

The connections percolated in my mind. I decided to call my editor with Reuters International News Service in Houston to see if he might be interested in a story about the wolf. The next night I was on the phone to Gerald Maestas, who was irritated when I asked him about the ABC "too stupid to survive" comment.

"No, I didn't say they were too stupid," Maestas responded. "That was the newspaper that said that." He went on, "I said they weren't smart enough to survive in the wild . . . . I don't know why it raised such a ruckus."

Maestas explained that the few remaining Mexican wolves were zoo animals and that releasing them in the wilderness would require "extreme care" for each animal, and that care would cost the state money. Was releasing the wolves an expenditure he could justify? The claim that wolves bred in zoos have lost the ability to survive was disputed by both Bill Zeedyk, Regional Wildlife Director for the Forest Service, and Kent Newton, Mammal Curator at the Rio Grande Zoo, where two wolves are being kept in hopes that wolves may be put back in their native habitat.

Anyway, none of this mattered, Maestas said, because the Game Commission would never hear the matter in the first place. Introducing the wolf into the wilderness was a dead issue, according to Maestas. The only reintroduction site, White Sands Missile Range, had already rejected a plan to have wolves on the sprawling military reserve in southern New Mexico because it would interfere with the Army's mission. Maestas insisted few people really supported introducing the wolf back into New Mexico. That was not what I heard from members of the New Mexico Wolf Coalition, the main group backing reintroduction, composed of fifteen to twenty members from organizations such as Greenpeace, the National Wildlife Federation, and the Sierra Club. They said public opinion in New Mexico favored wolf reintroduction. In fact, a telephone poll of six hundred New Mexico voters conducted by the Department of Game and Fish early in 1989 showed 48 percent favored wolf reintroductions. The coalition had raised some $15,000 over a period of a few years in their efforts to introduce wolves. They organized various events including several rallies and a "Bring Back the Lobo Week" in early spring of 1988. They had also rented billboard space on Central Avenue near the University of New Mexico backing the reintroduction program. "Bring Back the Lobo," read the billboard, "Extinction Is Forever."

Between Life and Death, a Thin Line

Since 1976, the wolf had been protected under provisions of the Endangered Species Act. The Federal Fish and Wildlife Service was charged with reintroducing the lobo into the wilderness. In 1979, the New Mexico Wolf Recovery Team was appointed by the Service. Three years later, Mexico and the United States signed a joint compact to attempt bringing the wolves back to their natural range south of the border and in southwest Texas, southern New Mexico, and southeastern Arizona. Educating the public about the wolf was also the responsibility of the Fish and Wildlife Service. Reintroduction proponents complained the agency had neglected its duty to inform the public about the animal.

"Why should we go through the trouble of conducting an education campaign about the Mexican wolf when White Sands has already rejected reintroduction?" a spokesman at Fish and Wildlife asked. According to the Wolf Coalition, Maestas and members of the Game Commission were "in the pockets" of the powerful New Mexico ranching industry. And ranchers despised the wolf with a passion that approached the irrational. They had their reasons. Given the thin profit margins many ranches run on, herd predation on just a few animals could wipe out an operation in just a season or two. It made a good story—plenty of conflict, both sides gripped in a deathlock struggle, two apparently irreconcilable viewpoints with little room for negotiations. But there was something missing from this controversy.

There are only thirty three Mexican wolves left in the United States and Mexico. Ranchers and bounty hunters had during the last century and through the late 1960s hunted the wolf with persistence. There was a missionary zeal to this campaign which had ended with the near annihilation of the lobo.

Why do people feel so strongly for and against this animal? Why such passion about this particular predator? What did eradication efforts say about us as a nation and a people? And what did they mean for the Southwest, this region that exercises such magnetic charm for the rest of the country through its natural beauty and its native cultures? Why such brutality here in this wild desert landscape prized for its almost spiritual magic? I was determined to find answers to these questions.

Face to Face

In the early morning one bright February day, I encountered my first lobo. I had been given an assignment for National Public

Radio covering attempts to return the Mexican wolf to the wilds of New Mexico, and now here I was at the Rio Grande Zoo in Albuquerque ready to meet my first wolf.

I was to interview Kent Newton, Mammal Curator for the zoo, about his activities as Chairman of the Captive Breeding Program which was established to keep the wolf genetically viable while debate about the wolf's return to the wild raged on between environmentalist groups and ranchers.

Newton is a taciturn man with a quiet sense of humor, graying dark hair, and a small moustache. As we sat in his office talking about the story, I felt a rising sense of anticipation as I considered my first time with the wolves. Even though I knew the image of this animal projected in myth and the reality were far apart, the thought of actually seeing a wild wolf face to face sent a thrill of fear mixed with anticipation through me.

In preparation for our interview, Newton loaded his tape machine with a cassette of wolf howls recorded by naturalists under the auspices of Robert Redford. His small second story office in the zoo education building filled with eery calls of the gray wolf as I held my microphone up to grab the sound.

The canned howls echoed like cries of ghosts bugling through his cramped room. An animal scent filled his cubbyhole of an office and clung around this man who seemed, in his subdued but powerful way, to be more comfortable with members of the wild kingdom than with people. The howling done, he popped the tape from his portable machine and leaned back in his desk chair.

Newton explained that, after the wolf had been declared an endangered species, the U.S. Fish and Wildlife Service approached selected state governments asking where wolves might someday be released back into their original habitat.

Texas refused even to consider the prospect of wolf reintroductions. Arizona suggested fifteen or sixteen possible sites, but continued to review these recommendations over time, putting off taking any substantial action. The New Mexico Department of Game and Fish provided the only solid recommendation site to the Fish and Wildlife Service—White Sands seemed in many ways an ideal location. Two reports were commissioned by the Service to analyze the missile range as a location. Both came back with extremely positive results, but the Army refused to go along with the plan, Newton said. The New Mexico Department of Game and

Fish named no other locations for reintroductions. "We don't know if the political climate might change either in Santa Fe or with the Army," Newton said.

The presence of biologists on the range posed a major stumbling block for the Army. The range commander contended wolf monitoring jeopardized the Army's national defense mission. Wolf proponents countered that other state biologists were already monitoring exotic species introduced years ago by the Game and Fish Department. Biologists were also monitoring mountain lions in the area.

Each year members of the public were also allowed in White Sands to conduct a special public hunt to thin oryx herds, the exotic African antelope (also known as the gemsbok) introduced back in the late 1960s onto the sprawling reserve. The reports commissioned by the Service said presence of prey species and water in the mountainous area above 4,000 feet made it an ideal location for wolves. Newton couldn't explain the Army's reaction. He shook his head and frowned.

Wolf Nature, Fact and Fiction

I wanted to know the character and nature of this animal. Newton noted that wolves are difficult to observe because they prefer to stay away from people. What has often been taken for cowardice by the ignorant who hunted wolves, in truth indicates their natural shyness. Someone wanting to observe wolves in their habitat might go for days, weeks, or months without ever seeing one.

"They know you're out there. They can tell a human being is there," said Newton. "A human being is the ultimate predator. The wolf will hightail it away from man."

Wolf behavior is complex, but not much insight has been gained into driving forces and motivations that lie behind wolf interactions. Over the past twenty years, though, much headway has been gained in observing wolves both in the wild and in zoos. Recent research conveys some interesting comparisons between humans and wolves.

Wolves enjoy strong family and group ties and they communicate in a socially sophisticated language of voice, body, and scent signals. Among their own kind they exhibit, like humans, an inborn friendliness due to their social nature. Behavior naturally varies from individual to individual, but the basic impulse of wolves is to be gregarious and they are well disposed toward other members of the pack.

"Sometimes I wish that human society could be as cohesive as Mexican wolves or other wolf species," Newton said. Contrary to popular beliefs, wolves are not the vicious, snapping, rabid beasts of legend. Newton said that the Little Red Riding Hood story had probably done more to encourage wolf annihilation than any other tale. Wolves rarely kill one another, according to Newton. L. David Mech, probably one of the foremost wolf biologists, cites some interesting examples of the wolf's dislike of violence.

According to Mech, John Fentress raised wolves with his farm dogs to observe their behavior, and noted that his wolves became very attached to the dogs. In one instance, Fentress saw a tame wolf become extremely upset when it witnessed its first dog fight, finally breaking up the row by pulling the aggressor dog away from combat by its tail.

Adolph Murie, a wildlife biologist, actually crawled into a wolf den after the female had run away in fear. Murie removed a pup while the female wolf barked and howled in the distance, never attacking him, even allowing him to take the pup from her den without responding. This is typical behavior. Wolves will allow men to invade their dens, take young, and simply stay away. They seem to know humans are stronger than they are and are dangerous enough to avoid despite their strong attachment to their young.

Another biologist in northern Canada captured some specimen wolf pups, experiencing the same lack of aggression on the part of the mother wolf. Late in the afternoon he shot some ptarmigans which he slung from his gun barrel over his shoulder. After dark, while he was walking to his tent, he heard something behind him. It was the she-wolf, her nose brushing the ptarmigans as they swayed back and forth.

Other Canadian biologists discovered they could pin wolves using a simple forked stick over their necks after they had been caught in steel traps. The wolves made no attempts to escape. Mech himself repeated the experiment using a similar forked stick to hold a nine-month-old wolf so he could tag her ear. Newton said that not one authenticated case has ever been reported of a healthy wolf attacking a human being. Barry Holstun Lopez, in his excellent book, *Of Wolves and Men*, disputes this, saying that Eskimos in the Northwest, indeed, report wolves have attacked and killed humans, but these incidents are rare.

The fact is, wolf nature is ambiguous and mysterious. There is no denying that wolves are predators that will attack sheep and cattle. Newton said that if wolves are isolated from human habitation, they will avoid contact and stay in the wild. Lopez cites evidence that wolves sometimes kill apparently for the mere sport of it. Usually the old or sick members of a herd of deer or other prey species are targeted for attack, but not always. Mech reports during observations of moose hunts by wolves that of 160 attempts he observed, only six kills resulted. Wolves test large prey. If the animal refuses to run, often the hunt is abandoned. Thus, a balance between predator and prey is maintained.

The Wolf as Barometer

"The wolf and its elimination are a barometer of our own quality of life," said Newton. "If we allow species to continue to be eliminated this world will be a barren desert like Ethiopia or other locations where desertification has occurred because of human activity." Newton stressed the role predators play in the web of life. Often we do not see that predators play a vital part in preserving the balance of all species. Disappearance of the wolf has meant a proliferation of coyotes in many areas of the Southwest. Subsequent attempts to eradicate coyotes have led to an upsurge in the rodent and small mammal populations in areas where coyotes come under attack.

We do not know what impact on the survival of other creatures (or even, ultimately, humans) elimination of wolves at the top of the food chain might have. Newton explained that wolves and mountain lions vied with one another as the most powerful predators in the Southwest ecosystem. Under certain circumstances, wolves even successfully eliminated lions. They also killed coyotes and other lesser predators. I wondered, thinking briefly of tales from childhood of voracious wolves who fool and then eat careless children, the three little pigs, the cruel wolf, the werewolf . . .

We completed the interview, and I packed up the mike and recorder as we prepared to visit the temporary wolf enclosure. We climbed into Newton's green golf cart and headed to the back area of the zoo. The pair of wolves participating in the breeding program were being temporarily housed there while their new expanded quarters were being freshly planted with native grasses and yucca and refurbished in preparation for the spring breeding season.

Rio Grande Zoo is one of several zoos in the United States involved in attempting to keep the wolf alive in captivity. The Arizona Sonora Desert Museum near Tucson has several wolves, and the Wild Canid Survival Research Center in Eureka, Missouri, also participates in the program, Newton explained. Alameda Park Zoo in Alamogordo and the Living Desert State Park near Carlsbad, New Mexico, have both cooperated in the breeding program. Eight wolves have been moved to four Mexican facilities where they are also being bred.

We drove up a small hill. Newton shut off the engine of the cart and we walked to a chain-link gate which he unlocked. We then descended a flight of steep stairs covered with snow. In my nervousness I slipped, almost falling down.

At the bottom of the concrete stairway, he opened a large chain-link enclosure, shutting another gate behind us. We walked down a narrow corridor surrounded on all sides with twelve-foot fences. The area reminded me of an industrial or factory setting, or perhaps a prison far from the wilds which were the wolves' natural home. We met two keepers who Newton mildly chastised for leaving open the final gate that led to the building where the wolves had their kennels, each with its own vertical slide door to the outer yard. Newton and I entered the building.

The animals rarely spent time in the enclosure where their food was prepared each day by keepers, Newton explained. They are extremely wary of the keepers and prefer the yard. Newton unlocked the final sheet steel door which led to the wolf enclosure.

We stepped from the darkness of the pens into the harsh southwestern light of the enclosure . . . and there he was, my first wolf, alert and crouching near the bunker which led to his kennel, the fur hackled on his broad back. He considered us, but stood his ground, chuffing and holding us with his gaze, hunkered down on his front paws.

Looking into the wolf's eyes, I saw an intelligence, a curiosity, and an apprehension. There we stood fifty feet from one another, each considering the other. He must have wondered what we wanted, these human intruders. His mate floated around, circling nervously at the back of the enclosure, moving with deft speed as the male continued his barking, still standing his ground.

I noted the male's gray coat, or pelage, tinged with black around the neck. The female was smaller, tawny almost like a coyote. "If they were in the wilderness, they would be ten miles away by now," Newton said. "They are much more afraid of us than we are of them."

We considered one another for a moment. It wasn't fear that I felt in regarding the wolf, but rather a sense of the complete wildness of this creature, the total "otherness" of this animal being, despite the zoo atmosphere. I held the mike out to try to record the low chuffing bark the wolf made. As I did so, he hunkered once more on his front paws, considering if he had any escape routes. The small barks made by the male were a warning to the female. If there had been a pack of wolves present, Newton said they all would be making that low rapid bark I call chuffing. The female continued to run around the back of the enclosure. I remembered Mech's story about men raiding the wolf's den and stealing her pups without any response from the female except her attempts to stay as far as possible from human intruders. There was another reason for the female's wariness. In a couple of months she would be having pups.

Wolf breeding season is in February. At the zoo during this time the main enclosure will be in use and the female digs her den about eight to ten feet into a hillock, Newton explained. She then excavates for another four feet in either direction at right angles from the main entrance tunnel. The whole structure is wolf-sized to ensure pup safety.

About two months following successful mating, the new pups arrive. For a few weeks they remain sequestered in the den and then they emerge. Within several weeks of their emergence the wolf pups are weaned and start to eat solid food regurgitated by other members of the pack. No distinction among adult animals is made in regard to regurgitation. All adults take part in feeding the young, who solicit their meals by nipping at the adult's jaw. In this way the entire group partakes in raising pups, Newton noted.

The male wolf still stood frozen, torn between curiosity and fear. I was overcome with a sense of sadness. Here was an animal, wild and free to roam over hundreds, perhaps even thousands of miles of woodlands and mountains. At one time not too long ago, the wolf was master of every ecological domain, known for its intelligence and its ability to survive, gregariousness with its fellows, and as a hunter par excellence. Now the few survivors had to make do with a little yard, a dank concrete block building and a small man-made hill where it could follow its most essential calling to breed pups.

We left the yard, closing the iron door once more behind us, mounted the steps from the temporary wolf area, and rode in Newton's cart to consider the expanded wolf area. Only two small viewing windows allowed the public to see the animals. This was a small concession to the wolf's love of privacy, these two windows cut in a wood fence set twenty feet above the main yard area where the wolves would soon run.

Two litters have been raised in this area, Newton told me as he started up his cart so we could head back to the main zoo building. Newton spoke about the old menagerie concept of zoo management and how that has now been changed due to worldwide efforts to avoid rapidly escalating extinction of many species. True to its eighteenth century origins, the idea of the menagerie was to have a collection of one or two of every conceivable wild or strange animal caged in order to display them for public exhibition.

"We don't have postage stamp collections of many species of animals anymore," he said. "Conservation and species preservation is at the leading edge of professional zoo keeping." Zoos all over the world are attempting to maintain viable gene pools through captive animals so that one day reintroduction into the wild may be possible.

Newton cited the example of the Arabian oryx that had virtually been eliminated from its Mideast habitat by soldiers taking target practice. Zoos have been important in reintroducing the animal to its original homelands. Newton also reported success with the bald eagle, which had just about been wiped out in the wild, but is now making a comeback. The Rio Grande Zoo has worked with the Fish and Wildlife Service in reintroducing the bird to Tennessee.

As we drove along over the zoo path, peacocks in full plumage wandered across our path. I thought of these successes and I wondered if wolf cries would ever be heard once more in the wilds of the Southwest instead of on tape produced and promoted by a movie star.

❂ ❂ ❂

By Wolf Light

That night I slept fitfully. Finally, toward dawn I had a dream that once again I stood inside the wolf enclosure. Newton was by my side.

"This time you have to go in alone," he said. He quickly slammed the heavy steel door. It closed with a metallic crash. I stood alone in the enclosure, fear mounting within me. Suddenly as if appearing from out of space itself stood a huge black wolf with a green fire that shone in her eyes. She regarded me with an indifference which created a surge of panic that raced up my spine. I considered trying to escape but the wolf had me penned in. We stared at one another. How human her eyes appeared, how intelligent and how dispassionate. We regarded each other for a long and solemn moment. Then she approached. My fear mounted to an uncontrollable frenzy. I considered ways that I might kill this wolf. I knew, though, that I was trapped. She sniffed the air, her nose prodding for scent. As my terror ratcheted she calmly strode over by my side.

"What you fear is the wildness inside you," she said in a very human voice full of calmness and compassion. "You will never understand me. It is the wolf within which you must come to understand." Then she licked my hand like a dog and smiled, her eyes glowing like green coals.

I woke drenched with sweat and shaking. It was early dawn. The light which shone through my north window I could name only as wolf light, gray and cold.

CHAPTER TWO

Brother Wolf

On the eastern edge
Wolf the hunter has come out.
With glittering paint
With white head feather tip waving,
He has gone
Bravely will I go
To get spruce,
Acquiring blessings.
—Acoma hunt song

Seen to the east from the Sonoran plateau that extends for miles in a gently sloping plain to the Rio Grande, the Sandia Mountains resemble a giant tortoise forever frozen in stone. This geological reptile rises ominously above the sere desert landscape dotted with dust green piñon, juniper, yellow-flowered chamisa, and the twisted spidery arms of cholla cactus.

For the Tewa Indian village of San Juan eighty miles to the north, these mountains are called *Oku Pin* (Turtle Mountain). This place marks one of the four corners of the Tewa world endowed with sacredness, site of a *nan sipu*, or earth navel and home of the Towa é, guardians of the Tewa universe.

At 6 A.M. on a day early in September, I'm the only hiker headed north on the Rincon Ridge section of the Piedra Lisa trail that leads up the northeast flanks of Oku Pin. Even this early, it is already beginning to get hot. I trace a route over a small sub-ridge toward the shelter of Juan Tabo Canyon where a trickle of water flows through willows, elders, and granite boulders worn smooth by centuries of wind.

From my cool sanctuary I spy the barren heights of 8,000-foot Rincon Peak to the west extending in a bow that comprises the front leg of the ancient tortoise—Rincon Ridge—my goal for today's walk. I stare at fluted spires and walls of stone fired pink by morning sun. A buzz of insects and my rasping labored breath penetrate the silence as I once again begin my ascent.

Soon I am among giant Ponderosa pine and gambel oak reading signs of this mountain's life in limestone and shale escarpments deposited some 300 million years ago by an ancient Pennsylvanian sea. Below the limestone crest lies a ragged layer of stone called by geologists the Great Unconformity because this expanse of tortured rock, lacking any fossil record, leaves an inexplicable million-year gap in the earth's known history. Below the Unconformity, a 500-foot stretch of vertical granite now warms in sunlight.

After negotiating several switchbacks, at about 8,500 feet I make ridgetop among spindle fir. I gaze east to Mount Taylor, and fifty miles away see the looming basalt tower called El Cabezon rising 2,000 feet from the desert floor. I scan the dusty burnt umber plateau of the Rio Grande Valley broken by a thin green slash of meandering river.

I imagine the Rio Grande Valley as it once was, the land wiped clean of the city below named Albuquerque that sucks life from the plain called in Spanish *el llano*. A few thin plumes of smoke drift south downriver from distant pueblos.

Here I am content to consider a hawk as it darts in and out from spires and buttressed aretes, listening to my heart thump. I attend to that moment between inhalation and exhalation where stillness resides . . .

Without warning, somewhere below a branch snaps. I whirl around. There on a bald flat a thousand feet above the creek a large gray wolf emerges from surrounding trees, eyes burning as he scans his territory. His pelage mottled dun, another smaller wolf emerges cautiously from surrounding trees. Finally a third wolf pads with nonchalance and ease into the gathering light. For a moment these three inspect this unprotected prominence and sniff the wind, noses held high, eyes slightly closed.

At some hidden signal a great jostling and bumping of wolf bodies ensues as the two latter wolves smile and touch noses with the first in an enthusiastic greeting full of wolf affection and good humor. With great dignity the first wolf breaks from his fellows. Lifting his leg, he urinates to mark this place with his scent. In imitation, his companions follow suit, lifting legs, micturating and scratching the earth once or twice. In an instant they are gone, vanished forever . . .

Only in my imagination do wolves emerge from these mountains where once they roamed. The Mexican wolf, grizzly, pronghorn antelope, elk, and even the prairie dog disappeared from the

Sandia Mountains long ago. Yet, while the Mexican wolf is gone from the wilds, it still exercises a tremendous pull on my imagination. So I see this small pack here, creating in my own mind a reality that will never again exist here in the Sandias.

As I stare at the barren spot where these imaginary wolves materialized and then disappeared, I think perhaps we humans at the deepest level share many attributes of wolves. Perhaps wolves and human beings emerged from similar circumstances in the distant evolutionary past and we carry shadows of this ancient heritage with us deep in our marrow. Is this identification? Are these old memories why wolf nature horrifies and fascinates us?

Indeed there are many similarities between how wolves mingle and how people interact, especially when the veneer of civilization is removed and primal cultures are compared to wolf society. There may even be a similarity between how wolves see their world and how we learned to view our circumstances in our ancient prehistoric past when we, like wolves, hunted animals and lived in small groups.

People have not always despised wolves. Some societies have learned from wolves and have even honored them, maybe because they saw similarities between wolves and humans. The view such societies have held of their world, though, differs markedly from our own.

Of Naked Wolves and Mental Maps

Researchers have often speculated about similarities between wolf behavior and the conduct and habits of primitive peoples. Roger Peters, a cognitive psychologist at Fort Lewis College in Durango, Colorado, for three years studied several wolf packs in Superior National Forest near the Minnesota-Canadian border.

Peters wanted to gain insight into the behavior of early humans. He theorized that wolves, like tribal hunters, made mental maps, noting significant landmarks, routes, and territorial edges. Peters based his ideas on theories developed by Carveth Read, an English logician born in the 1840s whose interest in human origins, superstition, and logic led him to study early human evolution to discover roots of primitive behavior.

Peters formulated what he called the "naked wolf model" for cognitive development. According to his theory, human learning abilities are the legacy of millions of years when our ancestors lived like wolves, cooperatively hunting for large animals over vast territory while their young and other related pack members waited at dens and rendezvous sites.

Such a way of life might lead primal humans to remember routes, geographic features, and territorial boundaries. Peters's investigations led him to note that wolf scent markings were complex and appeared to follow distinct patterns that seemed more than just random. He speculated that wolves might even navigate like birds using the sun, stars, or even earth's magnetic field to orient their travels, but he dropped this idea returning to his original formulations.

He carried out detailed observations of wolves as they urinated, defecated, and scratched the ground to see if he could note an overall organization to such scent markings. He paid particular attention to raised leg urinations (RLUs) and squat urinations (SQUs) to see if these behaviors signalled particular differences that might hold significance for wolf map-making ability.

So complicated did these behaviors seem that he was on the verge of giving up his theory. He began to compare maps drawn by people of the same region occupied by his wolf subjects. Peters noted in these hand-drawn maps a striking similarity between what people perceived as significant in a land area and what wolves saw as important in the same region. Though human-drawn maps varied in scale and detail, people seemed to select the same significant features and landmarks as compass points.

Then he noted that these were the same landmarks where wolves concentrated their scent marking. Wolves, like people, made distinct mental maps of their territories and they saw the same geographic features as having importance to their territorial navigations.

Peters also noted other wolf behaviors which appeared to be similar to tribal behaviors. The German ethologist Schenkel observed that each relationship in a wolf pack concerns every member of the pack. Nothing can happen to a pack member, and no pack member can take action, without affecting all the rest of the members. This dance of action and reaction shows an intimacy among pack members very similar to primal human society. Pack members bestow special recognition on other wolves whom they acknowledge. They snuffle only to another they see as a member of their own tribal group.

In his book *Of Wolves and Men,* Barry Lopez pointed out how deer seek safety in territorial boundaries where wolves spend minimal hunting time due to pack rivalry. In border areas between rival Plains tribes, Lopez noted deer sought similar safe havens because tribe members avoided these areas. Neolithic hunting groups ganged their prey just as do wolves. Strong family and group ties typify the hunting lifestyles of both species. Wolves and tribes even shared an ability to communicate through sign language and Plains Indians were fond of donning wolf skins to conduct bison-hunting forays.

Cultures Hot and Cold

Peters and Lopez are not the only authors who have noted a striking similarity between wolf society and tribal organization. R.D. Lawrence, who studied wolf behavior for over twenty-five years, observed that wolves preserve hierarchies astonishingly similar to social structures of closely woven small tribes.

Wolves also accept their social positions with neither complaint nor rebellion, whether high in rank or low in position. There seems a kind of built-in sense of overall group welfare, a sort of wolf consensus, which allays strife in favor of the overall good of the wolf pack. A similar sense of commonality can be noted in tribal interactions.

In tribal cultures everyone has a say in decision making. No one's feelings or opinions are ignored. Each person must come to feel aligned with the group decision before any action is taken. This ritual avoidance of social conflict and political dissension through consensus has led anthropologist Claude Levi-Strauss to call primitive tribal societies "cold" because they avoid social friction caused by strife. Like wolves they seek order and common good at almost any cost so that the group can survive challenges imposed by natural conditions.

In modern, industrial societies, social strife among groups, suppression of one group by another, and constant struggle between conquerors and conquered all create social friction. Continual conflict, inequality, and the disorder of competition generate entropy and "heat." The metaphor for such a society, in Levi-Strauss's model, is the machine.

Industrial cultures see wolves as snapping rabid beasts with rolling eyes and dripping fangs. We call wolves savage, and we mean by this characterization to associate wolves and tribal peoples. Perhaps these stereotypes are just evidence of our refusal to admit our own predator nature and our projection of these attributes onto the wolf.

The industrial world has managed to hide its predatory violence under a veneer of political, economic and social organization. We believe in a linear, chronological historical scheme. We record the progress of civilization as we subdue wilderness and convert nature's raw materials to manufacture through the mechanism of production. We consume nature's fruits as if earth's bounty was everlasting. We disguise and humanize these material gifts in elaborate sanitized packaging to remove us from the source of our abundance.

In societies that we call primitive, people participate in culture through collective ceremony and ritual that occupy a central place in community life. Goods production is of secondary importance. Time is cyclical just as seasons are cyclical. I call this ritual awareness of natural cycles "naked wolf time" because it celebrates human nature as part of overall essential wildness. One observer of Southwest Indian cultures has drawn some conclusions about Pueblo views of time that elaborate on this perspective.

After serving as Advisor on Trusteeship for the United Nations in London, John Collier, a longtime advocate for Indian rights in the 1940s and 1950s, wrote a small volume entitled *On the Gleaming Way*. Collier termed his book a watch and a vision.

As a kind of southwestern Thoreau, Collier compared Pueblo peoples of the Rio Grande to Ceylonese Buddhists who view linear time not as the only time and certainly not the controlling time. For Pueblos as well as for Ceylonese Buddhists life has a kind of interior spaciousness, an enduring future which draws the present on and on and an enduring past that melds with the present because the past is not the past, it is the present. Every phase or part of Pueblo life leads to all other parts and involves them all, Collier noted.

He said of the Tewa Indian pueblo of Tesuque near Santa Fe that it functioned along a razor edge of western time. He perceived ritual and ceremony as a bridge between eternal past and eternal future. In Western industrial society the only comparable experience he cited for such perceptions was to be found in personal mysticism. These observations will have particular significance in considering how industrial society and so-called primitive cultures look at the world of nature in general and the wolf in particular.

The organic continuity suggested by Collier's observations means that Pueblos, in philosophy and practice, regard nature and the human world as indissoluble, an ecological whole. In a peculiar sense, from this vantage point, there is no world of nature, or at least the word "nature" ceases to have any meaning from this perspective.

For instance, in the Tewa language, there simply is no word for "animal." Neither is there a word meaning "mammal" in use. The ways tribal peoples viewed the wolf show a whole different perceptual orientation than the white or white-dominated societies of our present time, which see the wolf as other, as split off from man-made reality.

Tribes that flourished in areas where the wolf was relatively common incorporated wolves as important totems representing qualities they wished to emulate in their struggle to survive as hunters.

Wolf Rituals of the Northwest Coast

Near the Straits of Juan de Fuca and the shores of Vancouver Island two Northwest tribes, the Makahs and Quillayutes, performed wolf dances that were an indispensable part of their ritual life. These rites were completed to gain power from wolves, which were the chief and most visible predators in the great forests of the northwest coastal regions. Wolves were sought as spirit helpers, not for individual purposes, but to obtain special powers and privileges from the wolf spirits for the entire tribe.

In the early 1950s anthropologist Alice Ernst, a student of Franz Boas, studied the wolf rituals of the Northwestern tribes at some length. Her detailed monograph that describes the various wolf dances says tribes chose wolves for their rituals because, as tutelary animals, wolves are the bravest and fiercest predators in the northwest region.

Being embedded within nature, the Native American view of animals is much different from our own view, which tends to alienate us from members of the animal kingdom. Even the term "animal kingdom" suggests there is a realm separate from the human world occupied by creatures who, because they are different from us, are lesser than us.

This way of thinking, in which animals are less significant than people, denies the simple and obvious fact that we are animals and reinforces the distinction between wild and civilized. Scientific descriptions of the natural world, as beautiful and articulate as they are, with their logical descriptive categories for plant and animal worlds, when reduced to popular conception, reinforce a sense that people exist apart from nature. Being able to use scientific descriptions as pigeonholes, or even knowing such descriptions are available, has given industrial cultures a comfortable sense that understanding descriptive systems of the natural world is the same as knowing nature.

Wolf Way of the Hunter

To the Native American mind, animals may be seen as members of other tribes or other peoples with their own special abilities and powers from which may be learned secrets to follow in life. There was no idea of a hierarchy of importance among animals in the Indian way of thinking, just as there was no religion split off and separated from other aspects of life in the Indian mind. The Buddhist idea of sentient or conscious being perhaps is closer to the kind of radiant animism that filled all creatures, plants, and even rocks in the Indian conceptual framework. The earth itself was viewed as a living being, a sentient consciousness upon whom all life depended. Given this interdependency, it seemed to the Indian way of thinking quite appropriate that everything that existed participated in this mysterious living spirit.

People were not seen as more important than other creatures, but simply members of the human tribe. The tribal group might call itself "the People" because group identity and survival were considered most important. For an individual to feel he or she was more important than others implied being out of balance with all the forces and phenomena equally participating in the great mysterious web of life.

When the Northwest tribes observed the wolf and incorporated in their rituals the wolf as a tutelary animal, they did so with a profound knowledge that they were dependent on prey animals for their existence. Killing was necessary for human life to be sustained. Yet balance had to be maintained. Balance as opposed to imbalance—not good versus evil—was the life principle for Indian traditions.

Life was ultimately considered as a mystery because so many things happened which could not be controlled or explained rationally. Life was tenuous and subject to forces that could be neither explained nor examined. To ask why there was suffering or disease, or why rain came one day and not another, or why a hunt was or was not successful simply was not a meaningful practice when all life was considered to be embedded in what we call nature.

In a world where progress and the machinery of production are significant, questions are the main mode of learning. In a universe where most things are manufactured by people, origins and causes yield readily to the process of explanation. The habit of mind in such cultures seeks to explain, order, categorize, and interpret experience and events.

Learning, Mystery and Power

In many tribal cultures, asking questions in order to learn was considered either rude or simply stupid. All phenomena and things were perceived to be interconnected. Learning occurred by paying close attention through much patience to the weather, the world, and all living things to seek the subtlest level of awareness leading to a sense of wonder, power, and mystery.

This mystery and power resided not only in all things observed through such attention, but could be sought in specific animals, plants, and phenomena. Either individuals sought power or a whole tribe attempted to participate in the qualities represented through a particular animal, such as in the wolf ritual of the Northwest.

Since life was tenuous, people sought beyond themselves for power and courage. Animals were bringers of vision and givers of power. In a culture reliant on prey for survival, hunting was the most important activity. Reliance on hunting created a keen awareness that a tribe's survival was at the sacrifice of the prey's life, reinforcing a philosophy of sacredness and interdependence.

Wolves test large prey and for unknown reasons often break off the hunt. In approaching a moose or other large animal, wolves will often stare at their prey, engaging the other animal's gaze. Some observers term this a "conversation of death." This phenomenon is not fully understood any more than the language and full significance of howling is comprehended. Barry Lopez speculated that the brief exchange between wolf and prey allows for some kind of subtle exchange of information leading either to termination of the hunt or hot pursuit. Young wolves have also been seen chasing deer, not to kill them, but to sharpen their prowess, to train themselves.

Doubtless, Indians observed this testing of prey by wolves. It is reasonable to speculate they incorporated these observations in their belief that prey "give themselves" to the hunter just as prey give themselves to the wolf.

Ritual, ceremony, and legends incorporated modes of teaching and ways of relating to the world in which tribes found themselves. In wolf rituals of the Northwest Coast, the warrior spirit of the wolf fostered bravery and endurance. By fasting, bathing or swimming in icy waters of the Pacific, or other means of training, wolf power could be gained. Seeking access to the mountain home of wolves was one way to learn the secret of their strength.

One such legendary seeker, *Ha-Sass*, went to find the source of wolf power, according to Northwest Indian legend. Because of his strength and personal power, wolves gave him the war club or *Che-to'kh*. They also taught him guile or wisdom.

As in other tribal stories and legends, the tools and abilities to survive are acquired through the agency and intercession of beasts and not simply invented by clever, productive people. The war club is a gift of the wolf, not a human invention. Even guile or wisdom as a habit of mind is not attained through human agency but is a gift of the wolf.

Individual cleverness or ambition were not viewed as positive attributes, but threatened the overall good of the tribe, because self-seeking attitudes and egocentrism were viewed as evidence that an individual was out of balance in expressing his self-importance. Gifts to the legendary hero were gifts to the entire tribe. The hero represented communal inheritance of the advantages necessary for survival.

Reflections on Wolf Nature

In his autobiography, *Memories, Dreams and Reflections*, psychologist C.G. Jung described a visit he paid to the Taos Pueblo in northern New Mexico. Jung told how the special vantage point he enjoyed by being a complete outsider to the Pueblo culture allowed him what he felt was a particular sense of insight into this foreign culture.

Jung observed that the Pueblo communities were absolutely secretive about their rites and ceremonies. He quickly abandoned any attempts at direct questioning as a mode for learning about this secret knowledge. Jung knew disclosure of these mysteries threatened the power of Pueblos to resist domination and intrusion by the white world. Disclosure could rob the mysteries of their ability to maintain order and could bring about collapse of the community as well as individual downfall.

He met there a Taos man named Ochwiay Biano (Mountain Lake) who spoke to Jung about the mystery that penetrates all of life. While both were seated on the pueblo's roof watching the sun as it tracked across the sky, Ochwiay Biano began to speak.

"Is not he who moves there our father?" asked Ochwiay Biano. "How can anyone say differently?"

Jung was astonished at the depth and power of the Taos man's emotions as his eyes filled with tears and he revealed his reverence for the beauty and mystery of the sun's simple journey to distant horizons.

Ochwiay Biano pointed out to Jung how cruel whites appeared with their rapacious eyes, their thin lips, and sharp noses. He wondered why white men seemed always to be wanting something, always uneasy and restless. He told Jung they thought with their heads and not their hearts. These observations caused Jung to plunge into a deep and despairing period of contemplation.

In his mind he saw images of conquering Roman Legions, the chiseled features of Caesar, the dominance and conversion of the Gauls to Christianity and subjection of a thousand different cultures and peoples. Colonization, missionary zeal, and the spread of civilization seemed then to Jung to have all taken place under the cruel and watchful eyes of some terrible bird of prey. The ensign of our culture seemed to him to be all the predatory creatures that had adorned European coats of arms.

If we humans share a common ancestry and patterns of behavior with wolves, if we ourselves were not once naked wolves, is it not this very link that magnetizes us in a dance of attraction and repulsion with the wolf? Native American tribal cultures rarely killed wolves, but viewed them as having power and mystery. They came to terms with the fact that they had to hunt to survive. They lived within the cycles of nature.

Other cultures have feared the wolf, but they have not sought to eliminate him. Instead, they have honored wolves and attempted to learn from them secrets to live better, fuller, and richer lives. In the story of the Mexican wolf's eradication and in continued persecution of wolves are more clues that reveal much about our deepest human nature, secrets that until recently we have preferred not to hold up to the light of inspection. Jung, in his soul-searching disclosures made during his visit to Taos, saw that civilization was the thinnest veneer covering our predatory nature.

What it means to be a predator is a more complicated issue than we might be willing to admit. On one hand society condemns and punishes predatory acts. Murder, rape, and violence against others are considered the most heinous crimes, yet in war or conquest social prohibitions are violated with impunity. When seeing a wolf in the wilds bring down a young fawn, an observer might be filled with horror and repugnance at such a seemingly violent and brutal act. A wolf's successful kill is violent and brutal only through human eyes. During warfare society readily condones behavior far more savage than the wolf's simple and natural quest for survival.

In musing on the destruction of other cultures and ways of life, Jung uncovered in himself a deep and abiding sadness. Jung's penetrating insights into human-predator bonds leads me to ask if, in attempting to destroy the wolf, we are not trying to wipe out our knowledge of our naked wolf ancestry? Is it any wonder that we feel sorrow? In wolf eradication are we not attempting to erase the beast within us?

The wolf is neither good nor bad. It is we humans who give the wolf meaning and so we try to destroy him because of his supposed evil, or we seek a power we impute to him that he has only in the human mind and spirit.

The remorse that now is coalescing as groups organize to bring back the wolf to its natural habitat shows some of us are mourning the disappearance of this fierce and mysterious animal from what remains of our wild country. We have vanquished the wolf and we have subdued wildness for our own civilized purposes only to discover that we haven't come to terms with that secret and dark wilderness within ourselves. We want to make peace with the wolf whom we have sought to destroy perhaps because he reminds us that not long ago we ourselves were naked wolves. The urge to hear wolves call once more is a cry from deep in the human heart, a howl of longing for our own primitive and ancient past.

CHAPTER THREE

Great Beast God of the East

So he went out and came to a
large court. He was in an upper
story with somebody. Below
them were different kinds of
animal—mountain lion, bear,
wolf, fox, wildcat, dragonflies,
also bees, the big and the little
ones. He was frightened. They
said, "We are your friends."
They jumped up on him and
scratched him. They had power.
—Elsie Clews Parsons
Tewa Emergence Myth

Early in March, I phoned anthropologist Alfonso Ortiz to discuss
my wolf book. I told him I was interested in discovering what the
wolf meant to Pueblo tribes. Originally from the Tewa village of
San Juan, Ortiz is one of those amazing people who has in a single
lifetime spanned two cultures, maintaining a foothold in both the
Indian and white worlds.

He referred me to some basic readings and graciously agreed to
meet with me in two weeks after I had time to study the works he
suggested. I immediately obtained the two or three books he recommended and began to scour them for material relating to the wolf.

My research was disappointing. There were few references to
the wolf and those that I managed to uncover were obscure and
difficult to decipher. My search seemed to be going in a confusing
circle. I felt less and less sure of my direction. I wondered if I even
had the right to be considering such an enormous and demanding
undertaking.

On a cold blustery day, I headed across the University of New
Mexico campus to meet Ortiz at his second story office overlooking
an open courtyard of the anthropology department building. His
door was open as I approached and I could hear he was on the
phone. Cautiously, I knocked.

White Man's Thinking

"Come in, come in," he said. "So, you're the wolf man." His booming, melodious laugh filled the room cluttered with books stacked in random piles in and around his desk. I thought, if I am the wolf man, Ortiz is the bear man. Large, but full of energy, he seemed constantly on the verge of exploding with the excitement of discovery. He wore his hair long in a traditional Tewa *chungo* wrapped at the nape in a figure eight with a piece of yarn. He motioned for me to sit.

"Well, what have you learned?" he asked, pushing his glasses back on his nose.

I told him I had discovered that the wolf was the Beast God of the East.

"Maybe in Zuñi," he replied. "I've thought about your problem driving back and forth from Santa Fe. There's nothing on the wolf that I know of, and if there is, you'll have to talk to men who are in their eighties now . . . men who were hunters. There's a lot on the coyote, but nothing on the wolf . . . Nope, nothing."

He explained that the coyote was an intermediary. I mumbled something about heaven and earth and asked if the wolf being Beast God of the East meant the same thing to Pueblos as to Plains Tribes. Ortiz scowled.

"That's white man's thinking," he said. I felt foolish and embarrassed.

"No, I think you misunderstand," I said. "I meant if the Beast Gods are the same to the Plains Tribes and Pueblos."

"*I* misunderstand!" he said.

I asked Ortiz why he thought the wolf had been exterminated by ranchers and the government. He compared the fate of the wolf to genocide and continued persecution of Indian tribes. He commented that wildness in any form had to be eliminated by the white culture. He paused, his brow furrowed in thought.

"If there is something on the wolf," he said, "you can find it by going west to Zuñi or Acoma. Don't go north or south. You'll waste your time."

"I have some contacts at Taos," I said. "Maybe I should try going up there."

"Maybe," he said. " But I think you'll find it's a waste of time. Head west if you want to learn about the wolf. I wish I had more for you, but you'll have to talk to the old men. I've thought about your problem a lot and this is all I can tell you. I'm sorry. I wish I could be more helpful. Go west and maybe you can learn something." We shook hands and my encounter with Alfonso Ortiz was at an end.

I was deeply disturbed and baffled by our meeting. I stayed awake most of the night turning over in my mind our meeting. On the one hand, Ortiz had expressed genuine concern for the project. On the other, he seemed impatient, secretive, and defensive. Then there was the issue of our misunderstanding and his comment about my white man's thinking. I felt ashamed and vulnerable, my efforts to make a favorable impression obviously unsuccessful.

Clarity Emerges

Not only was I confused by my encounter with Ortiz but I found my research continually perplexing. I knew prey animals were associated with the cardinal directions and that each direction, in turn, was associated with a color. The color for north was yellow, for west it was blue, for south it was red, for east it was white, and for zenith and nadir it was black or variegated. Plants, trees, animals and birds likewise had this directional association— mountain lion with north, bear with west, badger with south, eagle with sky, mole with underground . . . and wolf with the east.

Plains tribes had similar associations between animals and directions, but the wolf was associated with the color red. Interchange between Plains tribes and Pueblos was common, so it seemed reasonable to assume the Pueblos could have adapted this way of thinking. I pondered what these associations meant. Could animals, directions and colors be elements in a secret system of symbols which was totally closed to outsiders?

Two weeks after my meeting with Ortiz I read in one of the most extensive studies of Pueblo traditions published in 1939 by anthropologist Elsie Clews Parsons that a certain doctor by the name of Kroeber had been given the name Onothlikia, or Oriole, by the Zuñis because he had originally come from the north and had worn khaki clothing. According to *Pueblo Indian Religion*, the two-volume study recommended by Ortiz, the oriole is the bird of the north and yellow is the color associated with the north.

In Pueblo legend, Wolf Boy, suitor of Yellow Corn Girl lived in the east as is to be expected because this direction is associated with the wolf. Suddenly, Alfonso Ortiz's advice came back to me. He had suggested I go west in my searches for wolf knowledge. How appropriate his suggestion seemed.

If I arrived from the east and told residents of Zuñi or Acoma I was interested in the wolf, chances for a good reception were enhanced. I would be arriving from the east, the wolf's direction.

I decided to open my investigations to a whole other mode of thinking that seemed to be emerging for me. Ortiz had given me my first instruction and demonstration in Pueblo thought modes, not through explanation and question-answer format, but through demonstration, participation, and example.

He was right. My mind was so bound up with my white man's presumptions and my reporter's questions that I was failing to take seriously the subject of my inquiry and I was failing to understand, honor, and respect the traditions I was studying.

Ortiz's instructions had been a vivid example of one phase or part leading to the whole and involving all other parts. A more vivid example of this principle came from Ortiz's penetrating exposition of Pueblo life and thought, entitled *The Tewa World: Space, Time, and Becoming in a Pueblo Society*. The wolf plays an important role in the Tewa's most important myth, the emergence story.

As revealed in the previous chapter, questioning and discovering the origin and causes of particular phenomena or events is not seen as a way of learning in Indian thinking. The sacred infuses everything and is akin to a kind of sentient-being spirit. In Judeo-Christian beliefs, God is an outside agency, a kind of grand mover who shapes the universe. The creation story is for European cultures, therefore, very important because it explains *how* and *why* the world was created.

Interest in origins or explanations is not the central focus for Tewa mythology. The Pueblo world is multidimensional, extending in at least six directions. The gods are not "above," and down is as important as up. Humans are in the middle and the village is in the center of the Pueblo universe.

The most important story for the Tewa is the myth of emergence, just as it is for many Native American tribes. In emergence stories, people, animals, divine beings, and others originally lived in a world beneath the present world. Often this ancestral underground universe is described as a place of darkness and social chaos. In the

Tewa story the underground universe is located beneath a lake.

The collective unconscious with its dream images and subterranean archetypes may be compared to pre-emergence existence in which animals, gods, and humans can communicate. The pre-emergence world is the realm where the dead go and the magic place where shamans descend in their soul travels. The universe before this one is the womb-world. By intercession of a hero or powerful animal the people climb through a hole or up a tree into the present world.

The analogy to the birth experience or parturition has been noted by anthropologists. Emergence stories may record mythological memories of an ancient past when ancestral prehumans had yet to take the first tentative steps on the long journey of human discovery. These myths record the evolution of human awareness and dawning consciousness. In this sense emergence myths trace the birth and growth of social awareness. In some Pueblo traditions humans emerge from four womb-worlds into the present world. In each world social chaos, imbalance, and disorder erupt and the people repeat their initiation in another universe until they emerge in our present world.

The emergence of humankind is not a creation in the Tewa myth. Humans are seen as already existing. There is little if any interest in telling how or where humans or the world came from or ascribing such origins to a moral, purposeful God who rules the world from on high. Myths serve as a way of instructing people about habits of mind, tradition, and ways of doing things that are in accord with the sacred which infuses everything, not just in explaining how or why things evolved they way they have.

Of particular importance in the Tewa emergence myth is the role played by the wolf and other predators in the entrance of the People from the previous world into the current world. The wolf teaches predator lessons and survivor skills, and bestows hunting tools.

When I first read this story of Tewa emergence, I felt only my usual confusion. The legend seemed to yield to me no meanings whatsoever, like a dream half-remembered the next morning after a fitful sleep. I decided I would let the story speak to me without forcing meaning from it. I resolved to read the legend over and over, to memorize, it and to repeat it to myself, allowing whatever meanings to surface in my conscious awareness by emerging from deep within my own mind. My process was intended to imitate the

very story itself. Like the ancient hero who undergoes rites of initiation to journey from the realm of darkness to the world of sunlight, I struggled toward insight by abandoning my reason and rely-
ing on intuition.

I drew pictures of the myth with colored pencil and I imagined
the story over and over until the legend saturated my experience.
What emerged from my studies gave me a deeper knowledge than
my initial confused readings of this myth, in which the wolf as
predator plays a most important role, a crucial part in the development of an awareness that infuses all of Tewa life.

According to Elsie Clews Parsons, who conducted her detailed
studies of Pueblo life in the early to mid-1900s, a white woman
asked a man from Taos Pueblo what Indian religion was.

"Life," he answered, meaning that religion was a means to life,
that it covered life as a whole and that everything of meaning was
alive and vibrantly part of religion. It is in this sense that the myth
of emergence must be understood. The Pueblos form analogies for
everything they see and life is permeated with sympathetic magic
which informs all experience.

A Dawning Consciousness

Far to the north of the present Tewa world located in the Rio
Grande Valley of New Mexico there was a large lake called *Ohange
pokwinge*, or Sandy Place Lake. The "lake of the dead" is an actual
place located in the Sand Dunes National Monument northeast of
present day Alamosa. It is a forbidding site, a place of death.

In 1892, an old rancher who lived nearby in the Sierra Blanca
said the lake was about a hundred yards in diameter, the water
black, the shore surrounded by a perpetual ring of dead cattle that
had mistakenly drunk the waters.

In the primordial time before this world people, animals, and
supernaturals lived beneath this lake in a place called *Sipofene*.
This world was dark, and time and death were unknown. Two of
the supernaturals, Blue Corn Woman (the Summer mother of the
people) and White Corn Woman (the Winter mother), asked one
of the men to go forth and discover a way through which everyone
might be able to leave the lake.

Three times the man pondered this request, and, on each occasion he refused. Finally, after a fourth demand, he agreed, going

first to the north. He found only mist and haze, saying the world was unripe (*ochu*) or green. On successive tries he went to the west, then to the south and east. The two mothers instructed him to go to the above. He came to an open place and here he saw gathered all the *tsiwi*, or predators.

The wolves, mountain lions, coyotes, foxes, vultures, and crows were there waiting for him. He was afraid. On seeing him, the predators rushed him, knocked him down, and fiercely scratched him. Then they told him to get up, that they were his friends. His wounds disappeared and they bestowed on him a bow, arrows, and quiver. They dressed him in buckskin and painted his face black and they tied feathers of carrion-eating birds in his hair.

"You have been accepted," the wolves and other predators told him. "These things we have given you are what you shall use from now on. You are ready to go."

The Tewa emergence story recounts a shamanic initiation journey of an anonymous hero who represents the entire people as he travels from the darkness of unconscious underworld existence where only a pale moonlike dimness resides. Here the people grope about lost in social chaos.

According to Santa Ana tradition, beneath our world there were four womb-worlds, each of a different color, from which humans and animals originally emerged. The Tewa version seems a condensation of four worlds into one. In no way is the underworld personified, but the womb analogy seems a most apt description. Emergence from the dark womb-like underworld can be seen as a kind of journey of human consciousness as it travels from dim semiawareness toward self-knowledge and social conscience in the upper world, where the sun resides and blesses all life.

The corn mothers, associated with winter and summer and agricultural cycles, give birth to the people, but ability to survive comes from this journey of initiation. The teachers who bestow survival knowledge on the hero are Wolf and other archetypal predators who test him by scratching him. Knowledge comes with pain. Perhaps by scratching him, the predators make the hero aware of his own frailty, his own mortality, and his dependence on the prey he must hunt and kill for his own survival.

The knowledge that Wolf and other predators give to the Tewa hero is not knowledge of good and evil as in the Biblical story of Adam and Eve, but knowledge of life and death and the interdependence of animal and human life cycles. It is an ecological knowledge.

The Tewa call the world *'opa* which includes all that is. Their universe is considered as a living being and is worshipped as Universe Man.

The Tewa, when asked why they practice certain rites or why they do certain things, say that such practices came up with them in the emergence. They also say that in the beginning they were one people and that they later divided into Summer and Winter people. This explains how the Tewa divide themselves into moieties or primary subdivisions of the people into two seasonally identified parts. At the same time they recognize the essential wholeness of the people. Thus, they are simultaneously both divided and "at one." Their traditions and this mode of thinking, they say, stems from the time of emergence.

As a part stands for the whole, so hunting practices are reflected in the emergence myth. The hero's initiation by predators allows him to be given magical tools of the hunt. He has proved himself worthy. The relationship Pueblos developed with prey species is based on identification with wolves and predators.

Animals in their mortality resemble humans, but they are more closely associated with gods because they are considered to be ultimately mysterious. They have powers not possessed by men. Predators and the wolf play a special role in Pueblo life because of their spirit power. Due to their power, they bestow hunting knowledge on men. The talismans of this special knowledge—bow and arrow, quiver, dress made of animal skins, black face paint, and feathers of carrion birds—are given to the mythical hero ancestor at the dawn of this world as a sign that he has been provided with the power to hunt. All Tewa hunters from this time forward get their power to hunt from the mythical ancestral hero who led the people from the world of darkness into the world of light and who was given hunting magic and ritual by Wolf and the other great predators at the beginning of this world.

The successful hunter who led tribal communal efforts to kill deer depended on a spirit helper such as the wolf that was possessed of special hunting magic. Predator power, as pictured in the emergence myth, was evoked in tribal hunting practices when the hunt chief relied on the wolf or other prey animals to give him power and knowledge.

Ritual dances to stimulate vision power for the hunt leader

were enacted during communal hunting rites. Sexual continence, proper eating and personal conduct were carefully observed to ensure successful hunting. Through his vision power a hunt chief might locate a herd of antelope or charm them to tameness after beaters had scared them from the chaparral into a corral where they might be shot.

Deer magic was conjured at camp before the hunt so prey would give themselves to the hunters. Rituals, offerings, dances, and display of sacred objects ensured the arrival of Wolf and other hunt gods known as supernaturals. Individual ritual behavior was believed to please prey. For the Zuñi and Keres, supernaturals invoked through proper rites, eating, and behavioral observations were the beast gods of the four directions, including the Wolf of the east. Prey gods were considered guardians of the prey. In other Pueblos a deity called Mother of Game Animals was evoked. Rites, dances, and prayers culminated in the appearance of Wolf and other prey animals.

Soft Words and Spirit Animals

Quarry, when hunted successfully, were believed to return to an animal spirit world where they reported on the treatment they had received. Others of their kind were encouraged in this way to undergo giving their lives to hunters who honored them through ritual and ceremony. Dances and rites involving the Wolf of the east, the Game Mother and other supernaturals were also held to promote the general good will of prey species.

During these rites dancers imitated animals and supernaturals. In singing ceremonial songs involving the Wolf god of the east, other supernaturals, and prey animals, so-called "soft words" were used to avoid offending prey by using their direct names. The wolf, coyote, and crow were often given secret allusive names. To what extent the spirit wolf was an independent being or a helper or intercessor is hard to tell.

The nature of spirit wolf identity was confused by the tendency to preserve social integrity through keeping exact traditions secret or deliberately lying to outsiders. The spirit wolf and other prey animals are sometimes known as "pets" or spirit companions. Anthropologist Elsie Clews Parsons thought spirit animals participated in a collective identity. Perhaps such confusion arises because of the desire not to offend prey by referring directly to the supernaturals or prey.

Among the western Pueblos, killing deer without damaging buckskin held special value. It may be that the value and power obtained by such hunting practices came from imitating the wolf. The wolf was observed to run after his prey, while the mountain lion killed by springing on his quarry. Indian hunters ran down the deer until it fell down exhausted and they smothered it. This practice may account for many of the running games so popular among Indians of the Southwest.

These traditions evoke mindfulness of the total dependence people have on resources provided through earth's bounty. Understanding that the earth freely gives a harvest of corn is an obvious reason for seeing earth as a powerful living being. Game animals give themselves to hunters and require propitiation for their sacrifice. Compassion for animals who are hunted, suffer and die is embodied through elaborate ritual conduct and ceremony so participants are always reminded of a fragile balance preserved between species.

Wolf of Legend, Wolf of Myth

The association between use of prayer sticks and the wolf is strong among Pueblos. Prayer sticks were used almost universally by Pueblos except in Tewan and Tiwan villages. They were buried under trees or shrubs, or in other propitious locations, sunk under water, carried to mountain tops, placed on altars or in kiva or house walls, or they were simply stuck in the ground or "planted."

In one Pueblo story, a boy cuts prayer sticks in honor of Yellow Wolf. He brings them to Wolf's house and presents them to Father and Mother Wolf and their sons and daughters.

"It won't do to have him [Wolf] living near us. We shall have to send him away," says the boy who presents prayer sticks to the Wolf family. Then he commands Father Wolf to go north, Mother Wolf to go west, the Wolf Boys to head south and their sisters to head east. This is said to explain why wolves were found in all the hills in every direction. In this brief story ambiguity about wolves and wolf nature leads the boy to desire to keep Wolf at a distance. Despite reverence for Wolf's power, wolf nature embodies the dangerous and unpredictable that produces antipathy in the human spirit.

Wolf was not viewed as the most powerful Beast God as he was portrayed in Wolf Ritual stories of the Northwest. Anthropologist Ruth Benedict related a Zuñi tale about the Beast Gods who were angry with people because they didn't know how to make prayer sticks or offer prayers.

Wolf, Bear, Mountain Lion, and the other Beast Gods were living in Ice Cave thirty miles east of Zuñi. They held a council there and they were very angry because, if the people did not know the use of prayer sticks, their ceremonial omission would upset vital balances that preserved harmony essential to the well-being of the entire universe. They sent Wolf down to the village each night to kill the women and girls. Wolf's attack represents this imbalance through powerful sexual symbolism. It might be tempting to explore Freudian interpretations of this story, but perhaps more meaningful in the imagery of Wolf's attack is the sense of a world turned upside down because of a seemingly unimportant oversight or lack of knowledge. How dire the consequences of this imbalance are is manifested in the terror of Wolf's attack, which overturns all social order and wreaks havoc and destruction through the murder of women and defenseless girls.

The men were afraid to go out. Local priests bathed a virgin girl and boy and made from the slough of their cuticle a fetish of Ahaiyute, War Patron. Thus empowered, the fetish was sent to protect the village from Wolf's ravages. When the image of Ahaiyute confronted Wolf, he retreated to Ice Cave.

"There is someone down there who has more power than we have," Wolf told the other beasts. "I do not think I can go there any more." Badger rebuked Wolf for his cowardice, choosing to go himself, but he was chased back to Ice Cave by Ahaiyute who fearlessly challenged the Beast Gods. White Bear, when he saw Ahaiyute coming, told the animals to scatter.

This, according to the legend, is the reason why predators were to be found everywhere and why they no longer attacked people. Both these stories also seem to be dealing with the dread that predators have always evoked in humans. Cowardice when presented with danger, or outright panic when confronted with wolves in the wilds, was to be avoided if calm heads were to prevail and survival was to be secured.

As a hunter, the mountain lion was considered to be more powerful. This may be because of the prominent role mountain lions play in the Southwest ecosystem. Wolf's reduced stature in

Pueblo beliefs may also be because as myths and legends circulate, characters may change in importance, while content remains relatively stable.

A writer about Pueblo mythology, Hamilton Tyler recounts that Wolf and Mountain Lion were considered to be companions and that they visited each other constantly and talked about hunting. Wolf was thought to make his kills rather directly and easily. Mountain Lion could not run as swiftly, and did not kill as many as Wolf. He sang a song and sprang on his prey, while Wolf pursued his quarry and never gave up the chase.

In one story, Mountain Lion and Wolf held a contest to see who was a greater hunter. Wolf chased some deer without fatigue, but Mountain Lion hid himself and waited until the deer that Wolf was chasing passed his hiding place. Then he sprang out and quickly dispatched the deer. This happened several times and Wolf was left to gnaw the bones and other leavings of Lion's kills. Tyler suggests Wolf's lesser position in Pueblo mythology was due to wolves that could often be observed cleaning up lion kills.

Wolves are capable of killing mountain lions and will try to eliminate them as competitors, just as they will more effectively eliminate coyotes. Given Tyler's theory, the Pueblos would not have known or observed how wolves play a pre-eminent role in the predator cycle. Provided the emphasis in Pueblo thinking on close sense observation of all natural phenomena, obvious predator interaction like the relationship between wolves and lions probably could not have escaped their notice.

Just as the story of Ha-Sass in the previous chapter credited Wolf with superior guile, considered a mark of wisdom, in this story Mountain Lion outsmarts Wolf and shows the same trait. Guile as a component of survival wisdom seems to be the lesson to be learned from this tale. Other attributes such as strength, endurance, and concentration perhaps were less important than such cleverness. In a version of the White Bison myth, Zuñi legend credits Wolf for being a steadfast guardian of the young hero who gives Wolf an eagle feather that he covets. As a reward, Wolf guards the boy all night, wakes him, and taking his leave, trots off into the east from where he has come.

Tyler compares the wolf with coyote and fox, an association that probably would not enter the minds of Pueblos, or at least might not interest them. Pueblo nomenclature recognizes differences, not relationships. Pueblos are not given to the habit of classifying animals by species, order, and family except in the most obvious of cases. Usually an animal is considered a distinct creature not related to any others.

Power Wolf and Medicine Societies

Much of what can be surmised about Southwest Pueblo wolf beliefs relies on information gathered through the early part of this century. With the increase of non-Indian populations, the larger game animals such as the deer, elk, mountain sheep, and antelope either were greatly diminished or disappeared from the wilderness entirely. The wolf as an important predator was also being rapidly depleted.

As the population of prey species diminished, so did the importance of hunt societies and traditions. By the late 1930s, the hunt society had become virtually extinct in Keresan and Tewan towns. What is known of Wolf must be told from the faintest outlines sketched in the anthropological accounts of Elsie Clews Parson, Ruth Benedict, and other observers.

These hunting traditions, which were once central to lifestyles developed by Pueblo and other Southwest Indians, show how predator magic typified by the wolf was vitally important to their beliefs. The Tewa emergence myth taught how predators gave the people their hunt magic. The wolf and other predators were honored for their knowledge, but the prey animals themselves were also honored. Everyone, through myth and rite, was led to constantly be reminded of the dependence people had on the game animals who gave themselves in death that the people might live. Wolf and other prey animals were also associated with war, especially in the west and at Jemez.

Wolf, as a power animal, also played an important role in Pueblo medicine, as did the other prey beasts. Disease was cured through an agent, or an animal such as Wolf, having power for good or ill over disease. Shamans having vision power belonged to societies devoted to curing. Priests and temporary healers also served to cure patients. Disease in Pueblo cultures of the Southwest, however, was defined differently than in Western medicine tradition.

Maladies were brought about through intrusion of objects into the sufferer's body, loss of soul, spirit possession, breaking taboos, or

sorcery. These causes were assigned to all disease. Shaman medicine societies each had their power animals with control over disease and their own distinctive songs and rites.

The spirit wolf and other prey animals, as patrons of medicine
societies, had quite independent identities. The bear was considered
the most powerful sponsor, but wolf and the other prey animals also
had healing powers. All beast gods had their home in a mythical
place called *Shipap* in (Zuñi *Shipapolima*) in the East despite the association each beast god had with a primary direction and color.

During Zuñi medicine society initiations, predators were imitated, and, reminiscent of Tewa emergence, clawed and bit the initiate like wolves. Eastern Pueblo medicine societies involved re-
birth rituals. Animal images were used by the Tewa in such rites.

Breach of hunting rituals or disrespect for remains of prey was
thought to cause disease. At least two animal societies in Zuñi
were thought to have the power to create disease. This idea appears not to have been as well developed in other pueblos.

Pueblo ideas about disease were closely tied to traditions about
witchcraft, which often involved the wolf. Doctors possessing animal powers could transform themselves into animals. Witches,
having the same power, could do likewise. Doctors could over-
power witches or sorcerers through the same means. Essentially
witches, like doctors, were thought to know all, but they used
power improperly for personal gain.

Elsie Clews Parsons defines *nagualism* as the transformation
into wolves or other animals and receiving power from animals.
Parson's definition is more narrowly focused than that found in
other cultural traditions of the Southwest and Mexico, in which
the individual human becomes identified with a particular spirit or
animal counterpart. Nagualism is practiced either by individuals or
collectively through societies. Even witches sometimes belonged to
societies but most often operated alone.

Of Witches and Wolves

Nagualism and the practice of witchcraft among the Pueblos
was shot through with Spanish influence. A witch was considered
to possess all the traits people thought to be antisocial. Anyone
who was cantankerous, assertive, or quarrelsome could be subjected
to accusations of witchcraft. Insomniacs who wandered at night

were also under suspicion. In accusations of sorcery lie the dark side of Pueblo tendencies to sacrifice individualism for the social welfare of the entire group.

Witch baiting and trials were conducted by Pueblo alcaldes and war captains. Where proximity to Hispanic villages was common in New Mexico, witch lore was more fully developed. European ideas associating witches and wolves influenced Pueblo beliefs, making it difficult to distinguish Hispanic ideas from Pueblo concepts. Accusations of witchcraft and nagualism were used by both Spaniards and Pueblos for social control. Popé, instigator of the Pueblo Rebellion of 1680, was accused of witchcraft. After his release, following pressure from Tewa warriors he began his rebellion against the Spanish.

The growth of witchcraft and absorption of Spanish concepts began the negative association between wolves and witches. Werewolves and witches were minions of Satan in the European mind. Pueblo terms not originally associated with witchcraft became so. For instance, the Hopi runner called Wolf Boy became known as Witch Boy in the east pueblos.

Intertown antagonism or suspicion between Pueblos often took the form of imputing witchcraft. In the early part of this century, Taos Pueblo secretly referred to Tewa as Wolf Dung and the Tewa in turn called them Taos Rats.

As late as 1906, Laguna war captains executed a woman named Tsotsi as a witch after a wolf skin with tie strings and paws made into moccasins was found nailed to her wall. She had been known as particularly quarrelsome and as a gossip and braggart. She and her husband, like many another accused of witchcraft, always seemed to have plenty though they were known to be poor. In the 1920s during Parsons's extensive study of Pueblo culture she developed contact with a Pueblo individualist accused and subsequently persecuted as a witch.

Transformation into wolves was thought to be effected by either wearing a wolf pelt or by passing through a hoop or ring and in this way the witch was said to turn over and assume wolf form. A witch who practiced nagualism could be identified because the wolf's snout could be seen pressing against the witch's forehead.

While belief in witches certainly existed before the arrival of the Spanish, their appearance marked the infusion of European ideas about the wolf which spilled over into Pueblo beliefs about nagualism and the negative association between witches and wolves. Witches were a manifestation of social imbalance and personal misuse of power. They were not seen as extensions of evil. The association of witches and satanic forces is a European idea, an idea that has marked the relationship with the wolf ever since that belief was brought to this continent.

In Pueblo culture the wolf was a spirit animal who bestowed his power on hunters or those who sought his aid in curing diseases. The Great God of the East, the wolf stood at the door of the world when time began and taught humankind hunting secrets and served as guardian of deer, antelope, and other prey upon whom life depended. Close to nature, indeed, embedded in the natural world, the Pueblos saw Wolf as a great teacher, sometimes frightening, but always to be honored and respected.

CHAPTER FOUR

Wolf Way, Skinwalkers, and Shape Changers

He goes out hunting
Big Wolf am I
With Black bow he goes out hunting
With tail feathered arrow he goes out hunting
The big male game through its shoulder that I may shoot
Its death it obeys me
—W.W. Hill
Navajo Stalking Way Song

During late fall before the first full moon in December, Navajo Wolf Way was planned. The northwest New Mexico sky shone brilliant blue. The air was crisp and chill. In preparation for mating season the deer were fat and sleek. Each day those volunteers who had chosen to participate in ritual hunting according to Wolf's Way untied knots made in a string to mark the time before departure day arrived.

During preparation, each hunter cleaned and inspected his rifle, made new moccasins with thick soles, and fashioned gray leggings, shirt, and pants. To wear red or black was forbidden. Each avoided any mention of hunting, as words of killing and death could hurt women, children, and stock animals whose bones were soft. Only corn meal and corn bread could be taken so the Keeper of Game would know the hunters were in need of meat and they would be allowed to kill deer.

Finally the appointed day arrived. River stones were buried in a hot fire which burned all day long. Three sticks with forked ends were made into a tripod. Two straight sticks were joined in the east at the apex to form a door over which blankets were hung. Sticks and boughs were placed over the framework covered with cedar bark and mud until a sweat lodge had been prepared to mark the beginning of Wolf Way. As afternoon shadows quickly lengthened, four men entered the lodge.

Songs to invoke the assistance of Big Trotter or wolf, Black

God or crow, Talking God, and other hunting deities and animal companions were sung as rocks glowing red hot were brought in the lodge. Round after round was sung as steam-laden air seared the men's lungs and boiled their skins. Those who were faint of heart kept their faces close to earth to breathe, but those who were intent on accruing hunting power only sang with more ferocity.

As the ceremony progressed, a change came over those whose voices reverberated in the close confines of the lodge. A strange reversal was taking place among these hunters, whose eyes gleamed in the dim preternatural light of the lodge. They were no longer men, these hunters, and their songs were no longer just songs, but wolf howls rising, wavering and dying away. The flap door of the lodge was thrown aside and these hunters loped into the carmine glow of gathering dusk.

For the next two to fifteen days they were transformed, eating as wolves eat, running as wolves run, thinking and feeling as wolves think and feel. In this way the power of wolves entered them so that they ran with tremendous speed without faltering even at night. They slept on their sides with their knees flexed so their campfire would not weaken them by entering the soles of their feet and they dreamed of killing or the chase, relating their visions to one another before they sang morning hunting songs, blessed their weapons, and sought the deer.

Two of the hunters hid, crouching on their haunches at a canyon outlet. There they waited in ambush as their companions chased the lead deer. As the deer passed, each hunter howled like a wolf. Eyes wide and glazed with fright, the deer stumbled and turned. One of the wolf hunters who lurked in ambush loaded his bow. He aimed and shot an arrow true to its mark. The deer fell, exhausted and in panic, rose briefly and fell again for the final time. Now the hunt could begin.

The signs were good. Many deer would fall prey during the Wolf Way that year.

Finally, after all the rituals were observed and the hunt was over, they returned as wolves to the sweat lodge and once again a transformation occurred. Through ritual and ceremony they sloughed off the predator skins of wolves. They donned their own human skins and everything to do with hunting was put out of mind. They became men once more. Again they could sing Blessingway songs that are the backbone of Navajo ritual and affirm their bonds with a life of peace and human fulfillment. Once more they walked in beauty . . .

Wolf Way

For those of us who have always lived in the modern urban world, such Wolf Way beliefs may seem arcane and incomprehensible. That people who are little different from us, equipped with the same human bodies and brains, can believe in such a radically different universe is a source of wonder. Who were these hunters who believed they could transform themselves into wolves and what did such an act of transformation mean?

The answer to this question lies in the history and development of the Navajo. Three thousand years ago ancestors of present-day Navajos crossed the Bering Strait and migrated to North America. Some linguists think their language was descended from a family of Asian tongues called Sino-Tibetan, which evolved into the Native American Athapascan languages.

The Northwest coastal tribe of the Tlingit speak a dialect of Athapascan. Other tribes spread along the Northwest and northern California coasts also speak Athapascan dialects. These tribes were familiar with wolf ways and often incorporated wolf into their ritual life. Prevalence of Athapascan language groups is taken as evidence for early separation and wandering by these related peoples.

These immigrant nomad Navajo ancestors had observed wolves during their wanderings. As roaming hunter-warriors they saw the kinship between their lifestyles and wolf ways. In a manner of speaking, the early Navajo followed the ways of wolfmen.

Sometime around 1000 A.D., when the Anasazi pueblos in Chaco Canyon were still being constructed, the Dineh, or People, as they call themselves, came to settle in the area the Navajo consider their ancestral homeland, Dinehtah. Bounded to the north by the La Plata Peaks in Colorado, to the south by Mount Taylor and the Zuñi Mountains, to the east by Pelado Peak near Jemez, New Mexico, and to the west by the San Francisco Peaks near Flagstaff, Arizona, this land of flat alluvial valleys, piñon and juniper groves, mountains and mesas became home to these fierce wanderers.

While by the early nineteenth century the Pueblos and Spanish traded with the Navajos, the latter conducted predatory raids on their neighbors, stealing sheep and other livestock as well as taking women and children as slaves who were quickly absorbed into Navajo tribal life.

The Navajo were careful not to destroy or burn out those they raided, wishing to allow their victims an opportunity to refurbish their goods so they might be attacked again. Even if raids were conducted against enemies for revenge, the aim was not to murder and decimate a foe. The object of raiding was to show predator prowess and bravery in the face of danger. Using wolf stealth and guile was considered a mark of honor.

The Dineh established their lifestyle as sheepherders, weavers, and warriors par excellence, making them hated and feared by the village-oriented agricultural Pueblos. The Hopi called them *Tasuvah*, head pounders, because they smashed the skulls of their enemies with stone axes.

The Navajo, while they chose to raid many pueblos also absorbed many Pueblo traditions and beliefs. Relations among the Spanish settlers, Pueblos, and Navajos was a complex dance of attraction in the form of trade and repulsion in the form of raiding and warfare.

Wolf Power and Naatl'éétsoh

A life of raiding and warrior and hunter prowess meant wolf ways were consciously employed during ritual hunts like the one described at the beginning of this chapter. Hunting rites reflected Navajo beliefs in a primordial time before men and animals had assumed their present forms and had "put on their own skins."

Religious historian Karl Luckert has cited this hunter ideology as evidence of belief in what he calls prehuman flux. Animals, humans, even trees, rocks, lakes and rivers, and stars were all considered people in the mythical time before this world began. All beings spoke the same language.

Examples of a period before the beginning of time when beings shared this fluid identity can be cited from many cultures in many locations throughout the world. The Pueblo emergence myth shows evidence of such a belief. The Tlingit as well as the Navajo also believe in a pre-emergence world when men, animals, and all beings shared a fluid identity and kinship with one another.

This sense of kinship is the origin of many Native American stories about marriages between animals and humans. The act of hunting was therefore fraught with peril and guilt because hunters pursued, killed, and ate the bodies of their kin. Death ways and hunting were naturally opposed to life ways and birthing. The emergence myth as a collective birth metaphor fixed human and animal identities in their current forms.

Perhaps due to the significance of hunting among Navajos, a separate myth recounted the hiding of game animals from other primordial hunters by Black God or Crow. During a mythical sweat lodge, Black God, the keeper of game, removes his crow skin and enters the lodge where he is found out by Wolf and the other predators and power hunters. They can see him as the thief of game because they are all without their skins and so stripped of their separate identities. The primordial predators were thus able to free the game animals through trickster deceit.

When a Wolf Way hunt began, going into a sweat lodge allowed post-emergence humans who followed human life ways to magically reenter the pre-emergence world of fluid identity and assume the demeanor of wolves.

All predators were called *naatl'éétsoh*, or wolves, by the Navajo. Sweat baths were not used for purification, as is popularly assumed, but were an effective means for allowing people to break the bonds of daily time and enter the world of mythic pre-emergence time, taking on predator power embodied by the archetypal hunting companion animal, the wolf.

Hunters during the Wolf Way did not just imitate wolves, but actually assumed wolf identity. Hunting success was assured by stalking like a wolf, giving chase like a wolf, and participating as fully as possible in wolf ways. The only appropriate means of communicating with other hunters during this magically altered period of the hunt was through howling in the language of wolves.

By assuming wolf identity and becoming predators, hunters could absolve themselves of the burden of killing their deer kin. Through following elaborate behavioral proscriptions during the hunt and then participating in a sweat at hunt's end, they once again assumed their identity as men. Fluid identity established in myth allowed hunters to take on wolf ways and to resolve the dilemma of either going hungry or facing the guilt of being forced to kill their kin to survive.

The wolf was considered to have some of the attributes of a god. He was a powerful intermediary. For the Navajo, gods could easily assume animal shape and did so often as *naatl'éétsoh* or wolf beings. The distinction between gods and power predators is, therefore, blurred. The Judeo-Christian hierarchy of being descends in importance from God to humans and then to animals. Our habit of seeking to categorize levels and kinds of being doesn't work in considering Navajo ideas about fluid identity.

Big Trotter and Little Trotter

Anthropologist W.W. Hill, whose Wolf Way accounts researched in 1933 and 1934 form a basis for this chapter's inception, briefly mentions nonritual wolf hunting. Wolves were slain only when a shaman wanted to use the tail sinew, dewclaws, bladder, or gall for medicine. They were also killed when caught preying on sheep.

My interest in studying Navajo relationships to wolves is due to the fact that the Dineh are avid shepherds. There are so many European folktale associations between sheep and wolves that it seems quite reasonable to assume the Navajo would often recount through similar means their reaction to sheep predation by wolves. The little boy who cried wolf, the wolf in sheep's clothing, and other folk stories have recorded this relationship between voracious wolves and victim sheep.

Such occurrences must have been a rarity, however. Navajos spent much of their time watching over their flocks. The presence of shepherds would have been a powerful deterrent for wolves, who naturally desire to avoid confrontation with people. The wolf was known as *ma'iitsoh*, or big trotter. The Navajo called the coyote *ma'ii*, that is, slim-trotter.

Elaborate precautions were observed by Navajos when killing coyotes that were caught preying on sheep. Nonviolent methods were employed and coyote's tracks were carefully sprinkled with corn pollen, symbol for long life and health. Similar methods must have been in use when wolves were killed, but these instances are rarely recorded. Navajos avoided such kills because coyote's power might be turned against them. Coyote and wolf predations on livestock placed both animals in direct competition with people.

The wolf effectively vanished from the southwestern ecosystem in the 1920s and 1930s. He remained a powerful animal, however, evoked by werewolf traditions. The coyote is still present for Navajos as a biological creature *and* as a powerful sponsor of werewolf transformations.

Wolves will kill coyotes, effectively controlling the coyote population in areas occupied by both species. Elimination of wolves meant that coyotes flourished. By the 1960s, anthropologist and journalist James Downs recorded that coyotes, despite their power, were routinely killed because they were considered a serious threat to people and livestock.

Such routine killings were no doubt made necessary since the wolf, the coyote's natural enemy, had been decimated by then. Without such an important environmental foe as wolf, coyote predation must have become much more prevalent. While the mythology of game animals and predators still left its traces on the Navajo mind, when Downs observed the Dineh, ritualized hunting had all but disappeared. Downs observed that hunting had become necessary in terms of animal husbandry and also was now considered a source of "fun," an idea that most certainly would seem bizarre or even repugnant to the followers of Wolf Way.

Familiar with the larger and more impressive wolf from their historic wanderings, the Navajo associated wolf and coyote. Both were endowed with predator power. But coyote they viewed as a defamed trickster upon whom they heaped scorn because he was thought to be a bungler and a rogue, his tricks constantly backfiring on him. Coyote attempted to turn the world upside down. Wolf, as chief embodiment of hunter power, was viewed with great respect.

Navajos classified living things by their ability to move. Swift movement was a sign of spirit and life power and indicated an animal's importance. Living things were divided into things that move and so-called unusual animals that were alive only during summer.

Of the things that move, the Navajo further categorized these animals by their means of locomotion. There were the human two-leggeds. Then there were those that trotted on four legs. Among the four-leggeds were the "dangerous animals."

Domestic animals were regarded not as sentient beings but as property. Despite their usefulness, horses were considered possessions that were the tally of a family's wealth. Sheep, because they furnished wool and meat, were regarded more highly than horses, and dogs were treated with disdain. Game animals, as already discussed, were accorded great reverence and respect. Wolf and coyote, as predators invested with mythical significance, were both considered dangerous and powerful animals.

The faster a creature was in getting from place to place, the more power and mystery it held. Wolf and coyote moved with great swiftness in addition to their mythical predator attributes. Coyote and wolf are also associated in the Navajo mind with witchcraft. Coyote, the arch trickster, is the patron of witchcraft.

When Wolves and Men Merge

One of the most intriguing ideas Navajos hold about humans and wolves involves a witch's ability to transform himself into a wolf. Navajo beliefs about werewolves called "skinwalkers" combine many of the concepts introduced here. If boundaries between human ways and wolf ways are permeable, then power to assume animal form can be exploited for personal gain as well as for communal welfare through hunting practices.

At first glance, the Navajo skinwalker looks very much like his European werewolf counterpart. In wolf form, he roves at night wreaking havoc and destruction on his enemies. He participates in bizarre rites appearing much the same as a witch's coven, but superficial likenesses are deceiving in the case of the skinwalker. The philosophical underpinnings of skinwalking express a whole different constellation of beliefs from the European Christian ideas about werewolves as minions of satanic evil. The Navajo skinwalker is a totally indigenous creation, not an expression of satanic evil.

The skinwalker distorts the Navajo world order and turns everything upside down. For the Navajo, all beings have inner and outer forms. Power beings are the inner forms that animate individual expressions of natural phenomena. For example, the Predator Wolf or the Power Wolf finds expression through each individual wolf animal. In an encounter with a wolf, a person must deal with inner power which is given form through the particular animal.

This power is certainly different from the notion of an individual soul, in the sense that Great Being Wolf gives "wolfness" to all animals sharing attributes of wolfhood. Great Wolf is the source of a particular wolf's power, and this mystical bond is what makes the individual animal dangerous. Wolves, like coyotes and bears, were called *naaldlooshii báhádzidii,* that is, "dangerous animals."

✪ ✪ ✪

A Most Dangerous Animal

The power of a wolf is linked back to the pre-emergence world when animals, supernaturals, and humans communicated and shared magical powers. When hunters transform themselves into wolves in the sweat lodge, boundaries between wolves and humans evaporate. When wolves are confronted as individual animals people are subject to all the powers inherent in Great Wolf.

When a person dons a wolf's skin, his inner form takes on the outer form of Wolf and a dynamic transformation occurs, a frightening and powerful mixture of human, animal, and god.

The Navajo creator, Changing Woman, made the different tribes when she rubbed skin from various parts of her body. In the last chapter we saw how an image of Ahaiyute, Patron of War, was created from a virgin's cuticle to defend the village of Zuñi against Wolf's ravages. Whether originally a Pueblo belief or originating with the Dineh, the idea of skin as a power substance is a typical Navajo idea. Skin is not only a creative and protective substance, but may be used for ill as well.

Navajo witches, finding a bit of dried skin, may use this against a victim to cause sickness or death. Coyote, in Navajo legends, had the noisome habit of throwing his skin at people to make them ill. Navajo witches engaged in the most powerful taboos—incest, necrophilia, and cannibalism—while in the skins of wolves.

Social harmony, order, stability, and balance are always reaffirmed through Navajo ritual and myth and are among the highest values of Navajo life. The pre-emergence existence typified by mixed or uncertain categories of being, social chaos, or darkness, such as in Pueblo emergence stories, may have influenced Navajo beliefs about witchery as an expression of confusion and chaos.

Witchery Way

In the post-emergence world, negative intentions and acts summon disharmony. By putting on wolf skin and becoming a *yenaldlooshi*, the skinwalker invokes the negation of order. Yenaldlooshi means "he who trots along here and there on all fours with it."

According to traditional Navajo belief, the skinwalker dressed in wolf hide climbs on top of a Navajo hogan or house at night and drops pollen made from the ground bones of dead children down the smoke hole. Contact with this powder brings the sleeper illness, bad fortune, and even death. Dirt falling into a hogan from the smoke hole, loud dog barking, or unusual noises are taken as signs that a Navajo wolf has been lurking. If the Navajo wolf is tracked and caught, he will beg for mercy and offer to bribe his captor.

Shooting a wolfman, so informants say, will result in the discovery of a Navajo who has been wounded in the same place as the wolf and at the same time.

The ways of witchcraft and wolf walking can be learned just as a medicine way may be learned. These deliberate practices are aimed at specifically chosen victims. Usually a relative teaches witchery ways to a willing student.

Yenaldlooshi gather in caves at night where they initiate new members and plot against their victims, according to tradition. They sit in a circle surrounded by mounds or baskets full of corpse flesh. Naked except for masks and beads, they create inverse rituals and sing songs backwards, or create sand paintings on which they spit or urinate. While ritual was created to make cosmos from chaos, Witch Way ritual is made to create chaos of cosmos. Widespread belief in skinwalking may also have played a part in the decline of Wolf Way as a ritual hunting practice. Defamation of the wolf because of the harmful association between wolves and witchery possibly meant that Wolf Way hunting practices fell into disrepute.

A World Upside Down

Anyone who uses personal power to turn the Navajo social world upside down is in danger of being considered a wolfman. The overly rich, the politically powerful, ceremonial singers, and the aged all may be suspected of witchcraft.

In the confines of Navajo society, people who live at a distance and are not well known are often accused of being yenaldlooshi. Belief in human wolves acts only partly as a social prohibition because witchcraft is viewed as a natural and even necessary part of life. Navajos who have been witched by a wolfman try to restore balance through enacting proper rituals, not through punishing the antisocial or uncooperative individual. Navajos prize individuality. Coercion is generally considered inappropriate and highly repugnant.

The yenaldlooshi, then, acts out all of the proscribed behaviors most feared and hated by Navajos. Ignoring all social rules, the skinwalker moves between the human and animal worlds with a swiftness that betrays his enormous yet ambiguous power.

Through incest, bestiality, and sexual excess the Navajo wolf turns sexual taboos on their ear. Running through graveyards at night dressed in wolfskins, the yenaldlooshi is said to have intercourse with dead bodies, invoking the great inverse power of this symbolic act.

Navajos loathe having anything to do with the dead because once a person has died the spirit remains with the physical body and must be avoided at all cost. The Navajo wolf seeks the most intimate contact possible with the dead, destroying the boundaries of social propriety and occupying the netherworld between animal and human existence. Breaking taboos against cannibalism, the human wolf smashes the greatest Navajo transgression of all and eats the flesh of the dead, thus altering or even destroying the bounds between life and death.

Wolf, Sacred and Profane

The Navajo conceptual world presents a complex picture of human experience. Everyday life is ordered and predictable, but the seeds of chaos have been planted in this world, brought forth from pre-emergence existence. The word chaos is Greek in origin and refers to the disorder of formless matter, confusion, and disarray said to have existed before the ordered universe.

The modern world hardly knows or intuits what both Greeks, Navajos, and other tribal peoples so clearly express in their mythology. For the Dineh the chaotic pre-emergence time before time is not just an idea, but a working principal on which all of life is based. Humans, through sweat-lodge ritual, can transcend everyday time and return to the pre-emergence world when all beings shared a common identity and a common language. They do so through Wolf's agency, through predator power, in order to overcome guilt and remorse they face because to live they must hunt their animal kin who give up their own lives.

This sacrificial relationship is permeated by beauty, compassion, and tragedy. These beliefs keep people ever mindful that their lives continue at the expense of animals who give their bodies that humans may exist. These animals are not "other," but are considered kin. No bond is as strong to the Navajo as kinship and no taboo is as strong as the ban against cannibalism. To subsist on the flesh of those to whom you are related and to do so through necessity are horrifying ideas. Prey have a terrible power that must be propitiated for hunting to be successful.

In this manner, Wolf serves as cosmic redeemer, absolving hunters of the horror of killing their relatives by facilitating sweat-lodge transformation of everyday men into wolf hunters. Magically, Wolf allows them to return to the pre-emergence condition, to the time before time. Following the mystical, shamanic, and communal journey of the hunt, men can take off their wolf skins and return to human life-ways through sweat-lodge ritual transformation.

The concept that identity and time are fluid and that all beings have outer forms that express inner power means the world is fraught with mystery and danger. Boundaries between humans and animals are permeable. Internal power for good or ill easily conveys to other beings. Forms shift and change. Time is but a transparent membrane that can be penetrated and crossed through sacred or profane ritual to invoke chaos.

The defamed trickster exemplified by Coyote is the patron of witchcraft. Coyote turns everything inside out and backwards. He breaks all the rules of sexual and ritual conduct, doing exactly the opposite of what is socially appropriate. Little Trotter or Coyote in the Navajo mind is associated with Big Trotter. While some witches transform themselves into coyotes or other animals, almost invariably the term used to describe a witch is "man wolf" or "Navajo wolf." This association may be due to Wolf as chief power predator who can facilitate the return to prehuman fluid identity.

While Wolf Way is conducted for the good of the entire people, profane use of Wolf power for an individual's personal gain under the auspices of defamed trickster Coyote invokes the power of Witchery Way. In these Navajo beliefs, sacred and profane are balanced in a way those of us from Judeo-Christian backgrounds may find difficult to understand.

In Christian Biblical traditions, when Satan is expunged from heaven and cast into hell by God, the forces of light and darkness and good and evil are set to war with one another. At the end of time the forces of light vanquish the forces of evil and darkness.

No such opposition exists in the Navajo mind. Order and disorder are two sides of the same coin. Both express the way things are. The animal, human, and sacred worlds can all be called on to bestow their power, whether for the good of all beings through life-way ritual and song or for personal gain through profane ritual and song.

By throwing together this dangerous mix of animal, human, and god, the yenaldlooshi, he who walks on all fours in the wolf's skin, turns the Navajo world inside out, calling on the power of reversal and chaos to do his bidding. It is a spirit that rouses dread in the Navajo's deepest being. The Dineh do not try to make war against these chaotic forces or vanquish evil by punishing the evildoer, even though witchcraft is considered a powerful and perverse transgression against social order. Through ritual, song, and ceremony the Navajo try to reestablish the balance and harmony set awry by witchcraft.

Recognition of both sacred and profane wolf nature by the Dineh suggests that a profound psychological and spiritual insight into our own human predator past has been incorporated into the Navajo tradition to describe and redeem human experience.

The shadow of a mysterious predator has fallen across the path we humans have so carefully carved from our experience to create order and light from darkness. Through the modern industrial world's denial of our own amorphous and ambiguous predator past, we have attempted to shove this shadow wolf back into the darkness and wilderness of our own spirit. Denied, the wolf of destruction has risen from within us, not disguised in wolfskin, but in human form. Driving creature after creature into extinction, ravaging forest, desert, plain, mountain, and air, Manwolf stalks the earth.

CHAPTER FIVE

Lobo Misterioso

We stand on a peak of consciousness,
believing in a childish way that the path
leads upward to yet higher peaks
beyond. That is the chimerical rainbow
bridge. In order to reach the next peak
we must first go down into the land
where the paths begin to divide.
—C.G. Jung
Psychology and Alchemy

My story begins in southern Europe during the 1500s. Colonists were leaving Spain and arriving in what was to become New Mexico. They brought with them a strange treasury of beliefs about wolves that reflected what was happening in their homeland and throughout Europe at this time.

The late sixteenth century marked the end of the Middle Ages and the beginning of the Renaissance. The old mythologies that had dominated the Christian medieval period were starting to crumble. The seeds of what was to become the Age of Reason were being planted in the European mind.

In 1543, Copernicus published his paper on the heliocentric universe and in 1616 Galileo was condemned as a heretic for daring to challenge the common supposition that earth was center of the cosmos. As elsewhere in Europe, the Inquisition in Spain was at its height. Religious nonconformists were persecuted with crazed persistence. Author Marc Simmons, in the only book written about New Mexico witchcraft, *Witchcraft in the Southwest*, writes that the persecution of witches differed to some degree in Spain when compared to France, Germany, Scotland, and England, where butchering witches proceeded at a fevered pitch.

In the Province of Navarre in the early 1500s, inquisitors decided during an outbreak of witch fever that most confessions were the product of delusions suffered by local peasants. Civil authorities ignored the call for leniency and conducted mass executions anyway. During 1538, inquisitors were sent to the area to moderate the popular belief that witches destroyed crops.

Early in the 1600s, five witches were put to death in Navarre. Other forms of heresy that went under the label of Judaizing, such as studying Kabbalah, were less tolerated. In 1492, Ferdinand and Isabella expelled Jews from Spain. In 1569, the Office of the Inquisition was established in Mexico to oversee the northern territories and to prosecute cases involving commission of heresy. The Inquisition often accused suspected heretics of using demonic sorcery to change into wolves.

These intrepid settlers who came to the Southwest believed people actually had power to transform themselves into wolves and that wolves possessed a terrifying power in themselves. These beliefs were part of a whole complex of ideas that expressed fundamental tensions occurring in the European psyche.

For us, wild wolves and werewolves are the stuff of Grade B horror movies, but for the medieval Spanish conquistadores, werewolves and dark magic were as real as space rockets and atom bombs are to us. Many Spaniards either had personally experienced incidents involving wolves and werewolves, or at least knew wolf and witch lore. The three hundred year Inquisition, intent on rooting out any sign of heresy, concentrated its efforts on trying those accused of witchcraft and sorcery. Many stood trial as accused werewolves.

The Wolf Substrate

In 1541, a peasant near Padua, Italy, became a *lupo manero* (werewolf). He said he had grown wolf's hair, but "turned inside under the skin." At the beginning of the sixteenth century, English dramatist John Webster's mad Duke in *Duchess of Malfy* thought himself to be a wolf. Only a wolf's "skin was hairy on the outside, his on the inside."

French sheepherder Pierre Bourgot bargained with a strange horseman who promised him money and protection for his flocks through the help of his master. Bourgot met with others he did not recognize. Together they danced in a wood near Chastel Charnon and swore allegiance to Satan. Each held a green taper lit with blue flame. They kissed the stranger's black hand that was as cold as a corpse. After Bourgot had been rubbed with salve, he believed he had been transformed into a wolf. At first horrified by his paws and fur, he then discovered he could travel like the wind. Bourgot craved human flesh. He told his judges, appointed by the Holy Office of the Inquisition, how he murdered four children and an old woman.

Accused werewolves and witches, hung on the rack to consider the gravity of their heresy, soon confessed to any act, no matter how bizarre. Some were actual witchcraft practitioners, others were probably mad and, no doubt, yet others were completely innocent victims.

Fear of wolves was to some extent justified. In southern Europe during the 1500s, rabid wolves roamed the hills and mountains and probably accounted for many attacks attributed to werewolves. People who had rabies were also most surely accused of being werewolves. They were said to suffer from terrible thirst, a symptom of lupine rabies.

Terror of wolves and of wolfmen, associated in the medieval mind with Satan, gave darkness, fear, and evil a tangible form. Wolf madness burst out all over Europe. Trials for heresy, witchcraft, and lycanthropy amassed tomes of werewolf evidence and confessions extracted through the usual Inquisition methods—agonizing torture.

Haunting Questions

Lycanthropic incidents surged during the sixteenth century. As I researched this chapter, I began to ask myself questions that haunted me. Why should fear of wolves and supposed transformation of humans into wolves provoke the slaughter of thousands of people in the name of the Holy Inquisition? Why should wolf terror approach epidemic proportions during this period?

Historians, with rare exception, have simply dismissed the belief in witchcraft, lycanthropy, and like notions as ludicrous superstitions not worth the attention of serious scholars. Yet, wolfmen and witches were very real to the sixteenth century. Physiologically, emotionally, and mentally we are not much different from our sixteenth century ancestors, but their responses seem bizarre and foreign to our own perceptions. What accounts for such dissimilar experiences of the world?

Equating objectivity with truth is typical of our time, though we hardly recognize this predilection for the rational and scientific as a characteristic of our age.

For the purposes of this book, I take fear of wolves and the belief people can become wolves as psychological truths that had tremendous influence over people's lives. Dread of the wolf and the idea that people can transform into this fearsome creature are inextricably linked in the human psyche. Only when we take other people and their perceptions seriously and only when we try to understand exactly what motivates others to behave as they do can we overcome our prejudices.

Lycanthropy and lycanphobia (fear of wolves) express deep-rooted beliefs stretching back to the Stone Age and even further, back to the origin of human consciousness.

In the first two incidents I recounted at the beginning of this chapter, I mentioned that those who became wolves believed that the hair they grew was turned inside under the skin. This idea, so typical of late medieval werewolf accounts, suggests that whatever else this transformation was, it was most certainly at root a psychological process, an internalization of emotions and thoughts expressed as a physical awareness.

The hair werewolves grew was turned under the skin and so was invisible. This hair, which could not be seen by others, was experienced as a physical sensation of extreme discomfort. The process of becoming a wolf in southern Europe during the Middle Ages surely must have involved imagination and magical visualization and also involved acute physical sensation.

Assuming many people did so willingly, to become a wolf must have meant some very essential needs that people were denied during this time were being met through this transformation. To risk systematic humiliation, torture, and death, these needs must have been strong indeed.

Werewolves, Witches, and Lycanphobia

The story of lycanthropy in Europe during the late medieval period is, I think, an account of mass denial—rejection of human animality and the assigning of animal traits to others, the subsequent torture and brutalization of those assigned Otherness in the name of righteousness and reason (God's law).

European beliefs of this time about wolves and wolfmen mirrored a fundamental change in the way people experienced reality. This revolution in consciousness meant rational thinking was emerging as the chief means of interpreting and determining reality.

When French mathematician and philosopher René Descartes

(1596–1650) wrote, "I think therefore I am," he perfectly expressed the rising awareness that rational thinking is reality. What is real is what can be thought reasonably, logically, and scientifically. Anything else that is "unthinkable" gets thrown away and denied. The irrational aspect of experience becomes unreal. This reliance on the authority of reason was entirely new in human experience.

One of the primary archetypes of the irrational, animal side of human nature was the wolf. So, what I am really talking about regarding the wolf in the Middle Ages is wildness and animality, and the European way of dealing with Otherness, wildness, and animality during the waning medieval period.

In discussing lycanthropy in native Southwest cultures, I've already shown how the Navajo wolfman represents imbalance. Sorcery, even dark magic, has a place in the Navajo universe because without darkness there can't be light. In seeking to right the imbalance caused by acts of wolfmen and sorcerers, the medicine man or singer performs rituals to restore harmony. The Navajo wolfman himself is not pursued, forced to confess through torture, and then executed.

In Pueblo agricultural societies the wolf is respected. As we've seen, the earth is revered and there is no perception of separation between humans and nature. Under Spanish influence, lycanphobia was used as a means of social control and subjugation. Medieval Spanish ideas about wolves and werewolves easily changed original Pueblo notions, instituting a Manichean dichotomy separating Christian verities from evil and black magic associated with the primitive, the wild, and the animal.

In the medieval European mind equating the wolf with animality, darkness, and evil accompanied the rise of rationalism and suppression of the irrational. Suppressed animality burst forth in lycanthropic incidents during which all participants were infected with wolf madness.

In 1598, for instance, a French girl named Pernette Gandillon believed she was a werewolf. She attacked another girl picking strawberries. When the girl's brother defended her with a knife, Gandillon tore the blade from him and severed his throat. Enraged villagers seized Gandillon and ripped her apart.

In effect, these crazed townsmen themselves became wolves. Such lycanphobic frenzies had ancient roots in ecstatic Classical and pre-Classical religious practices that relate to long-held wolf beliefs. Indeed, the whole three-hundred-year Inquisition period was a dark descent into predatory blood lust denied and ascribed to those accused of witchcraft, heresy, and lycanthropy.

In typical Inquisition fashion, the maddened villagers extracted a confession from Gandillon's brother and nephew who said they transformed themselves into wolves through aid of a magic salve. After being thrown into prison, the two crawled on all fours and howled. Pernette's niece confessed she had given herself to the devil who had appeared to her as a black goat. Satan was also given animal attributes, pictured as half man with a goat's head, legs and a tail. In this defamed form, Satan assumed the ancient characteristics and attributes of the Paleolithic god of fertility and sexuality. The old god became the despised Christian anti-god.

The Power of Unconscious Imagery

As psychoanalyst C.G. Jung realized, the Middle Ages marked creation of the unconscious mind accompanied by ascending rational awareness. With this growth in rational thinking, anything associated with the irrational was banished from conscious attention or projected and exteriorized.

The reservoir where this denied material became stored, or rather hidden, Jung named the unconscious. Images of the body itself, because of its sexuality, animality, and carnality, submerged into the unconscious. Repressed elements burst forth in unaccountable behaviors.

The tremendous upsurge in lycanphobia during the 1500s bears witness to the great power the wolf image held in the nascent European unconscious. Accompanying the wolf, feminine imagery and witchcraft were similarly suppressed during the Inquisition. Women, by no means always old crones, were the target of choice for accusations of witchcraft. Compare this to Southwest Indian sorcery practiced in large part by men.

The association of the feminine, wolves, and magic is an extremely ancient one and relates to Paleolithic beliefs. Simone de Beauvoir, in her revolutionary book *The Second Sex*, showed how the Great Goddess of the Stone Age became, with the rise of patriarchy, an embodiment of "Otherness," as did woman herself. The Goddess (Gaia) represented earth, agriculture, and the feminine generative principal associated with the serpent. Traces of the Great

Goddess remain in the classical deities Demeter and Persephone.

The Goddess also possessed another aspect associated in Classical mythology with wolves. Diana/Artemis, called Artemis Lykeiæ (Wolf Artemis), the virgin goddess hunter, was joined in her predatory pursuits by nymphs, the most beautiful of whom was Kallisto, daughter of Lycaon. Zeus turned Lycaon into a wolf after he fed the god human flesh to test his divinity. Hence, he was the first werewolf.

The followers of Artemis were Lesbians. Apollo Lykeios (Wolf Apollo) seduced Kallisto by appearing to her disguised as one of the nymphs. Apollo, only later associated with the sun, was first linked to prophecy and poetry. His name derives from a more ancient form of the jackal-headed Egyptian god of the dead, Anubis.

The Maenads, nymph attendants of Bacchus/Dionysus, god of wine and madness, also exemplified the wild feminine Other. The word Maenad means lupine madness or rabies. The Bacchantes were the rabid or raving women called the "coursing bitches" who, during the Bacchanalia, engaged in wild nocturnal chases through the woods tearing apart deer and young fawns or kids. Human rabies or lupine madness was thought to celebrate Dionysian rites. The ancient cure for rabies was to don a wolf pelt and rave, then shred the pelt to purify oneself.

Dis Pater, Soranus, or Feronius, Roman consort of the Sabine goddess of the underground, Feronia (called Mother of Wolves), was the Roman wolf god. Feronia was identified with Lupa Romana, the she-wolf who suckled Romulus and Remus. Propertius Romulus, son of Lupa, wore a *galea lupina*, that is, a wolf's helmet. The Roman velites, or light soldiers, according to Greek historian Polybius, wore similar wolf helmets in honor of this association. Lupa, the She-wolf, purified Sabine cities when young men dressed in wolf skins participated in the Festival of Lupercalia.

On February 15, these luperci, acting as wolves, slaughtered goats, dressed themselves in the skins of the sacrificed animals, and chased through Roman towns, beating those they encountered in the streets with leather thongs or tongues cut from the goats they had killed. The chosen victims of such ancient wolf hunts were women who were attacked "for fun and in a lascivious way (per ludum et lasciviam.)"

❂ ❂ ❂

Of Women and Wolves

These practices and ideas were not only known in the Middle Ages, but vestiges of these beliefs infected the medieval mind with fear, hatred, and suspicion of woman, wolf nature, and Otherness. Stories like the Gandillon episode were common during the 1500s. In the Knight's Tale, Chaucer tells of a maiden devoted to Artemis who loves to hunt and fears marriage and the birthing of children.

De Beauvoir mentions that the medieval *chanson de geste* relates how noble women were raised crudely and had to partake in rigorous physical exercise. At maturity, the chatelaines or mistresses of the castle hunted wild beasts like their Classical predecessor wolf women. Negative associations between women, witchcraft, wolves, and werewolves erupted during the Inquisition when suspected witches were persecuted and slaughtered.

Witchcraft, lycanthropy, and allied beliefs and practices, as I've suggested, stretch back to the Stone Age when Great Goddess worship flourished. The rise of Christianity meant brutal suppression of these ideas.

Morris Berman, in his study of the relationship between body and spirit in the history of the West entitled *Coming to Our Senses,* traces the outlines of an intriguing hypothesis linking the evolution of tameness, wildness, and human history to our own individual psychological experience and growth.

In Chapter Two, I discussed how Roger Peters and a few other investigators are interested in the links between wolf behavior and the behavior of early man. I suggested that perspectives in Pueblo and Navajo beliefs invested wolves with mystery and power.

Berman says that such power is derived from the Paleolithic view of animals as sacred Others and that it was likely that the boundaries between natural and supernatural were blurred in these ancient hunter-gatherer cultures. Belief that people transform into animals goes back to these times. Why, though, should wolves be invested with such power? Why should Otherness hold such importance in the human psyche?

In the gaze of animals, and particularly in the look of wolves, as one of the creatures most different and separate from man, such power resides because this animal stare serves as a mirror that is totally unlike the look of another person.

In the wary countenance of the wolf, primitive people became conscious of themselves returning this look. In this distance and silence resides the nonhuman mirroring power of animals. Berman argues that mirroring is one of the most important features of human experience because the moment of self-recognition occurs when a child first sees it is separate from the world and from other people. During early childhood, at the moment a baby sees its mother, is severed from itself, a perceptual gulf opens.

This shift from body, somatic, or kinesthetic awareness to visual awareness and separation represents a terrifying chasm which comes to differentiate the individual from the world. This coming to consciousness ruptures the continuity that once existed between the self and the world. Through this awareness develops the vague sense that "something is missing," and that one is split or empty.

What Berman calls the Basic Fault is a modern perception that really becomes prominent from the sixteenth century on. He links the first widespread manufacture of mirrors and the "rise of the individual" that characterized the Renaissance with the evolution of this human perception. During this time the "irrational" and wild elements of the mind are finally banished from awareness and the unconscious mind is born. Here in the murky netherworld of the unconscious dwelled the irrational and bizarre elements not recognized by reason, which was becoming the major determining principal of reality.

A Separate Self

In the Paleolithic mind this sense of separate self, this gulf had not yet developed. The mirroring power of animals was sacred because humans began to behold themselves as Other. This knowledge seemed marvelous and strange. This perception is evidence for human participation and nonseparation from the environment.

When agriculturally based societies began to develop, the idea of wildness was born in the human mind, or became certainly much more sharply defined, due to the distinction between cultivated lands and natural country. This difference extended also to animals, because, in taming the land for human purposes, people also domesticated animals to their own ends.

Those that were raised for human use, such as cattle and sheep, were the tame, good animals. Those animals that remained undomesticated were the wild, bad animals. The Otherness of animals was, then, not something that caused awe and reverence. Rather the gaze and aspect of wolves, as a primary example of wildness, became a source of dread. In part, this fear was based on the fact that wolves were competitors for the same resources as humans since the evil wolves preyed on the good sheep and cattle. Domesticating animals removed from them their magic mirroring capacity. Domestic animals were familiar companions, not Others.

Animals lost their power to create awe if they could be tamed. Dogs, the descendants of wolves, assumed a new domesticated identity, not associated with their wolf ancestors. The idea of wildness then became opposed to tameness. The savage beast, the wolf, that ravaged the tame beast and threatened human sustenance maintained his association with Otherness and also became associated with evil. Tameness belonged to the human sphere and was good. The process that associated wildness, wolves, and evil marked the gradual development of binary thinking that pitched humans against nature, good opposed to bad, heaven split from earth.

With the rise of binary thinking came a powerful urge to join what had been rent asunder. One of the chief ways of filling the ever-widening gap opened by binary thinking was to fill this void with creatures that were both human and beast, both wild and tame, or both Other and self. Therioanthropy, the creation of combination animals that were both wild and human, became a necessity to relieve the growing pressure in the human psyche. What creature was more wild and more Other than the wolf? Hence, lycanthropy, the combination of man and wolf, most symbolized the gulf that had opened in human consciousness.

The Spanish mind of the sixteenth century blended elements of Christianity and of earlier Classical paganism. Christianity had not displaced pagan beliefs but had usurped pagan elements in many instances with its own versions of earlier myths and beliefs.

By the late Middle Ages, when the Spaniards came to the Southwest, there was already this rich lore of wolf legends and beliefs inherited from the Greeks and Romans. These ideas comprised a kind of background awareness that these newcomers carried with them as part of their belief system.

✪ ✪ ✪

The Terror of the Abyss

With the rise of reason during the Middle Ages as the determining principal of reality, the chasm between Self and Other
opened into a terrifying abyss. What better reason for murdering
generation after generation of suspected Others? It is also during
the late Middle Ages that animals were routinely captured and
torn apart for amusement, a pastime that survived the era in the
form of wolf hunts and bear baiting.

Jungian scholar Robert Eisler, in his monograph *Man Into
Wolf*, showed how Biblical sources trace lycanthropic beliefs that
are the root of human evil. Eisler suggested that all peoples were
once peaceful vegetarians. The story of the Garden of Eden por-
trays this time in human prehistory when God made Adam and
Eve to till the soil and tend the Garden. The serpent (symbol of
the Great Goddess and feminine principal) tempted Eve. The
snake shares the amorphous qualities of combination beasts that
are neither predators nor domestic animals. I've mentioned the
medieval portrayal of Satan as goat and man. The werewolf also
occupies an anomalous position.

The serpent tempts Eve to know what God knows. Eisler inti-
mates that when the primal couple ate of the fruit and imbibed in
the knowledge of life and death, they learned the secret of predators. God then clothes the two in animal skins and banishes them
from the vegetarian paradise of Eden. The animal skins are not
only the mark of lost innocence, but signify lycanthropy. In knowing the forbidden secret of predators humans now are clothed in
fur, a symbol of their wolf nature.

What is this forbidden secret known by wolves? It is the knowledge of life and death. The death of prey nourishes the hunter.
Wolves sustain themselves through the death and suffering of prey
species.

The hunting knowledge of predators or wolves is how to survive by killing others. This knowledge is forbidden because it bestows the power of life and death on the hunter through the sacrificial flesh of the victim of the hunt. Hence, this forbidden knowing
is a source of shame and guilt.

In subsequent generations Cain kills Abel whose blood cries
out from the soil to God. Esau, elder twin of Jacob, is born covered
with red hair. Eisler says Esau, whose name means the hairy one, is

the archetypal lycanthrope. He is the hunter, who later vows to kill Jacob when his birthright is stolen by his wily vegetarian brother. The Jews were known as the children of Jacob, and were identified as a pastoral and agricultural people. Muslims were the children of Esau, and were known as hunters.

In the early 1500s Moslem mystic Muhammed ben Isa (son of Esau the hairy one) became the patriarch of a cult that practiced ritual dismemberment of animals. It was said of this saint that he tamed animals and snakes. Having only recently wrested Spain from Moorish hands in the early 1500s, the medieval Spanish were most probably familiar with Muhammed ben Isa.

Jesus is known to the Muslims as Isa bin Maryam, and as scripture says, when Jesus was born, he fulfilled the prophecy of Isaiah that the wolf shall dwell with the lamb. Paintings of this period show Jesus surrounded by animals, having tamed and subdued them. The Bible is replete with wilderness imagery. When Jesus attained special knowledge, he departed into the wilderness, place of wild beasts.

Many of the colonists who left Spain for the New World beginning in the sixteenth century were secret Jews who wanted to escape the terrors of the Inquisition. Jews were also considered Others, practitioners of mystical Kabbalah, or recent Christian converts who wished to hide their identity.

In the far away Southwest, the Inquisition was a shadow of the reign of terror that raged in Europe. Much of the oppression focused on Native Americans and lycanthropy was a popular charge brought against those suspected of heresy and rebellion.

Tales of Terror and Fascination

Most of the records documenting Inquisition trials for heresy in New Mexico were destroyed during the Pueblo Rebellion of 1680. What remains provides evidence for the prosecution of prominent New Mexico personages on grounds of witchcraft. For a couple of hundred years, the Inquisition in Mexico City vied with local authorities for power by continually leveling charges of heresy against local dignitaries. As already suggested in previous chapters, the Pueblos eagerly adopted to the new Manichean lycanphobia. Witch purges swept through Zuñi.

Little official documentation remains to tell the story of the early settlers' relationship with the Mexican wolf. A new cultural tradition, rich in folklore and influenced by Native traditions, was born and nourished in New Mexico.

Sheep and cattle ranching placed the Hispanic settlers in proximity to wolves on occasion. Sheepherders spent much of their time with their flocks, though, and the animals were not allowed to wander alone through the desert high country unattended. These practices mitigated against wolf kills because wolves avoid people and are extremely wary of attacking if people are present. Little remains in oral or written accounts of the early relationship with the wolf. Wolves were most probably scrupulously avoided because of their reputation.

This shy and wary creature also most assuredly avoided human contact. Only sheepherders and cattle ranchers encountered them, though their howls filled the New Mexico nights, causing people dread. There is also no record of systematic attempts to eradicate the wolf because of predation. Weaponry and other methods of elimination were comparatively primitive, and it seems little if any attention was paid to eradication. The Mexican wolf's natural prey still thrived in the days before Anglo settlement, and cattle had not yet exhausted arid grasslands in lower elevations and moved to higher regions where wolves roved. Since they had other food sources, wolves seldom confronted men.

The obsession with eradicating wolves developed only later in the history of the Southwest under Anglo rule. Avoidance was most probably the response people had to such a dreaded creature.

Hispanic culture also was influenced by Pueblo ideas and traditions as these many different people coexisted. In northern New Mexico, strong ties to the land developed, mixing Spanish ideas of land grant ownership and respect for *Tierra Madre* (Mother Earth). Stories about wolves in Hispanic tradition took several different forms.

Michael Jenkinson, in his work *Beasts Beyond the Fire*, tells how familiar werewolf tales were to the Spanish settlers who spun yarns around New Mexico fireplaces during the winter. Oral tradition blended rabies, madness, bestiality, and dark medieval magic to evoke terror and fascination in relating these tales. For local inhabitants of New Mexico, wolves maintained their reputation as a source of dread associated with sorcery and Satan.

Beyond the transformation of man into wolf, one typical form of the wolf tale survives even today in New Mexico Hispanic folk tradition. It is a common belief that Satan appears as a ball of fire swiftly traveling through the desert. This ball of fire often then transforms into a cat, a wolf, or an owl. The image of the wolf as it has survived in New Mexican folklore remains that of the dread Other.

In 1955, a resident of Cebolla, New Mexico, recorded a story about three men who were riding along the New Mexican desert plain late one night on horseback. They saw a small colt following them. Upon closer examination the colt changed into a wolf and then back to a colt again, but this time with fire spouting from its nostrils and wild eyes rolling.

Other Hispanic tales recently recorded by anthropologists suggest wolf stories relate back to the animal fable which paints a much more whimsical picture of the wolf as a fool, a dupe, and a buffoon. These Aesop-like tales comprise versions of the little boy who cried wolf, and footraces between the wolf and bees or fox in which the braggart wolf is outsmarted through the deceptive agency of either bees or fox. In another tale, a hungry wolf encounters a mother pig and her babies. The wolf tells the mother pig he will eat her, but the mother protests, saying her babes are not christened yet. She tells the wolf she will be happy to let him eat her children if first he will christen them.

They all go to a nearby brook and the mother shoves the wolf in, grabs her children, and runs into the woods to hide.

The wolf, continuing his search for a meal, meets an old mule who tells him she has a splinter in her hind foot. She wants the splinter removed before she agrees to be consumed. The wolf starts to remove the splinter when the mule rears back and kicks him, knocking him out.

The wolf comes to and is still hungry. He encounters a rabbit whose burrow is near the edge of a cliff. The rabbit convinces the wolf to race him to the end of the cliff. He dodges into his hole as he approaches the edge, but the poor wolf tumbles to his death because he is racing so fast.

In another tale, a rabbit who has been told by his father to beware of man encounters a wolf. He asks if the wolf is a man. The wolf agrees to help the little rabbit find a man. Just then the two are snared in a trap. The rabbit escapes from the trap, jumping free on the wolf's head saying, "Now I know what daddy meant when he said to watch out for man."

Perhaps these tales proved popular as a way of defusing fear people felt about wolves, Otherness, and animality. These and other Hispanic tales from New Mexico reflect much older folklore traditions extending back to the days of early Greece, but the underlying construct regarding the wolf remains fear and avoidance.

Michael Jenkinson argues that it was not the dread and fear of wolves that eventually accounted for the largely successful attempts at eliminating this sophisticated and intriguing predator from the American wilderness. Jenkinson says wolf eradication was simply a matter of displacement as was the virtual elimination of the buffalo and the reduction of elk, deer, and other species as Anglo culture came west. I think, though, that we have to look at reasons why "simple displacement" of natural species was not only viewed as an acceptable practice, but was considered a laudable activity during the westering of America. In subsequent chapters this subject will be developed in greater depth as an overlayer interacting with the "wolf substrate" that evolved during the Middle Ages.

Shifting Awareness

Surely we must look at what happened to Europeans during the shift in consciousness that occurred throughout Europe in the Middle Ages. Such changes, which have recently been called "paradigm shifts," have profound consequences for us all, and, because they occur largely unnoticed by people, they have a profound and far-reaching effect that often passes unseen.

Denial of our own predator nature and projection of these negative traits onto the wolf has had terrible consequences for our country, including species and environmental destruction, genocidal warfare, and the unconscious practice of predatory cruelty that we have kept hidden from our conscious awareness. Perhaps it is time to start asking why we continue to act as we do, especially in a world where the natural world is suffering real damage because of our actions. Really though, it's not nature that we are destroying today—it is ourselves.

I feel that in our own era we are undergoing a deep awakening to the forces that we have denied since the Scientific Revolution cast out elements of unreason from our awareness. Never before have people in such numbers felt that cruelty to animals, or environmental destruction, or saving the wolf were important enough to act decisively. Awakening to these issues is awakening to our own Otherness.

Recently, certain segments of the environmental movement have emphasized a unified vision of the natural world, stressing that all creatures, plants, and even the soil itself have inalienable rights similar to the rights we grant to humans. This reorientation of values means that animals are equal to humans and the old anthropocentric view of the world is no longer valid.

If we see animals as "other people" this means that we may be becoming aware of animals as beings equal to ourselves. They have feelings as we have feelings. Loss of faith in technology and science as an answer to our problems has possibly meant a rediscovery of unconscious imagery and our identification with our own animal nature, because if animals can be regarded as other people, we can see ourselves as animals. The knowledge that we *are* animals may be a somatic and kinesthetic rediscovery. Or perhaps, we are simply so out of touch with ourselves that we want to make these animals our pets.

In awakening to our kinship with animals we face the grave danger that we once again create Others whom we must attack in order to preserve our sense of internal integrity, because this awakening is deeply terrifying. Polarization between rabid environmentalists and committed ranchers who view each other as enemies, no matter how attuned to underlying felt senses and awakened truths, can only enact again the basic split which separates us from ourselves.

We must come to see again the wonderful and miraculous mirroring power of the wolf. We must embrace the wildness and Otherness we find there because, in truth, it is ourselves we see in the silent gaze of the wolf, our own Otherness and separation reflected in the eyes of the wolf. More than ever we must embrace our terror.

CHAPTER SIX

And God Gave Man Dominion

Then God said, "Let us make man in our image, after our likeness; and let them have dominion over the fish of the sea, and over the birds of the air, and over the cattle, and over all the earth, and over every creeping thing that creeps upon the earth." So God created man in his own image, in the image of God he created him; male and female he created them. And God blessed them, and God said to them, "Be fruitful and multiply, and fill the earth and subdue it; and have dominion over the fish of the sea and over the birds of the air and over every living thing that moves upon the earth."
—Genesis 1:26-29

By the fifteenth century, when exploration became a serious business, Western Europe had long since established a pattern of thinking and a system of beliefs toward nature based on Biblical scripture. If myths are maps of the life spirit of various cultures, these Biblical beliefs stand in stark contrast to the myths of Native American cultures such as the Pueblos.

For Native Americans, the land and its creatures were sacred beings. The earth could be read as an intimate text which conveyed sacred meanings to humans through natural cycles that blessed and informed all of life. The Native American relationship with earth was personal and profound.

Belief in Biblical texts as the basis for religious conviction removed Europeans from intimacy with their environment. Seasonal and other natural cycles had no religious significance for those whose beliefs were founded in scripture. This sense of objectivity toward the natural world was further enhanced by Biblical sources themselves.

The history of the nomadic Israelites, who traveled through hostile and forbidding deserts, made the natural world seem dangerous and alien. The earth and its creatures were objects suited to man's domination and use, as ordained and sanctioned in the book of Genesis.

Gnosticism, with its emphasis on immanent, personal spiritual growth and mysticism, had since the third century given way to the belief in Jesus as redeemer of history who had conquered flesh through spirit. Other voices echo in Christian history, showing other possibilities inherent in Gnosticism. If Western society's relationship to nature generally found expression through dominance and cruelty against nature, other modes surface in examining European history as well.

I refer to St. Francis, who was said to possess the ability to speak to animals. Known today as the "hippy saint," "nature mystic," or the "ecology saint," St. Francis has provided inspiration for many contemporary ideologies and persuasions. His mode of knowing bears close resemblance to the perceptions expressed in Native American storytelling traditions. The context for his philosophy was thoroughly medieval, though the saint's ideas were more united in outlook to the Native American views described previously because they are rooted in a similar perceptual base.

A Somatic Echo

The perceptual organization, the somatic knowing St. Francis developed, was expressed through metaphor and evocations of experiential states. St. Francis and his followers bound themselves to "Lady Poverty," establishing thereby a lifestyle and an economy that emphasizes conservation and limited use of nature's bounty, as opposed to exploitation and plunder of resources. At heart the saint overthrew the notion of man's dominance over nature and established a philosophy of harmony with natural circumstance. This relationship to nature he expressed through the metaphor of marriage. In this manner, the saint conjured an entire emotional constellation meant to create in the hearer a somatic resonance, echoing the state of being and a relationship to the world of experience.

What can it possibly mean that the saint spoke with animals? Is this merely the invention of hagiographers who wished to express the saint's mysterious contact with God, or are we to take his talking with the birds and beasts as an actual behavior engaged in by Francis? His biographers are so shaped by their culture and time that it is difficult to separate the psychology of the man from inventions created by those who wrote of his life.

Is it not possible that an individual is so transfigured by his experience that he supersedes the ordinary boundaries which culture and belief dictate and enforce upon him? Is it not conceivable that such an individual can entirely alter ordinary perception, and through his act of transformation, become indistinguishable from that which he has created, disappearing into his creation?

Shamans as well as other Native Americans and tribal vision seekers have often been said to perform such an act of metamorphosis and to speak with animals, so why not St. Francis? If reality is determined by social consensus through acceptance of current fashion and fiction, then a person whose beliefs are molded by forces beyond the social periphery may indeed change the entire shape of reality.

Western society has never taken seriously the idea that men and animals can communicate. The notion that animals are man's equal has seemed ludicrous. The concept that animals can respond to human communication and that they have their own volition equal to human will, indeed that plants or even rocks or water respond to humans as equals—these notions are beyond consideration. Not so for St. Francis.

While he undoubtedly derived inspiration from earlier Irish nature mystics, who were also said to communicate with animals, the saint inaugurated a whole new way of seeing nature. He perceived nature as the language in which God expressed his thoughts. Hence, natural phenomena were extensions of the divine being in a way rarely before seen in the standard Christian context.

Quasi Silvestres Hommes

St. Francis's contact with his fellow creatures expressed mystical connection by reflecting inner meanings that were apparent to him through the observation of various forms of life and "inanimate" natural forms and events, though these meanings were hidden to others. He spoke, not only to animals, but to streams, fields of corn, rocks, the wind, and the sun.

To him, all these expressions of immanent being were his

equals, his brothers and his sisters. Rapt in his ecstasies of contemplation, he was "carried out of himself" so that the boundaries between the world and self dissolved. In St. Francis ecstasy is tinted with sadness and beauty to render us a stirring portrait—the saint playing his imaginary violin by miming the action of bow on string, dancing beneath the moon while singing in raucous French, carried away in transports of rapture.

This small saint who bound himself to mystery and renunciation was no ordinary man. The cost of realization was the total surrender of self. He was richer by virtue of what he could do without. In letting go of everything, Francis touched the core of life and embraced life wholeheartedly.

His biographers said that fire and creatures were obedient to him and venerated him. In this view they repudiated the prejudice that man must dominate nature. In truth the saint was so drawn to all creatures, plants, and any other expression of numinous being that, through the fires of compassion and rejoicing, he spoke to them with a voice tinged by inner joy.

He spoke to them as if they had reason and the world was so moved to respond. Each blade of grass, each drop of water burned with meaning and became a well of luminosity from which he drew his sustenance. He saw himself so unified, so dissolved in nature that he passed beyond good and evil. Thus, he threw his deepest being open to truth and joy.

Steeped in pacifism, repudiation of property, and communication with all of nature, St. Francis and his brethren were called *quasi silvestres hommes*, quasi men of the forest. Visitors described their sleeping places to be like the lairs of wild beasts. While animals in the Middle Ages were ascribed peculiar traits they did not possess in order to symbolically disclose divine truths, St. Francis opened himself to the possibility that all being praised the creative source. Most probably he was influenced by the Catharists—pacifist, vegetarian heretics who received their ideas from India. His mistrust of learning and his reliance on experience, action, and response grounded him firmly in somatic body knowing.

One of the most dramatic encounters the saint had involved a certain wolf that had been wantonly attacking the people of Gubbio. St. Francis, who happened to be in residence there, resolved to see this wolf. The townspeople hid in their houses trembling with fear while Francis walked the road where the wolf was often seen lurking.

Curious to witness the result, a group of brave souls ventured forth from the village and followed Francis at a distance. As St. Francis approached, the wolf opened his gaping jaws and growled ferociously, its eyes lit with savage fury. Just then Francis addressed "Brother Wolf." Then, so the tale goes, the wolf immediately closed his mouth and crawled meekly to rest at the feet of the saint.

Brother Wolf, Frate Lupo

Francis admonished the beast and bade him make peace with the people he had terrorized. He called the wolf of Gubbio *frate lupo*, meaning not only "brother wolf" but "friar wolf" as well. At this entreaty, the wolf showed his assent by signalling with his tail, body, ears, and a nod of his head that he was willing to comply with the saint's requests. In turn, Francis bound the townsfolk to feed the wolf every day, because the saint understood the creature had committed these atrocities only due to his hunger.

Once more the wolf nodded his accord, promising never again to harm any creature. As a sign of his pact, the wolf lifted its paw and the saint offered his hand. Then the wolf of Gubbio followed Francis to the town plaza as "meek as a lamb," while stunned and mortified villagers watched these two unlikely companions approach the square. Thus converted by the saint's love, the wolf of Gubbio remained to the end of his days a favored and celebrated creature who daily passed from house to house where he was fed and regaled. Even the dogs ceased to bark at his passage.

A variant of this tale appears in the New World. Toribio de Benevente, in his *Historia de los Indios de Nueva España*, told how the Aztecs enacted a play in which St. Francis spoke to the birds. As the saint preached to his rapt avian flock, an actor portraying a ferocious wolf rushed upon him from his hiding place in some nearby hills. The saint then made the sign of the cross and admonished the beast who was then led into town where the chiefs had gathered. Here the beast indicated his willingness to obey the saint through the usual gestures and signs.

This charming tale has antecedents stretching back to fourth-century Egypt. It is clear that the wolf of Gubbio is a fictional beast. Wild mammals, with good reason, shy away from human contact and the wolf is certainly no exception. There is more kinship between this fictional wolf and the beast of Tarascon, called the Tarasque, a dragonlike creature said to hide beneath a bridge approaching this town in southern France. St. Anne tamed the Tarasque that was cannibalizing the inhabitants of Tarascon.

The Wolf Tamed?

The taming of the wolf of Gubbio has several meanings in context of the saint's biography. Some interpreters have suggested that the wolf represents a brigand who was attacking Gubbio and with whom St. Francis arranged a truce. Medieval outlaws were treated like wolves. Criminals were sentenced with the words, "Let him bear the wolf's head." Like the wolf, he was then to be killed on sight. Likewise, wolves were treated like criminals. When caught, they were condemned and executed.

Such an interpretation places a literal weight that the story, on examination, probably does not bear. Rather, the saint, in taming the wolf of Gubbio, was making peace with the wolf within. By dissolving the boundaries between self and object, human and nature, Francis acted to resolve the fault which rents perception, the division between self and world created by human reason, treated as if rationality itself were truth. Animal, beast, and wolf imagery symbolizes the terror of the chasm that yawns in the human spirit. It appears the saint is able to heal the great spiritual rift by mystical union with terror and the forces of animality.

In the Christian context, the story of the wolf of Gubbio is a parable that relies on traditional imagery and well established symbolism to depict humans no longer opposed to nature, but at one with natural conditions. The story is the penultimate Christian vision—the reconciliation of man and nature through atonement. St. Francis acts as a conduit or spiritual channel establishing the "peaceable kingdom" or the "paradise on earth." The wolf lies at the foot of the saint "as gentle as a lamb," conjuring Biblical wolf-sheep associations. Francis himself also said that his enemies raged against him and his brethren like wolves against a small flock. When his merchant father physically assaulted him, the saint's biographers likened the savage onslaught to a wolf's attack.

Deeper forces rule our lives than we are perhaps willing to consider or admit. These wolf-taming stories come from ancient and hidden streams, indicating a fascination with the theme of making peace with the animal within and with nature. These stories and themes provide evidence of a somatic knowing that has long been active in storytelling traditions, whether of the Native American variety or the European variant.

A Perverse Alchemy

In the dominant interpretation accepted as a justification for political expedience and economic exploitation of subject peoples, Christian history was linear. The omega point was Christ's Resurrection, while mythical cyclic time, embedded in nature, reflected seasonal rhythms. European Christian mythology combined with psychological and spiritual factors discussed in the previous chapter to enforce an ever-growing illusion that humans were separate from nature. Man's preordained dominance over all of nature, sanctioned by scripture, became the justification for conquest and exploitation of the natural world and of those cultures that were embedded in nature.

Just as all creatures must submit to God-sanctioned human dominance, so other peoples who were compared to the heathen inhabitants of Canaan or to Egyptians or Sodomites—these enemies of the true faith too must submit to Christian dominance.

For the Spanish, expulsion of the Moors from their homeland just prior to the period of exploration, after six hundred years of occupation, seemed a sign of God's will and a divine sanction for their conquest of the New World.

In the eighth century, when the Moors invaded Spain, a legend circulated that told the tale of seven bishops who fled their homeland in advance of the Moors. These prelates were said to have established seven cities of gold somewhere to the west.

The persistence of this story fired the Spanish imagination. The relentless search for gold drove the Conquistadores to ruthless excess in their New World journeys. Gold meant riches, but as an archetype it also meant something much more to the European imagination.

Francisco Vásquez de Coronado financed his expedition to New Mexico in search of the Seven Cities of Cibola with the equivalent of $1 million, endured hardship and privation for three years, and yet gained almost nothing during his fruitless wanderings. The search for gold, the obsession for precious metals that posessed the late medieval mind, served other purposes besides the obvious desire for monetary gain.

Jung has shown how medieval alchemy exemplified spiritual growth of the individual. Gold represented, in this secret system of mystical ordination, the fruit of the spiritual search. Just as many failed alchemists did not understand the power of the alchemical metaphor and tried to create real gold from lead, so the Conquistadores in their relentless obsession for discovering gold through exploration and conquest misinterpreted the essential symbol of alchemical transformation from gross material to spiritual value. The invaders substituted material gain for spiritual transformation.

The same process was at work in medieval ideas about wolves and werewolves as it was with gold. Denial of human animal nature and displacing these denied traits on wolves became prevalent at the same time people mislocated the primary symbol of the inward personal spiritual journey, desiring instead to search outside themselves for power and riches. The European mind rejected internal meanings and placed greater significance on the external world. Alienation from self and terror at Otherness resulted in a ceaseless search to fill the spiritual void.

Those who lack true spiritual resources often demand that others agree with their own beliefs in order to assuage the ravenous doubts that tear at their souls. An obsessive attempt to convert native inhabitants to Christianity often accompanied the tireless quest for gold.

A Story of Estrangement

Cut off from their own bodies, estranged from the natural world and divorced from identification with other peoples and their mythologies, the Spaniards sought to indoctrinate all whom they encountered. Once subjected to reeducation, enslavement quickly followed so the new chattel might be impressed as rapidly as possible to obtain gold for their masters by toiling in the mines of the New World. So numb were the Spaniards to native peoples that they expressed confusion as to whether they were humans or animals.

The common stereotype of gold-hungry Spanish conquistadores belies the fact that European explorers in general expressed the same values resulting from a common psychology. As far as the natural world goes, the Spanish had no word for the wilds. Like other Romance languages, Spanish had to draw on particular traits the speaker wished to convey about the natural world.

The expressions *immensidad* or *falta de cultura* (lack of culture) captured aspects of wild country that the Spanish speaker wished to get across to his listener. The reason for this absence of terminology for wilderness is tied to northern European ideas about wolves. In the dark forests of these north lands, the wolf was more prevalent than in southern Europe and therefore more familiar to Germanic peoples than to southern Europeans.

The etymology of the word *wilderness* contains a secret history of the Teutonic relationship with wolves, building on and enriching the basic ideas about wolf nature that I have called the wolf substrate.

The etymological roots of the word *wilderness* are Germanic, indicating forest lands that are the home of wolves. The fact that the word *wilderness* appears only in Teutonic tongues links its usage to an area of northern Europe where heavy forestation occurred. The root *wild* may refer to *weald* or *woeld*, Old English for "woods."

Wildeor—The Wolf Unleashed

Most probably, though, the root *wild* comes from the same word as "will." This prefix was combined with the word *deor*, meaning "beast," to make the word *wildeor*, meaning "uncontrollable, self-willed beast." In Old Swedish, the word referred to boiling water, conveying a sense of the ungoverned and out of control. *Wild* also conveyed ideas of unruliness, disorder, and confusion, in this manner linking the concept to insanity. I've already discussed how lupine rabies, madness, and wolves were linked in the Classic imagination. The word *berserk* comes from Old Norse and refers to men who donned bearskins and assumed the power of bears, namely a frenzy of violence and wildness. Entranced in this way, they assailed their enemies. By dressing in bear skins, the wearer assumes bear power and becomes a bear. This transformation into wildeor and taking on the power of an animal by wearing its skin we have seen before in various forms when men become wolves.

That the beast referred to in the term wildeor was a wolf is made clear by one of the earliest uses of the complete word *wildeornesse* in the eighth-century Anglo-Saxon epic *Beowulf*. The Danes called the hero Beowulf, Scyld. They believed he came from the waters in a basket, like Romulus and Remus, adopted sons of the Roman she-wolf.

The popularity of the name Wulf or Wolf among Germanic peoples is a holdover from pagan belief in the sacred wolf totem. In the Beowulf epic the hero ventures into a dark forest region where crags and fens hide fantastic beasts. In this dismal land among "wolf-haunted hills" Beowulf seeks to slay two giant blood-drinking fiends who have beset his tribe. The bleak wilderness, home of wolves, is invariably associated with darkness, disorder, opposition, and deviltry, as is the wolf himself.

Wolf imagery tells us much about the northern European mind. Wodan, Wotan, or Odin, supreme god of art, culture, war, and the dead, accompanied by his pack of wolves forays into the night during his nocturnal hunts. In Teutonic mythology, time ends when the old gods must confront forces of chaos and darkness. Such a linear time scheme had its parallel in Christian views about Judgement Day and most probably made the Christian time sense more comprehensible to northern Europeans. The end of time holds no hope for humankind in Norse legend. The gods and their enemies destroy one another in *gotterdammerung* and all descends into chaos.

In German myth, handsome Loki, the trickster god who creates disorder and mischief, fathers Fenrir or Fenris, a wolf who each day grows in power and destructive capacity until the other gods decide he must be brought to heel.

In a challenge, Tyr, divinity of war, agrees to leash Fenrir. Fenrir, with eyes aflame, forces Tyr to put his hand in the giant wolf's maw while the war god binds him. The strand by which Fenrir is to be bound is woven from invisible earth power essences such as roots of mountains, breath of fish, and the noise of cats as they move. With this magical cord, as thin as a single hair, Fenrir is bound, but not before he mauls Tyr's hand, tearing it from his wrist.

This magic leash retains Fenrir until he breaks free and with all wolves consumes the earth, and even Wodan himself. After Fenrir is slain by Odin's son, the earth is again reborn.

The perceived kinship between wolves, darkness, and chaos meant that the wolf became archetype of wilderness, king of forbidding and strange lands where darkness and animality prevailed. Wilderness expressed a state of mind and a way of regarding the outside world that really exemplified an inner attitude of fear, hostility, and the desire to destroy external reminders of this inward state. As for the Teutonic gods, their names remain with us only in our days of the week.

The sense of alienation from the outside world and estrangement from natural conditions reminded early Church thinkers of the hostile deserts where Israel wandered. In the thirteenth century, Layamon, cleric and poet, was one of the first to use the word *wilderness* in *Brut*, a Medieval verse chronicle.

The word continued to be used by English Biblical translator John Wycliffe in the fourteenth century to denote arid and forbidding desolate lands of the Mideast. In the 1500s William Tyndale retained the term when he translated the Bible authorized by King James in 1611.

Howling Wilderness

By the time the Puritans described the "howling wilderness" into which they ventured in their New World pilgrimage, the association between wolf nature and the wilds had become so welded that they were virtually indistinguishable. The New World wilderness, where the Pilgrims found themselves, was a sinister adversary, home of tribal savages who practiced evil. The Puritans regarded wilderness itself as a howling beast, a wolf inspired by the Devil. In this desolation they sojourned and their journey reminded them that believers wandered in a world of sin, a spiritual wilderness replete with Godless enemies and insane beasts that wanted only to consume the righteous.

Puritan vision was built on dualism and assumed opposition, as historian Frederick Turner has noted. Without the battle of God's chosen people engaged in a holy war with the forces of darkness, Pilgrim myth loses meaning and power.

Since the Crusades and the Jerusalem massacre, the Word of God had informed those who committed serial mass murder in the name of holiness. The mythic primitive world from which the people of God had so recently emerged became an intolerable reminder of the mythic past when humans and nature were one. Thus cut off from nature, body, and emotive awareness, historical Christianity created enemies to destroy wild Otherness that in truth resided in the hearts and minds of those who numbed themselves to their own isolation.

Vanished was St. Francis's belief that birds and wolves were man's equal, and that all creatures possessed souls. Instead, as Puritan Jonathan Wigglesworth said, the land was " a waste and howling wilderness." Bostonian Edward Johnson in 1654 believed only the acts of the faithful could transform the "hideous thickets where wolfes and beares nurst their young." Cotton Mather sermonized in 1707 when he wrote of "Evening Wolves" as "rabid and howling Wolves of the Wilderness" that would wreak havoc on his Puritan flock. Only the "cleare sunshine of the gospel might dispel the thick anti-Christian darkness," as Thomass Shepard described the alien land and its inhabitants.

By the seventeenth century, use of the word *wilderness* evoked a whole realm of power and significance based on Puritan enthusiasm for typology in analyzing the Bible. Through typology, events and people in the Old Testament prefigured happenings in the New Testament. Thus the Old Testament wilderness through which the Chosen People wandered preshadowed the wilderness where Christ withdrew to be tested by Satan during his forty-day journey into desolation.

A Darkness Within

Christ's dual nature as man and God gave significance to His divine intrusion into human affairs. If the Old Testament prefigured the New, then the New Testament prefigured events in the New World. Biblical interpretation determined how Puritans interpreted their own situation, tinging their perception of the New World with their own dark beliefs about wilderness as repository of evil wolf nature.

Instead of attempting to harmonize with their circumstances in the New World or learning of their new circumstances from those who found a home in wilderness, the Puritans struggled to keep from being absorbed by vast, all-surrounding desolation of the natural world. Fear of wilderness, terror of wolves, denial of wildness, and the battle to stave off encroachments from the natural world were combined with a desperate need to control what could not be controlled but could only be destroyed.

The wolf and elk were soon driven from the East along with the turkey and prairie chicken. Native American tribes, as simply another type of wildeor, or viewed as enemies inspired by Satan, were confronted and slaughtered, or reduced to a twilight existence begging at the fringes of the new white world. Systematic humiliation by misappropriation of Native American cultural meanings and symbols, derision, ridicule, and contempt drove surviving tribal peoples to accept a meager life at the edges of frontier society.

The Divine Mission of conquest coupled with Calvinist predestination of the elect formed a ready justification for eliminating the damned, who were forsaken of God's grace.

Born from the spirit of eighteenth century mercantilism and nationalism, the colonies were founded on a belief in commercial pragmatism. Everything was viewed in terms of its usefulness to the chosen people. Such interpretations had already been sanctioned by scripture, which gave man the right of dominion over all God's peoples and creatures. The God who disposed early Americans to believe in their inborn right of domination was a God of Reason. Isolation from the very ground of being itself meant not only a hatred of the flesh, but ascendancy of Reason as a prime determinant of reality.

The settlers sought first to pacify the land and then to discover profit in nature's resources. The scriptural justification for exploitation came once again from Genesis and the reference to man's dominion and mastery over the earth and all her creatures. Frontier restlessness came from such an emptiness of spirit, fear of confronting meanings, and the displacement of these fears on the outside world.

There were others who rejected this continued process of exploitation, who came West to follow their own greater personal destinies, to seek elbow room, and to live with the land. But the overall effect of westward migration meant eventual despoilation of the land and its resources.

The American Disease

Psychiatrist Viktor Frankl has noted that the perception of meaninglessness seems primarily to be an American disease which arose during the process of industrialization. To strike out for new turf appeared the only alternative to suffering the emptiness of such restlessness of mind and spirit. This expansion followed shooting the animals, subduing native inhabitants, clearing forests, and establishing European agriculture where only elk and wolves once roamed. Very few questioned this restlessness of spirit. The battle cry was to move on, go west, and subdue the land. Denial of the barbarous cruelty accompanying westward movement and ascription of savagery and barbarism to native inhabitants insulated the settler against remorse.

Alexis de Tocqueville in 1831 noted that American frontiersmen thought him mad when he wanted to go into the wilds simply to enjoy nature. The Americans, he said, had only one interest in wilderness and that was for land speculation or lumbering. De Tocqueville found the settlers indifferent to all except their obsessive enthusiasm for tramping across the wilds, draining swamps, diverting the course of rivers, peopling the solitude, and subduing nature.

This economic model soon replaced the perverse remnants of medieval alchemical thinking which had lingered in the European imagination, imbuing gold with a magical and horrible significance that confused and confounded Native Americans who encountered early explorers. Now exploitation and economic determinism brought a new sense of objectification to the insatiable conquest of these lands. Scriptural and economic justification disguised an insatiable predatory lust for turning all of nature to man's use. This greed for domination, exploitation, violence, and rapine, hidden from awareness, was quickly ascribed to the wolf who was seen as a savage brute, a flesh render and creature of Satan that had to be eliminated or driven further back into the dark wilderness fastness.

The Cancer Economy

The mindless consumption of resources that has occupied America for the past three hundred years resembles the spread of a cancer—a cancer which now threatens to destroy the host.

In the mid-1800s, land grabs fueled by preemption and grants of land to settlers who wished to "domesticate" the West typified the push to subjugate the American frontier. All that these newcomers might have gained by learning from those who had lived in America in relative harmony for the past thousand years now became subsumed in the press to subdue wilderness. The cancer economy in America was in its inception.

Coupled with the establishment of agriculture, lands were parcelled and platted in neat rectangular sections for quick sale. The new inhabitants were in this manner further divorced from the natural landscape, because, of course, the true meaning of such wholesale harvesting of natural resources and the cruelty that accompanied it had to be hidden from the perpetrators' conscious awareness and disguised under a rationale of a greater good, a Manifest Destiny that clothed and masked an emptiness of spirit as vast as the American desert. Beginning in the 1840s, restless expansion, and with it the conquest and domination of nature and the original inhabitants of the American continent, seemed to fulfill the commandments of the "Father of the Universe" that the Anglo-Saxon nation must extend its dominion over North America. This apparent idealism disguised racist, imperialist, and mercenary motives that underlay the rationale for conquest. Greed, violence, and terror were instead ascribed to the Indians or to the wilderness itself and its creatures, especially the wolf.

In the late 1840s, Bostonian Francis Parkman set forth on the Oregon Trail into the "desolate wilderness." The howl of wolves signalled that darkness soon would engulf the prairie. Night fell across the land and the spirit of darkness also filled the hearts and numbed the spirits of those who had assumed their mission of destruction under banners of reason, destiny, and the will of God.

Indians who behaved like wild children or "thorough savages," Parkman said, would soon be "scattered and broken" and the buffalo upon which they fed destroyed due to the great changes that God had sanctified the white man to carry out in the name of divinity and progress. Parkman, like others who wrote of the frontier, expressed sadness and nostalgia for the beauty of this disappearing world they themselves were destroying. In the 1870s, after an initial period of settlement, European agricultural methods and animal husbandry were instituted in southwestern desert areas so unsuited for cattle raising that native flora were displaced.

The profound depth of this process of denial, the emptiness of soul accompanying barbarous destruction of the land and its inhabitants, hid beneath a veneer of prophecy and civilization. These civilized pioneers who reaped a harvest of destruction from the land had assumed the aspect of predators, and in justification of their bloodletting and exploitation, they accused both beasts of the field and native peoples of being Godless savage *wildeor* deserving of their fate.

Deceit, Brutality, and Denial

The psychology of werewolves had assumed new dimensions in the vastness of America's frontier. Now man had turned into wolf and denied responsibility for this act of self transformation, instead ascribing to his victims the qualities of wolfishness he refused to own. How deeply this process of alienation has extended and how important to its success is the careful hiding and obscuring of underlying motives and intentions.

Child advocate and psychologist Alice Miller has unmasked the hidden cruelty of accepted pedagogical modes that are typical of Western society. A child's natural spontaneity and creativity must be crushed through a carefully contrived system of deceit, brutality, and betrayal enacted by parents to instruct children through what Miller has termed "poisonous pedagogy."

Such oppressive child-rearing techniques are typical of American as well as German child rearing practiced during the late eighteenth century and are still a preferred method of raising children. Thus, adults are masters who, godlike, determine right from wrong. Children, who are seen as little more than animals, small wolves, or wildeor, must be subdued and broken and are held responsible for parental anger and violence because parents themselves were raised with such methods.

Humiliation, denial of affection and natural emotional response, a heightened sense of duty and obedience, and disgust and loathing of the body all prepare children for a world determined by ideologies such as Manifest Destiny or Fascism. Wolf imagery surfaces from unconscious grounds so fertile for sprouting seeds of such pedagogical oppression. Adolf Hitler, who was subjected to such child-rearing techniques, favored and evoked the wolf in describing the S.S., whom he admired for being numb and without pity in the face of suffering, privation, humiliation, and death.

Elaborate justifications for violence in child-rearing practices and the blunting of emotions are simply another facet of estrangement from motivations that are too painful to expose to the light of recognition. Historical justification for America's westward push relied by the end of the nineteenth century on evolutionary ideas. The analogy between inevitable biological development and historical imperatives put the final scientific gloss on America's drive to civilize the continent.

Midwest historian Frederick Jackson Turner, who studied at Johns Hopkins, accepted evolutionary historical premises in writing of the conquest of America's frontier but rejected the Germanic and European origins of American democracy. Instead,

America's forest wildness was seen as the birthplace of expansionism. European settlers conquered wilderness, but in their struggles the conquerors were themselves changed by America's wilderness. Turner, who said the frontier closed in the 1890s, viewed with suspicion the veneer of industrialization and urbanization which overlay the wolfish wilderness.

Cattle Kingdoms

The establishment of American ranching in the Southwest followed a typical pattern. In the late 1860s, construction of the Union Pacific railroad bifurcated the great American buffalo herd. Railroad workers, miners, travelers, and sundry adventurers took their pleasure slaughtering the bison. Buffalo Bill Cody alone killed four thousand buffalo in eighteen months while employed as a hunter for the Kansas Pacific line. Men like Cody and George Causey, who later settled in New Mexico, became heroes for slaughtering as many bison as they could.

Taking potshots at bison became a popular sport and the animals were left to rot on the plain until a Pennsylvania tannery discovered in 1871 that buffalo hides served as a source for leather. Hides rose in price from $1 to $3 apiece. In the two years between 1872 and 1874, three million bison were killed. Four years later the southern herd had disappeared forever. George Causey and his brother John killed over 10,000 buffalo in 1877 and the following spring sold 11,000 hides, 6,000 tongues at a dollar apiece, and 45,000 pounds of dried salted meat.

By 1886, only six hundred bison remained, having retreated to the Canadian wilds. Successive gold strikes and land rushes contributed to the decimation, not only of the bison, but of other natural game animals as well. With decimation of prey species, wolves were forced into increasing contact with humans, as lands once devoted only to the tribes were taken for ranching and farming. Drastic reduction of game meant starvation for the tribes. The fate of Native Americans closely paralleled that of the wolf.

Hispanic settlers had designed the bridle, bit, saddle, spurs, and lariat and had engaged in cattle ranching, but they never branded their animals, allowing them to roam and graze. Historians have claimed that Spanish ranching practices were desultory. These claims may have originated as a rationale for stealing cattle belonging to Mexican ranchers. After all, what better excuse for stealing another's property than that he is careless and lazy? Anglos who drifted into Texas commonly branded cattle they found there on the range, claiming them as their own. In the 1850s, Texas cattle kings drove their herds north through New Mexico to Colorado. Native New Mexicans preferred sheepherding, and with their flocks pushed east as far as the Llano Estacado and Texas and north along Rio Hondo and other areas where plentiful grass and water provided forage.

Contemporary accounts describe encounters with wolves, though often these sightings made no distinction between coyotes and wolves. In the 1850s, Mexican ranchers already laced fresh predator kills with strychnine. The pelts were then worn.

Taking a wolf's skin had since the Paleolithic period become a well-established method of robbing a creature of its power and appropriating that animal potency. Derived from the berserker and werewolf, the meaning of such a symbolic act was lost on nineteenth century ranchers who, dominated by dictates of reason, capital, and progressive thinking, failed to recognize the significance of this ancient practice.

Cattle ranchers drifting into New Mexico from Texas soon began to compete with sheepherders for pasturage. They found a ready market for their beef at Bosque Redondo Reservation, where General James Carleton imprisoned nine thousand Mescalero Apaches and Navajos who had been forced into surrender by Kit Carson at Canyon de Chelly and made to undertake the Long Walk, a disastrous forced march to the reservation.

Confined together in this concentration camp, the two tribes, who were traditional enemies, endured great privation, bad water, and poor provisions. Anglos forced the tribes to till the ground like white men, but few crops grew in the bitter soil of Bosque Redondo.

Two ranchers, Charles Goodnight and Oliver Loving, had helped provision the reservation. In 1866, they drove their cattle up the Pecos River Valley. The Goodnight Loving Trail was pushed north into Colorado later when cattlemen sought shipping markets for their animals. In the 1870s, John Chisum, a friend of Goodnight and Loving, established a cattle kingdom near Roswell which employed a hundred cowboys overseeing eighty thousand head of cattle.

New Mexico mining camps had sprung up, offering a new market for beef. The invention of barbed wire in the 1870s brought ranchers in conflict with dirt farmers who, inspired by the Homestead Act of 1862, pushed west to undertake the final act in subduing the western lands by fencing the open range.

In the late 1870s, the Desert Land Act allowed "nesters" to settle on 640-acre plots for minimal payments if they agreed to irrigate the land. The arid ecosystems of the West proved intractable. Cattlemen registered thousands of acres under the names of their cowhands to grab as much country as possible. A series of like acts fed land acquisition fever. Real estate speculators were ubiquitous, always on the scent, tireless in their predatory hunt for new prospects.

Philip Ashton Rollins, in his book *The Cowboy* (published in 1922), recounted how the disappearance of the buffalo and other natural prey species forced the wolf into preying on cattle. It was the regular duty of the "outrider," in encountering wolf kills, to bait the offending wolf with poison. When wolf kills became more than cowhands could rightly handle, ranchers hired a "wolfer" to pursue and destroy the hated wolves. Along with Indians, wolves were ranked as the most loathsome, despicable creatures.

Like individuals, cultures determine their meaning. Restless and driven, cut off from wilderness and the land, the New World Anglo-Saxon culture imposed its own forms and meanings, obliterating the land and the peoples who had inhabited the land, hiding guilt, greed, and rapaciousness under the guise of destiny, God, and progress.

Ranching was simply an extension of this process that viewed restless expansionism as an inevitable journey toward total dominance. Occupation, settlement, and development of the Great West was seen as a romance in the history of "civilization." European agricultural methods and the imposition of millions of exotic bovines in a wilderness suited to snakes, buffalo, Indians, and wolves seemed merely another step in supplanting old meanings with the new progressive spirit. Even when the earth proved hard and unyielding, the Indians stubborn and uncooperative, even after the last bison was shot and the last fence post was strung with barbed wire, few pioneers questioned the cancerous economic drive to squeeze each and every resource until the land might appear as a bleached and bloodless corpse. A ravenous wolf born in this anguish of spirit, nurtured by denial and conquest, subsumed the young American nation.

So began the first act of a drama that spelled extirpation for the Mexican wolf. The wolf had found its symbolic home in this wilderness of spirit, a profound emptiness at the root of consciousness, a desolation and isolation that yawned in a great chasm separating Western man from natural circumstance, and from this dark and bottomless abyss shone the eyes of the wolf.

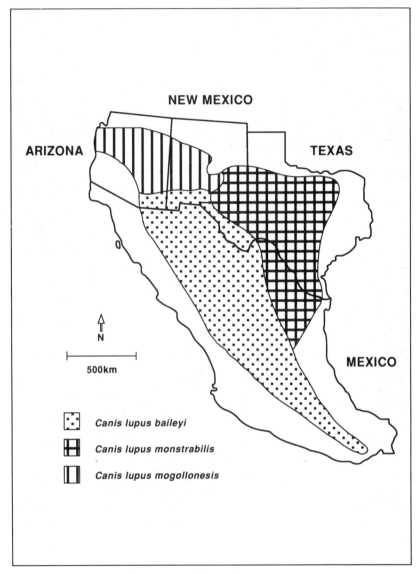

Historic distribution of Mexican wolf populations.

Mexican wolf. *Photo courtesy of Tom Smylie, U.S. Fish and Wildlife Service.*

A passel of Mexican wolf pups. *Photo courtesy of Kent Newton.*

Rare photo of Mexican wolf pups in a naturally excavated den. *Photo courtesy of Kent Newton.*

Wolf pups at Rio Grande Zoo. *Photo courtesy of Kent Newton.*

Wolf in winter at Endangered Species Foundation, near Golden, Colorado. *Photo courtesy of Ron McFarland.*

A wolf pack investigates a male wolf upon reintroduction to the pack, after a separation of several months to prevent breeding. Note submission postures of two wolves on left. *Photo courtesy of Kent Newton.*

Following reintroduction to the wolf enclosure, the dominant male reasserts his dominance with each pack member; he is shown here with a beta female. She takes on a passive submission posture. *Photo courtesy of Kent Newton.*

Wolf societies express aggression primarily through display; rarely do fights erupt. From 2 to 10 percent of wolf behavior involves aggression. *Photo by Jim Burbank.*

Mexican wolf showing territorial scratching upon being approached by humans. *Photo courtesy of Kent Newton.*

Male wolf presenting a dominant broadside dsiplay to rest of pack. Note hackles and raised tail, and upright posture with head up and ears perked. *Photo courtesy of Kent Newton.*

Dominant alpha male wolf: observant, challenging, and wary. *Photo courtesy of Kent Newton.*

CHAPTER SEVEN

Too Stupid to Survive

*That man is, in fact, only a
member of a biotic team is shown
by an ecological interpretation of
history. Many historical events,
hitherto explained solely in terms of
human enterprise, were actually
biotic interactions between people
and land. The characteristics of
the land determined the facts quite
as potently as the characteristics of
the men who lived on it.*
— Aldo Leopold
A Sand County Almanac

In the Southwest, wolf eradication took on the force and demeanor
of a crusade. In few places has human land use been at such variance with wolf ways.

By the 1880s and 1890s, agricultural practices had transformed
arid southwestern regions into one vast ranch. Where native grasses
had once grazed the bellies of passing horses, now desert scrub and
denuded soils cut by arroyos created a depleted landscape transformed by cattle ranching and sheep herding.

The Coues white-tailed deer, the southwestern wolf's natural
prey, had been reduced by unrestricted hunting, and the deer's natural forage had been exhausted by browsing ungulates. We will
never know what the Southwest looked like before ranching altered and degraded the now-barren landscape.

How the wolf lived and what habits it possessed shall remain
permanently sealed in the book of time. No studies of the vanish-
ing lobo occurred while wolves roamed free through southwestern
mountains and plains. We don't know if wolves killed neighboring
coyotes or if the two species co-existed in the same ecosystem.

We don't even know exactly what kind of damage wolves
wreaked on ranchers. Contemporary reports, tinged with hatred and
aversion, said wolves exacted a constant, steady tax on ranch herds.

Others claimed that wolves primarily attacked calves, young sheep, and animals that were infirm and unable to defend themselves.

Still others said wolves savaged twenty and thirty cows at a time, seemingly for sport, leaving the fresh kills to bloat and rot in the sun. Perhaps all of these reports are true. Wolves, like people are individuals. Few questioned the incongruity of implementing European agricultural methods in an area totally unsuited to bovine husbandry.

"Thin the Varmints Out"

The rationale of conquest and dominion over nature demanded the wolf be attacked and driven back into what remained of the wilds. Ranchers hired professional hunters to "thin the varmints out." In using such terminology the cattle man invoked colloquial usage for the Medieval word meaning worm (vermin).

Wolf, as psychological symbol of spiritual wilderness and the dark chaos of emotion, had been suppressed and denied. Since reason and economic objectification had become the sole means of interpreting experience and human cruelty itself was likewise denied, the next "logical" step in this progressive divorce from negative emotive truths became the ascription of these rejected images onto reality.

Thus, Native Americans were viewed as vermin (varmints), just as wolves were assigned the same meaning. During the years that followed the so-called settling and pacification of the Southwest, hunters sought not to control wolves, but to wipe them out, to rid the range of this lupine pestilence.

In 1893, New Mexico/Arizona Territory passed a bounty act allowing counties to raise money in order to pay wolfers for their services. In 1909, the New Mexico Territorial legislature provided a $15 bounty for lobos, which was the highest predator pay available. Counties were authorized to levy taxes in favor of the "Wild Animal Bounty Fund."

Economic significance joined with symbolic ancient meanings when bounty hunters were requested to present the scalp of each dead animal, or in the case of the lobo, the entire skin to the county clerk to claim pay for their services. Taking an animal's skin meant robbing him of his power. Throughout the period when bounty hunting was the preferred method of wolf extermination, payment for wolf hides confirmed the economic imperative as the only recognized conscious worth wolves assumed.

Problems of Mutual Interest

Thinning out wolves in these early days meant wolfers resorted to shooting, poisoning, and trapping. Stalking wolves or waiting near a recent kill were slow and time-consuming methods. Wolfers frequently laced wolf kills with strychnine. Upon ingesting the crystalline alkaloid derivative of *nux vomica*, the animal skulked away to die in agony far from the bait.

Many wolves and other animals died in this fashion without being discovered. Trapping also became a preferred method of wolf killing. The double-spring Newhouse trap, developed in the 1890s, featured offset jaws, sometimes with teeth that proved highly effective in catching wolves. Traps were baited with a noxious recipe of rotten glands, wolf body parts, urine, and feces reminiscent of medieval alchemical potions. Set on well-known trails in advance of approaching target animals, traps held their prey until hunters arrived to inspect them. In the event of a successful catch the wolfer then beat the animal to death with a "numbing club" which comprised a standard part of the bounty hunter's kit.

Denning was also a favorite wolfer method. After locating a wolf den, a hunter removed the pups and dispatched the litter. Problems with the bounty system meant wolfers tried to sell the same hide twice in different counties to increase their profit. Wolfers often let pups go during denning to assure a reliable crop of animals for future extermination activities, assuring their continued livelihood.

Stockmen became increasingly obsessed with wolf control. In 1914, ranchers put pressure on Congress to enact legislation in order to involve the U.S. Biological Survey in conducting predator control experiments. In November of that year, forty New Mexico cattlemen met with Gila National Forest Supervisor Hugh Calkins and his rangers to discuss "problems of mutual interest." Subsequent to this meeting the group decided to form the New Mexico Cattle Grower's Association. Uppermost in the ranchers' minds was elimination of the wolf. Three months later the Cattle Grower's Advisory Board voted an additional premium of $25 as an incentive for bounty hunters.

Canis Lupus Baileyi

Hunters were also organizing to promote predator control. In the same year, sportsmen banded together in the New Mexico Game Protective Association. They sought to involve the Federal Government in predator control as their primary objective.

Canis lupus baileyi, the Mexican wolf, bears Vernon Bailey's name. Bailey had primary responsibility for wolf elimination efforts in the Southwest during the early biological service days. One way of stealing power from the wolf was to bestow wolf races with the names of those who sought most ardently to exterminate them. *Canis lupus youngi*, the intermountain or Great Basin wolf, was named for Stanley P. Young, a senior biologist for the survey who became so intrigued by wolves that he wrote an early definitive book, *The Wolves of North America*, in 1944. Those who were often the most dedicated wolf killers grieved his disappearance. It was the kind of mourning that set in after slaughter and annihilation had eliminated the source of terror and left only haunting sadness to fill the void remaining after so much death and destruction.

In 1914, charged with establishing a wolf program in the Southwest, Vernon Bailey, senior biologist for the service, delegated the wolf control task to his protege, J. Stokely Ligon. Every bit the son of a sheep rancher, "Stoke" Ligon stood 5'8" tall and weighed less than 150 pounds. Square boned, with hammer-fingered hands and a face that revealed weathered pioneer resolve, he was born near Buda, Texas, in June 1870, the fourth of ten children.

As a small boy, he spent hours observing birds. Ligon learned to identify them by studying pictures emblazoned on his mother's baking soda boxes. While still a youth, he took copious notes on his observations, a habit he was to preserve throughout his life. For two years Ligon attended a small teacher's college in San Angelo called Justice Academy, and he studied biology for a couple of years at Trinity College in Waxahachie, Texas.

In 1900, after his family had moved to Pecos County, Ligon and one of his brothers constructed a raft. With a mail-order box camera he had purchased, Ligon and his brother drifted down the Pecos to the Rio Grande and then across the continent to the Gulf of Mexico. They hunted, fished, studied wildlife, and photographed the raw and open southwestern landscape through which they passed.

Seven years later he set out for New Mexico with a wagon loaded with tools for repairing wells. Ligon established close relationships with the ranching community in southern New Mexico after he began work as a crew member at the sprawling Bar Cross spread. Obsessed with recording everything, Ligon continued his meticulous wildfowl observations, cataloguing each location he visited through his numerous photographs. His notes and his pictures reveal a mind concerned with accuracy and detail but lacking in originality and aesthetic intent.

Ligon's field notes came to the attention of officials at the U.S. Biological Survey, forerunner of the federal Fish and Wildlife Service. They hired him in June 1913 to study and record nesting habits of New Mexico birds. His notes were to form the basis of his authoritative book on the state's birds, which Ligon worked on over a ten-year period just before his death in 1961.

Ligon got on well with the service. In 1914, he mapped prairie dog towns on the Becker Ranch near Springerville, Arizona. August Springer offered to pay Ligon a $10 bounty for every wolf attacking his cattle.

Then he received the assignment that was to change the course of history in the Southwest. Vernon Bailey conveyed to the young Ligon a sense of urgency and dread in his new task as chief wolf killer for the biological service, and he introduced him to his partner, Aldo Leopold, seventeen years Ligon's junior.

A Deep-minded Clarity

The two men could not have been more different. Open-faced, thin, and with a ready smile, Aldo Leopold was born of a wealthy family in a Mississippi River railroad town of Burlington, Iowa. He attended prep school back east and then Sheffield Scientific School at Yale. After obtaining his Master's degree in 1909, he joined the newly formed Forest Service where he was assigned to the Mogollon Rim–White Mountain border area between New Mexico and Arizona. He immediately became entranced with the Southwest.

Keen minded, Leopold displayed an avid passion for nature that blended scientific curiosity with penetrating insight. Leopold's intelligence was tinged with a poet's sensibility. As a writer, he was to develop in later years a deep-minded clarity of style that conveyed originality and a genius for detecting and discussing in lucid language the interlocking complexity of natural systems.

Ligon and Leopold, despite their differences, shared a mutual love for hunting and their passion for observing wildlife. Both men agreed to commit themselves to destroying each and every wolf until the final lobo breathed his last. They swore to destroy the lupine plague so that these "vermin" never would gain a foothold on the southwestern range again and New Mexico would be cleansed of the wolf scourge forever.

In September 1927, Ligon was to write in the *New Mexico Conservationist* that wildlife had always been a decisive factor in the "conquest and development of the nation." He saw wild creatures as valued solely for their ability to provide humans with recreation and a healthy lifestyle based on hunting game.

In the same article, he noted with concern what he called a great increase in game predation when compared to the past. For Ligon and for Leopold (at least at this point in the latter's life), the only good wolf was a dead wolf. The philosophy of total eradication, with its straightforward rationale, provided a compelling logic based on dominion over nature and conservation management. The key factor in maintaining and increasing an abundant supply of game was to wipe out the wolf. Hence the deer would multiply and hunters could then control the game populations.

The Old Hatred

Beneath the surface of such reasoned appeals lurked the old hatred and fear of wolves. As prophylactic against the true meaning of the predatorial binge, wolf hunters kept scrupulous records to detail, measure, and weigh each kill. The size, pelage, and color of each animal were carefully noted. From fifteen to twenty-five skull measurements were taken. The slaughter had to be objectively and scientifically recorded because wolf eradication was not the carefully planned massacre of another species, rather it was merely seen as a logical extension of game management.

Stoke Ligon and Aldo Leopold began their venture with enthusiasm, rallying support for predator control as they traveled around New Mexico speaking to local Chamber of Commerce meetings and groups of hunters and ranchers. The two were enthusiastically received.

In 1915, Stoke Ligon became the first inspector for the Bureau's Predator and Rodent Control program in New Mexico. The program received the acronym of PARC, conjuring a mental image of wide open spaces, managed for man's benefit.

Ligon retained a staff of seasoned wolf hunters with his $20,000 budget. From 1916 to 1924, he reported to his supervisors and constituents the progress made toward eventual wolf extinction. Stoke Ligon was a man with a mission and a tireless, efficient, and dedicated worker.

He needed a rock-solid argument to justify his program so the "wolf work" might continue unabated. What factors could he rely upon to form an undeniable appeal in support of his program? Ligon discovered and revealed in his first report an argument that blended eminently practical logic with a seemingly undeniable recourse to necessity—Ligon sought economic justification for PARC's wolf work because economics was the one reality that took precedence over all other American realities. Dollars and cents, he reasoned, had more persuasive force than any other logical or emotional argument in favor of wolf eradication.

Economic justification was a stroke of genius capitalizing on a thoroughly rational approach to exterminating the wolf. This eminently reasonable, objective appeal Ligon was to develop to a high art. Every program designed to control predators or other animal "pests" would find its inspiration in Ligon's increasingly inflated estimates of the damage wrought on livestock by wolf predation.

In the first year of operation, PARC destroyed sixty-nine wolves in New Mexico and Arizona, over half of them pups and fetuses. Ligon estimated in his year-end report that some three hundred adult wolves roamed the New Mexico range. If each of these wolves killed cows, horses, or sheep valued at $30 apiece, then it cost $324,000 for damages wrought against livestock by wolves.

Livestock losses from various sources, including wolf kills, were indeed a serious problem for ranchers. Ligon estimated that on the V-T spread in the Gila and Datil Forests, from 600 to 1,000 cows were killed by wolves each year. Why such a wide variance in the number of wolf kills? Almost apologetically Ligon wrote that, due to their wide range, wolves were not "noticed as much as if they were confined to smaller areas," therefore he found it difficult to estimate actual damages. He went on to say that it was a well established fact that wolves preferred only the very best meat and that they hungered for it constantly.

A Diabolical and Malicious Element

PARC hunters began to perfect earlier wolf killing methodologies to a high art. Various sizes of Newhouse leghold traps, with or without offset teeth, were located at scent posts where wolves marked their territory by urinating. Special attention was allotted to assuring human odor was carefully disguised. Wolfers spread the noxious mixture described earlier on the traps. Standing or kneeling on a piece of sheepskin or canvas, the hunter set the trap in a shallow hole disguised by plant debris and awaited results.

According to Gary Lee Nunley's report on wolves in New Mexico conducted for the Animal Damage Control Agency, the successor to PARC, "tallow-baits" laced with strychnine were frequently used to kill wolves. A small piece of hamburger was dropped near a recent wolf kill. The animal was thus encouraged to swallow the bait whole, the idea being that he would avoid the bitter taste of the strychnine.

Ligon described a sandwich bait of pork fat to disguise the same substance. Ligon recommended that the poison first be wrapped in waxed paper and then covered with pork fat. He also described a plug bait, of molded suet cubes laced with poison, but disparaged the time and amount of material required in the preparation of this method as well as the time required for the tissue type. Wolves had to be killed as quickly and as efficiently as possible.

In any case, the effect was always the same: the stricken animal slinked away to die far from the bait. No one will ever know how many wolves and other animals expired in this fashion.

Denning continued with enthusiasm as did the baiting of carcasses. Later techniques became more sophisticated. The "humane coyote getter" was utilized, a cyanide gun that fired poison into the mouths of wolves or coyotes after they pulled on a preset bait. Once again, the animal often traveled some distance from the bait and often died undetected.

More sophisticated poisoning agents were employed in the latter days of wolf elimination. Compound 1080, banned by the EPA in the 1970s, was used to bait carcasses or was placed on driftways or wolf trails. Compound 1080 worked very slowly, so that target animals usually went a long way from the scene of the poisoning.

A diabolical and malicious element resides in these poisoning techniques. The unsuspecting animal, whether guilty of predation or not, gulps the bait and dies in convulsive fits far from the witnessing eyes of its killer. The fact that wolves in their private death agony were unseen and that this was viewed as an advantage to poisoning raises some serious questions about wolf poisoning.

These death techniques reinforced the image of wolves as a disease that had to be eradicated and distanced the killers from the effects of their actions. Poisoning was clean killing at its best, despite the fact that many other untargeted animals must also have expired. The killer was thus protected from the knowledge of his actions. Also, this methodology served to further humiliate and degrade the victims that were not even accorded the attention necessary to deal with the aftermath—the bodies were never recovered.

Child psychologist Alice Miller suggests that in humiliating and "training" children to behave through "poisonous pedagogy," parents trick children into feeling degraded, ashamed, and responsible for parental cruelty.

In the case of wolf poisonings, the victim is fooled into taking the bait and subjected to ultimate humiliation—the animal wanders into the wilderness to die in invisible, unrecognized agony. The killers don't even bother to locate and deal with the corpse. This combination of surprise, degradation, lack of responsibility, and trickery shows thinly veiled hatred for wolves served as a surrogate for expiating unrecognized and buried negative emotions on the part of hunters. I expect many readers will dispute my interpretation of wolf elimination. They will argue that getting rid of wolves was necessary. Perhaps they will call me a "wolf hugger." So be it.

A Destructive Frenzy

I wish to respond by questioning the whole way in which our Western society imprinted its meanings on this continent, the land, its creatures, and the people who were native inhabitants here before European white man imposed himself on the New World.

It is the lack of responsibility for these actions, the denial and suppression of emotional meanings and ethical implications in predator slaughter which I find deeply troubling. Buried emotional and unconscious meanings erupted in a destructive frenzy for which our society has never claimed responsibility. I seek not to place blame so much as to embrace the terror of these meanings, to name this fear and hatred, and in this act of naming, to make peace with the wolf within.

Wolfers were no more cruel than anyone else, though one must ask what called them to perform such work. They expressed the general desires of their society and time. They were men doing a job, a task that society had assigned them. That mission was the carefully planned and executed extermination of the wolf, who was viewed as an impediment to human economic progress. It might be tempting to think of Stoke Ligon as a monster, but in truth he carried out the dictates of his time.

Stoke Ligon loved wildfowl and in his later life established a bird sanctuary, which he and his wife operated from his home in southern New Mexico. For Stokely Ligon, wolves were a disease that infected the land, but he loved birds and wildlife. He sought considerable justification for the perpetration of mass wolf death. Each year his estimated economic toll increased until the figure reached the millions of dollars.

Each year, wolves in Arizona and New Mexico were killed in increasing numbers until eradication efforts reached their peak in the early 1920s, when over a hundred animals were dispatched in both states. Suffice it to say that efforts increased annually, though through the mid 1920s fewer wolves were found. After a jump in killings late in the same decade, destruction methods yielded a consistently smaller number of wolves until, during the 1950s the wolf was all but gone. The last wolf carcass found in New Mexico was discovered in the Peloncillo Mountains in 1970.

I don't want to spend time detailing this destruction, stacking wolf bodies like so much cord wood. For those who want to quantify and measure the extent of wolf eradication in the Southwest, I recommend David L. Brown's book, *The Wolf in the Southwest*, which provides all the figures, charts, documentation, and statistics one might wish for, along with a well-developed discussion of wolf-killing methodologies. Let those who wish to quantify the eradication of the wolf do so.

There will also be those who say that it's fine for me to sit in my comfortable warm room in front of my computer terminal writing of an animal I have rarely seen or experienced and a time posing challenges I have never had to face. Ranchers have told me with fear in their voices of the terrible devastation wolves wrought against cattle. They have described to me their absolute opposition to wolf reintroductions and they have done so with conviction and determination. They have said that we don't know where our meat comes from, that we are divorced from the process which supplies us our food, that we are cut off from nature. I think maybe they are right in saying we are cut off from the real world of nature, but not for the reasons these adherents express.

The Green Fire in Her Eyes

I speak now of an awakening that occurred to one man who was a wolfer, and a committed wolfer at that. This transformation was to have bold and far-reaching implications for our time. His was a reawakening to principles which had long lay dormant and awaited the right person to make this rediscovery and to state with decisive clarity these long-hidden principals. That man was Aldo Leopold who, with Stokely Ligon, had continued his passionate support of wolf eradication.

At the inception of World War I, beef demand for the war effort was strong. In 1917, Ligon and Leopold relied on the justification of the war effort to increase their wolf rhetoric. PARC estimated over $2 million in predator livestock damages were made that year. This figure was used consistently in speeches to justify wolf killing.

While Leopold had been forced to give up his dream of conducting intensive field work due to a kidney infection he had contracted in 1913, he continued to hunt with a passion. Sometime during his early New Mexico days, an incident occurred that left an indelible impression on Leopold, though it was years before he understood the full implications of this event.

One day in the White Mountains, Leopold and his companions were eating lunch on a high rimrock overlooking a river. The men looked down at the water and saw what they thought was a deer emerging from the torrent. In climbing the nearest bank the animal shook itself in the distinctive way known only to wolves. Six other grown pups joined the she-wolf in a playful frenzy of tail-wagging wolf high-jinks.

Quickly the men grabbed their rifles, and in a second blasted away at the wolves. When they had emptied their guns they went to inspect their work.

"We reached the old wolf," wrote Leopold toward the end of his life, "in time to watch a fierce green fire dying in her eyes."

Suddenly there was something new to him in the eyes of the lobo.

"I thought," Leopold continued, "that because fewer wolves meant more deer, that no wolves would mean hunters' paradise. But after seeing the green fire die, I sensed that neither the wolf nor the mountain would agree with such a view."

Leopold's observation was drawn on many years of watching states eradicate wolves, an effort for which he was in large measure responsible. With their natural foe gone, the deer stripped every tree of leaves. In the end, the deer themselves died, the hoped-for hunters' paradise now a starving ground for the hunters' prey.

Hunting ethics had been a part of Aldo Leopold's life from the time he was a boy. His father, who willingly abstained from hunting in the spring, told him not to shoot partridges unless they were in flight. From 1915 until he left New Mexico in 1924, Leopold promoted game refuges, strict law enforcement, conservation, and management.

To others in the Forest Service he advocated protecting the remaining allotments of wilderness. The same year he left New Mexico to go to Madison, Wisconsin, his work paid off when the half-million-acre Gila National Forest was designated a wilderness area. Leopold took with him the manuscript for an ambitious book entitled *Southwestern Game Fields*. In this early work he revealed his penetrating insight into the "hair-trigger" natural balance he had discovered in the desert ecosystem of the Southwest. In Wisconsin, he worked at the Forest Products laboratory for four years and then quit the service to carry on the more rewarding work of surveying game in the Lake states for an arms manufacturing company.

Imponderable Essence

The stock market crash of 1929 and ensuing Depression ended his position and Leopold found himself jobless, supporting his wife, Estelle, who was a member of New Mexico's Luna land-grant family, and the five Leopold children. With considerable courage he persevered in writing a classic wildlife management textbook, *Game Management*, wherein he shaped and honed his ideas for what lay ahead. He was a natural negotiator and found himself balancing the concerns of wilderness and society's needs. The University of Wisconsin at Madison gave him a job teaching courses in the nascent science of ecology.

In 1935, he purchased a burned-out piece of farmland in the sand counties of central Wisconsin. Here, he and his family retreated on weekends while Leopold wrote, observed the country, and brought his farmstead gradually to life. His observations were to form the backbone of *A Sand County Almanac*, which has become an American classic.

Yet it was the she-wolf Leopold remembered and that long-ago day in the White Mountains which informed his work and brought him to a new realization about the meaning of homo sapiens' relationship with the natural world. Aldo Leopold recanted his beliefs about wolves. He had come to see the wolf as part of a great intertwining web of nature. In this discovery he sensed what the Pueblos, Navajos, and other Native Americans have always known.

Many other writers have been aware of the importance of Leopold's White Mountain encounter with the she-wolf and her six pups. In virtually every article written about him the green fire incident is recorded in full. Why?

This event lies at the heart of Leopold's thinking and informs all of his writings, underpinning a mind in search of personal meanings and ethical truths. His was a spirit fired by the green light shining in the she-wolf's eyes. Once extinguished, he saw merely a lifeless object lying still before him. The image of this dead animal recumbent in river sands—this wolf corpse—burned itself into his memory until toward the end of his life, Aldo Leopold came to know the meaning of this experience.

Leopold wrote of the "imponderable essence" of material things that "stands in contradistinction to *phenomenon* which is ponderable and predictable even to the tossings and turnings of the remotest star."

He speaks to the *noumena* in contrast to the shadow play of events and objects. The Kantian term *noumenon* is composed of two Greek roots—*noos*, meaning "mind" and *noein*, meaning "to perceive." The "imponderable essence" is the noumenon, what gnostics called the "depth" of all, or what existentialists have termed the ground of being shining forth, just as the imponderable green light shone from the she-wolf's eyes at the moment when death robbed her of her meaning.

Aldo Leopold's search for a "physics of beauty" led him to consider in the young science of ecology a view of history that grounds human beings once again in the mystery of life. He came to understand that American "clean" land management meant that the intricate and interdependent web of living plants and creatures had come to stand only for economic profit. Predators, as a pestilence, were being wiped away and imported plants, animals, and fertilizers were introduced to the wrecked and burned-out land in order to instill economic meaning to a wasted and ravaged earth.

Leopold called for a revolt against the tedium that had settled across America's landscape like a dull gray fog. This boredom, this ennui meant that land was just the "place where our money was made," not a living biota charged with the brilliant light of interdependent meanings.

The hunting culture of primitive peoples, he perceived, was based on wildlife. The predator instinct that delights in the sight and joyous pursuit of game trembles in every fiber of human being. Human wolf nature, Leopold so brilliantly saw, was a source of ecstasy and delight, a knowledge instilled in our being, a body knowing. Land, the earth, is by extension inextricably linked to this body knowledge. In short, the earth is our Mother and we have a living ethical relationship with her that implies love and responsibility.

Our connection to the land and its creatures is the stuff and substance of biotic history. The westward movement of conquest and dominion over this land, stained with darkness and blood, meant humans had misappropriated nature for exploitation and profit.

"The evidence had to be economic to be valid," Leopold wrote. Wolves, like ourselves are members of the biotic community, equals in every sense of the word, and no special interest has the right to exterminate them. The great pyramid of life, with its infinitely complex interactions of prey and predator, soil and plant, we can never successfully manage, because humans are but one link in this incredible and wondrous chain of living organisms.

The soft stirring of wolf paws, almost inaudible, the whistling of swift wings when the morning star pales in the east and gray light steals over hills, dawn wind rustling through old cottonwoods and over the ancient river sliding softly past—the music of Aldo Leopold's voice whispers over the land and the earth answers.

On April 21, 1948, while fighting a brush fire with his neighbors, Aldo Leopold suffered a fatal heart attack. He never saw his *Sand County Almanac*, that slim volume, come to life in print.

CHAPTER EIGHT

Beloved Wolf

*Life is, in itself and forever, shipwreck. To be
shipwrecked is not to drown. The poor human being,
feeling himself sinking into the abyss, moves his arms to
keep afloat. This movement of the arms which is his
reaction against his own destruction, is culture—a
swimming stroke. When culture is no more than this,
it fulfills its function and the human being rises above
his own abyss. But ten centuries of cultural continuity
brings with it—among many advantages—the great
disadvantage that man believes himself safe, loses the
feeling of shipwreck, and his culture proceeds to burden
itself with parasitic and lymphatic matter. Some
discontinuity must therefore intervene, in order that
man may renew his feeling of peril, the substance of his
life. All his life-saving equipment must fail, he must
find nothing to cling to. Then his arms will once again
move redeemingly. . . . Hence I no longer believe in any
ideas except the ideas of shipwrecked men.*
—Ortega on Goethe,
quoted by Austryn Wainhouse
Writers in Revolt

In the late 1890s, when Ernest Thompson Seton wrote about a wolf
he called Lobo, King of the Currumpaw, the wolf slaughter was just
beginning in New Mexico. Yet Seton's story captures what was then
occurring with the human relationship to wolves in the Southwest.

Seton recalled the incredible power of this wolf, who became
both outlaw and hero to the well-known nature writer. Ranchers in
the northern part of New Mexico where Lobo roamed noted his
preternatural strength and cunning, his uncanny ability to avoid
every means of trapping or poisoning and his love for his mate,
whom Seton called Blanca. Mingled with the usual loathing, Seton
expressed admiration for the great wolf's superior wile. Despite every
means to bring him down, the huge Lobo avoided death at the
hands of a series of bounty hunters as well as the author himself. A

French wolfer, who tried his hand at destroying the beast, declared that Lobo was a "loup-garou," a werewolf, half human and half beast. But it was love that ended the marauding King's life.

Seton, after attempting poisons and carefully disguised traps, finally managed to catch Blanca, the great king's mate. The nature writer and a ranch hand lassoed the she-wolf and strained their horses in opposite directions until blood burst from her mouth, her eyes glazed over, and she died. The forlorn King of the Currumpaw, in his despair, wailed in the distance as Seton planned to trap him, using his mate's body for bait. The great wolf, heedless in his mourning, fell prey to the ruse, and Seton discovered him, a trap on each of his four feet, glaring at the author with yellow eyes of hate. After the wolf became exhausted from his struggle to free himself from his bonds, Seton forced a stick through his mouth and tied his jaws.

Then he carried Lobo back to the ranch where he staked him out in a field with a collar around his neck. The wolf did not protest, nor did he fight or growl, but acquiesced to his fate. The author placed food and water for the King, but he did not eat or drink. He lay in the field and looked out into the distance as if deep in mourning. The next day Seton discovered the wolf king in this position, the life having left him.

How well I recall this tragic tale of wolf love and death. I grew up with Seton's *Wild Animals I Have Known* on my bookshelf at home, having inherited the original edition from my father who was entranced by Seton as a boy. I have the battered volume on my desk before me now as I write.

Despite the fact that Lobo was not a Mexican wolf per se, the story says much about what wolf killing did to the human spirit as the slaughter progressed, because the hunters of PARC grew to know and invest their prey with qualities, some of which belonged to the wolves, and some of which are human. The wolf became an outlaw hero as he passed from being an object of dread. Those who were most responsible for the extirpation of wolves experienced heart sickness that mingled the bitterness of hate and a deep longing that could only be called love for this adversary whose habits they knew so well.

❂   ❂   ❂

A Beloved Desperado

In the 1920s when wolf elimination was at its peak, hunters often gathered around the fire to tell tales about Old One Toe or Old Aguila, a she-wolf of renown. These wolves were invariably huge and possessed superior cunning and unusual habits distinguishing them from their more ordinary kin.

This peculiar blend of hatred, admiration, and affection expressed by wolf hunters for their victims reveals a deeper emotional substratum in the relationship between killer and intended prey, a bond that suggests meanings Western society has carefully kept hidden beneath a more palatable disguise of surface motivations.

Strip away economic imperative, pseudoreligious moralizing, and the veneer of scientific rationalism from the crusade to exterminate wolves and what appears is a visage of man the lycanthrope. These wolf hunters were but soldiers carrying out the task society had assigned them.

I have detailed the split between conscious reason and unconscious motivation, the chasm of terror and isolation from embodied emotional reality that resulted in exploitation and extermination of the wolf as Other, as well as the domination and conquest of the American West and its inhabitants. I have spoken of the masks and guises behind which these factors seem to operate in the southwestern historical journey. I have shown how cruelty and dominance were denied by perpetrators and ascribed either to other peoples or to the wolf, both of whom were victimized by this process of exploitation.

But, why in the very midst of this process of extermination did the killers feel such a strong bond with the animal they were eliminating? Was it merely that they knew the wolf and her ways so well that they yearned for her in a kind of sadistic bond between killer and victim, blending hate and love?

Jungian psychologist Robert Eichler has noted such an association between cruelty and love ascribed to wolfishness in humans. When humans look at wolves, a peculiar ambivalence also begins to emerge—hatred, admiration, and even love mingle.

Ernest Thompson Seton wrote his story of Lobo at a time when Charles Darwin's theory of evolution was being hotly debated in scientific circles. Seton seems to invest his wolf with human qualities: faithfulness to and love for his mate, Blanca, and despondency and hence carelessness when she is killed. For these reasons, and because of the wolf's superior guile in avoiding capture, Seton admires Lobo despite hating him because he is a cattle-killing predator. If Lobo is pictured as a destructive predator, Seton, through the brutal and grisly destruction of Blanca, shows how humans engage in great cruelty, which we excuse through the "necessity" of halting cattle predation by wolves.

Revealed through Seton's wolf story is an image of wolf nature that seems to mirror human nature. In behavior, the two species show a remarkable affinity to reflect one another. At the same time, the ancient aversion and repulsion is present in Seton's reaction to the wolf marauder.

This distinctive blend of affinity and aversion is more than accidental. Contemporary scientific investigations have shown that our ancient prehistoric hunter-gatherer ancestors and wolves shared remarkably similar lifestyles and behavior traits. Seton's story may be more than simple anthropomorphism. The emotional ambivalence of hate and love may be due to ancient parallel adaptations shared by prehumans and the forerunners of the wolf. Both species filled the same ecological niche as the most effective hunters in their respective ecosystems. Neither species had significant competitors except for one another. Perhaps the old antagonism has left traces that surface in an aversion and fear of wolves in humans and a similar attitude in wolves toward us. Our remarkable similarity in wolves may be present in an attitude in attachment and affinity to them.

The relationship is much more complex than a purely psychological interpretation of attraction-repulsion between wolves and humans might first appear because of the biological relationships between ancestors of wolves and humans. This connection has been obscured by popular and scientific trends masking our affinity with wolves. Darwin's suggestion that humans and apes shared a common phylogeny and evolutionary history has perhaps obscured this connection between wolves and our human ancestors. Not only have scientific investigators failed to perceive our link to wolves, but common misunderstanding of evolutionary theory has made our complex relationship with wolves more difficult to comprehend.

❂ ❂ ❂

Wolf Analogs

The popular misconception that we humans descended from apes is a distortion of evolutionary principles. Evolutionary theorists believe humans and apes evolved from common ancestors. This perceived commonality has led to a series of studies investigating likenesses with our almost-human relatives. The search for a common ancestor of both humans and apes, the so-called "missing link," has long preoccupied scientists. Due to a preoccupation with these similarities and our own view of our uniqueness, we have failed to see how similar our ancestors were to other animals that on the surface, at least, may appear to be quite unlike us.

Only recently have we begun to explore behavioral and adaptational analogs to early human experience in order to shed light on our hominid ancestors who lived as hunter-gatherers. Within the past fifteen years, studies of the analogous evolution of wolves and early humans have begun to reveal a fascinating picture showing that prehistoric peoples and wolves shared remarkable similarities. Could not these similarities, then, bond us to wolves in ways we have yet to understand? Could not this deep affinity create mysterious feelings of kinship and fellow feeling for wolves arising from an ancient and hidden place in the human spirit?

In 1978, a group of scientists from different disciplines published the results of their researches into the comparative relationship between prehistoric humans and wolves. *Wolf and Man: Evolution in Parallel* presented a remarkable summary of the findings of these anthropologists, biologists, and psychologists showing that the link between men and wolves was the domestic dog. Dogs carry the symbolic weight of both wildness and tameness. They serve as both real and psychological mediators between the wolf world and the human world.

A Parallel History

Ten thousand years ago, on some forgotten windswept savannah a group of prehistoric hunters and a pack of wolves may have pursued the same large ungulate prey. It is possible that a kind of cooperative relationship, a sort of symbiotic bond developed between them. Wolf ancestors of the modern dog and ancestors of modern humans began a relationship resulting in a strange history of parallel adaptation. Other examples of symbiotic relationships, including cooperative hunting, exist throughout the animal kingdom, so my fictional scenario, even if speculative, is not so unlikely.

Dogs become a kind of psychological intermediary, occupying a position somewhere between the wild and the tame. Dogs represent, perhaps, the human tendency to subsume wildness in order to serve our own needs to control beast nature in favor of human meanings. The guard dog turns its savagery outward to fend off the wild and dangerous creatures, and then cowers submissively to obey its master's command. This reflects our human need to make the wild tame and to bend that which is savage to serve our own human purposes.

In any case, the evolutionary transitions from hominid to human and from wolf to dog have followed similar paths. Dogs have shorter snouts, smaller teeth, and more prominent foreheads than wolves. Similarly, humans possess reduced jaws, more refined teeth, and larger foreheads when compared to our ancient ancestors. Thus, the link between wolves and prehuman hunter-gatherers show some interesting parallel developments.

The earlier view of prehistoric humans as inept lesser apes with the marginal advantage of having hands capable of grasping and a relatively high intelligence has given way to the view of our ancient hunting forebears as social animals like wolves—living in rather small family units, highly intelligent, and able to exert themselves over long periods.

Fossil remains of early humans show that our ancestors successfully lived at least four to one million years ago, indicating a tremendously successful and stable biological adaptation. These ancient predecessors proved to be highly proficient survivors, not evolutionary misfits lacking survival skills.

Cave paintings at Lascaux and Les Eysiex, France, as well as other examples of prehistoric art, in depicting deer, bison, and other prey species, show an extremely close attention to the behavior, gestures, and postures of these animals. Such detailed observations indicate these cave artists matched in detail and felicity the most recent anatomical drawings completed by technical illustrators. Their observations display an accuracy derived from the study of prey by highly proficient human predators who knew the ways of game animals intimately.

While phylogenetically humans and apes bear commonality, in

terms of lifestyle and solutions to ecological problems, wolves and ancient humans are strikingly similar. Both wolves and men weigh about the same. Ancient human ancestors and wolves hunted in broken forest or open country and pursued relatively large prey. Both animals are "apex hunters," that is, they hunt at the top of the food chain, having no other natural enemies or others competing for their biological niche—except each other.

Currently, students of evolution are debating where our ancestors first evolved. Early hominid development may have occurred in Africa, far from the range of wolves. When hunter-gatherers had advanced enough to range over great distances, they may have first encountered wolves, and perhaps engaged in competition for food resources. Hence, the antagonism towards wolves, based on our similarities, may have begun in the dim past.

Where intensive agriculture and animal husbandry have existed, humans have attempted to eradicate wolves. This old antagonism underscores the ancient relationship between human agricultural practices, animal husbandry, and attempted wolf extermination.

Because early humans and wolves sought rather large prey, they ranged over territories larger than those of other animals and they lived in small groups. Wolf packs range in size from five to sixty but the average is about seven. Hominid hunter-gatherer clans were approximately the same size. Wolf packs of ten members range five hundred to a thousand square miles. About twenty-five prehistoric hunters would travel a similar range in search of game. Few other animals hunted in such wide-ranging parties composed of few individuals.

No studies of the Mexican wolf occurred before near extinction removed her from her natural range. We may assume that Mexican wolf and other gray wolf habits and life patterns were similar. The primary natural prey of the Mexican wolf was the Coues white-tailed deer, a relatively small prey. Hence pack size among Mexican wolves is thought to be smaller than that of northern wolf groups that prey on caribou or moose. In general the size of wolf prey determines how big the pack will be. Beyond this one distinction we must be content to study other members of the wolf family and draw our analogies about the Mexican wolf from looking at wolves in general. Again, the parallels with human life history show a remarkable affinity.

Wolves and humans spend the same proportion of their lives in infancy and adolescence. Both consume a small but significant part of their diet as meat. Because meat is nutrient rich, hominids and wolves spent a larger percentage of their time hunting and socializing, compared to browsing or grazing animals. Wolves and hominid groups function with a division of labor, with hunter and non-hunter groups based to some degree along sex lines but also on age and ability. Wolves and early humans used a home base frequented by nonhunters where groups or packs shared food and social life.

Wolf Culture

The simple minded view of hunting peoples as wild savages and predators as raging beasts cannot stand up under the light of thorough investigation and scrutiny. Previously, under the influence of our human-centered ideologies and concepts, we have considered that only humans possessed culture. But why should not animal groups also share in those closed systems transmitted from generation to generation that we call culture—especially wolves who share some analogous behavior with humans?

Culture is the attempt of a social group to stave off destruction through redeeming ritual and ceremony. Our human-centered beliefs have concealed the fact that wolves have a sophisticated "culture" involving ritual and ceremony as complicated as human tribal cultures. Many human tribal cultures and wolf cultures have shared a long history of stable biological adaptation. Only in modern human social orders do humans believe themselves to be safe and protected from the abyss of nature. Modern human social orders, through such a false sense of security, are prone to disintegration and revolutionary change due to what Ortega has called "parasitic" and "lymphatic" accretion. Human tribes and wolf packs, though, remained remarkably stable and met nature's challenges over thousands of years. Ritual and ceremony are the connections joining wolf and tribal human society together.

Wolves, like many tribal human cultures, practice elaborate and sophisticated rituals. Like many humans, wolves engage in ceremonial greetings of their leader, gathering rituals, and singing before the hunt, after eating, and in the evening. In human tribal groups social organization is based on dominance. Dominance is not a simple concept based on physical size or strength, but on the magnetic attraction exerted between leader and group, which we often call charisma.

Wolves also respond to some hidden power possessed by their leader. The alpha wolf may indeed be physically inferior or lack the hunting prowess of other animals having an inferior rank in wolf society. Dominance and social order in wolf packs is fluid and maintained through consensus.

An alpha male and alpha female produce offspring who then assume subordinate social positions based in part on birth order. Alpha males do not always mate with alpha females and other wolves have been observed mating with fertile females. In any case, dominance seems to be maintained by mutual consent in wolf society. Alpha wolves rarely display their weapons and are infrequently challenged by other animals.

Powerful offspring may challenge an alpha male wolf, but are sometimes driven from the pack if they persist in their assertions. Such lone wolves are a relative rarity in wolf social groupings. These lone wolves, having no pack affiliation wander through wolf pack territories. If discovered by home packs intruders are often attacked, driven away, or even killed. Lone males may find lone females and mate in order to start their own packs.

In this manner, an assertive male offspring who challenges the alpha wolf's dominance can become the progenitor of a new pack, if when encountering a female, he couples with her and they produce offspring. Genetic diversity is preserved through the mating of lone wolves with females from other packs.

Scientists are currently debating what constitutes genetic diversity among wolves. Genetic diversity is especially important in considering wolf reintroduction programs, because investigators are unsure if captive breeding ensures sufficient genetic variability over a number of wolf generations. Since parents and siblings mate, this evidence suggests wolves preserve diversity despite interbreeding.

In terms of pack relationships, wolves display elaborate ranking patterns that are akin to human social orders. These fluid relationships, based on pack hierarchy, allow a minimum of tension and prevent violent disputes from destroying wolf society.

Dominance and submission are the behavior modes that scientists have categorized during extended wolf observation studies. These human labels for wolf pack ranking and dispute resolution reflect our own propensities, as well as our limitations as observers. What these behaviors mean to wolves we may only guess, but these interactions are nonetheless fascinating.

Subordination is shown either actively or passively. Roger Peters, in his book *Mammalian Communication*, notes that the wolf showing active submission crouches in approaching his superior. He pulls back his ears, and licks, nuzzles, or gently bites his superior's face. Occasionally he will raise a front paw and stroke at the dominant wolf's face and neck.

He holds his tail low and wags laterally, sometimes with great force, so that the hindquarters move; in contrast, the dominant wolf holds his tail high. The lips of the subordinate are parted in a "smile" and the face is turned toward the neck of a superior. Active submission displays of varying degrees take place during the greeting ceremony mentioned above when inferiors rush the lead wolf. Group ceremonies often happen when the pack has just located prey. The other wolves seem to entreat the alpha wolf to lead them in the chase.

In passive submission displays, ears and tail assume the same position. The subordinate wolf lies on its side or back exposing its abdomen. Often the superior responds by licking or sniffing the inferior's groin. Some investigators think passive submission imitates the position assumed by pups when adults lick them to stimulate elimination. Thus, the dominant wolf plays parent to the subordinate.

Active submission displays sometimes are misunderstood and produce a hostile response. The importance of tail position underscores the wolf's dependence on anogenital odor to convey complex information about an animal's condition and emotional state. The tail held low restricting anogenital access allows little odor emission. Peters has noted some ten tail positions indicating threat, uncertainty, social position, restraint, and power.

Wolf facial characteristics are likewise complex, highly expressive, and convey different shades of emotion. One interesting facial expression made by young wolves Peters has named the "play face." Play is for wolves, like other mammals, an important means of learning adult responses and behaviors. Games such as king of the mountain, combat, chase, and tag occupy young wolves, and even adults engage in play, though less frequently than pups. In signalling the desire to play, a wolf pulls back its lips in a smile and pants in eager anticipation.

Wolves share with humans a fear and distrust of strangers that may produce group rejection or even attack. By noting such similar behaviors, we may gain insight into xenophobic behavior that humans practice—which is inherited from our ancient hunting past, but which may no longer serve us. In and of itself wolf behavior is thus fascinating and variegated, showing an unexpected emotional and tactile richness we have perhaps reserved only for our study of humans.

Ritual preservation of social cohesiveness and distance among wolves regulates pack affiliation and preserves appropriate social distance. Food may be solicited and shared, likening wolf eating behavior to human groups that share meals together.

Wolves and our ancient ancestors engaged in so-called epideictic displays involving the sudden and inexplicable congregation of animals occurring at often predictable places and times. During these gathering displays, information is exchanged after which the group may break up or remain together to migrate, hunt, or engage in other instinctive behavior. Investigators speculate that some kind of magnet effect may occur in these displays. Individuals stimulate one another, inhibitions break down, and a kind of group, collective mind occurs. Among humans mob action, political demonstrations, and sports rallies all share in aspects of this display behavior. Among wolves howling, yelping, barking, greeting, submission displays, tail wagging and face licking, all akin to tribal dances, mark pre-hunt behavior.

Wolf Vocalizations

Formulated as extensions of the scientific paradigm, studies of captive wolf utterances portray these sounds as objects for investigation, not as subjects for reflection in order to determine greater meanings. In examining possible syntactic structures in wolf calls and other vocal behavior, elaborate systems to determine howl length, duration, intensity, and pitch have been developed by biologists. Yet we have obtained only a hint of what secret worlds wolf cries open to the lupine heart. In the rigors of scientific methodology lie its limitations as well as its insights. This fascinating animal remains forever an object and not a fellow being to whom we may draw close in order to learn its ways.

Biologists have defined whimpering, growling, barking, howling, and "social squeaking" as the range of wolf vocalizations. The soft, high, plaintive sound called whimpering is used by wolves most often near the opening of dens to express solicitude for offspring.

The wolf world is as complex and emotionally variegated as our own. When dominant females dance in heat, they whimper. Subordinates engage in the same behavior when threatened by a more powerful wolf, though obviously for different reasons. In this fashion submission and whimpering are linked to request friendship, favor, and even what we might call "love." To term certain wolf interactions "love" is, of course, a purely human interpretation. An argument for making such a determination may lie, however, in our natural similarity as fellow creatures and mammals sharing a common heritage. What such interactions mean to wolves we will never know. Wolves nonetheless display an extraordinary amount of affection and loyalty to one another, though there are pack outcasts and intruders that do not receive favor.

Aggressive growling, made by a dominant wolf, may be combined with what wolf observers call a "threat, bite posture" in order to display rank and assert position against an inferior. Deep, guttural, and coarse barking spells excitement, wolf alarm at potential intrusion by strangers, or a call to the chase.

The "social squeak" has rarely been observed in the wild and seems to be made as a special whine when approaching other wolves. The squeak may be a special gambit to establish openness toward another.

A Plangent Call

We have always been intrigued and repelled by wolf howls. These calls seem to stir the human blood like few animal vocalizations. Naturally, it may seem to the casual observer that the wolf howl and human speech may share some commonality. According to anthropologists Roberta L. Hall and Henry S. Sharp, editors of the *Wolf and Man* study I have cited, imitation wolf howls made by humans elicit more response from wolves than recordings of real wolf calls. We are perhaps less removed from wolves than we might suppose.

Howling also seems to warrant the greatest attention from wolf biologists. It is the most obvious and easily observed vocalization and one cannot ignore the peculiar impact wolf howls create in the human psyche. Yet for all this study, the precise reasons for howling remain mysterious, especially in regard to group howling.

The haunting quality of the wolf howl perhaps has influenced investigators to call one type of howl "the call of loneliness." Such cries occur primarily during December through February and are issued by individual wolves.

Less than a month after birth wolf pups begin to howl in the den. When left alone by adult pack members or when separated from siblings, pups also howl. Adults show the same behavior when separated from pack members. At the entrance of dens and especially when strangers approach, wolves bark and howl.

Wolves howl in chorus or in situations of great excitement such as dominance fights. Once an animal begins its song, others approach and tend to join in. The functions of howling, though, remain obscure.

Group howling seems to elicit great excitement and pleasure from wolves, who will run from great distances jawing and mouthing little cries of expectation as they hurry to combine their voices. Following chorus howls for fifteen to twenty minutes, pack members remain silent before engaging in another howl. Why this period of silence? Biologists say either they are physically incapable of howling or they won't howl. Given the great emotion created in wolves by the howling experience, perhaps this quiet time is an interval of reflection and contemplation.

Howling may also convey information about wolf behavior to others, whether the animals are lying, slow walking, or pacing and these unique vocalizations can also distinguish to other members of the pack which animals are engaged in calling.

Howling in and of itself is an intriguing and mysterious wolf function, beyond its eery and blood-curdling effect on humans. Scientific examination of wolf howls began only in the 1960s. Wolf experts Fred Harrington and David Mech noted that wolf howls begin on a strong low register note and rise in pitch favoring harmonically related overtones. Those who have spent time observing wolves at close range relate howling to human speech and often attribute to wolves an emotional complexity and range that makes them intriguing if not mysterious subjects.

Wolf biologist Mech observed that Lois Crisler, who formed considerable contact with wolves in the arctic, watched with fascination as a female wolf went through her howling ritual. Crisler noted that this she-wolf often whined and wagged her tail before howling.

The wolf threw back her head and drew her tongue back and forth in her mouth like a "trombone slide," ululating with intensity and pleasure. She formed her notes with her mouth so that her voice broke in deep waves against the cold still air, or she held a long and mournful note letting it die off gradually.

Crisler attributed to her she-wolf subject a sensitivity and perhaps an ecstasy that seems to me akin to the songs of poets in the human realm. Wolves avoid singing in unison, enjoying formation of chords, and their calls seem to summon from them great feeling.

Crisler called wolf whimpers "talking." She became deeply moved by them because the wolves sought her eyes, their own eyes luminous with emotion, and they uttered long and fervent choruses of plaints and "wowing" that trembled around a single pitch.

Humans have seldom observed wolf vocalizations in the wild in any extended or systematic fashion. Many observations of wolf speech lack the sympathetic response Crisler developed in her relationship with her wolf charges.

As interesting as these details about wolf behavior are, they show at the same time both the limitations and strengths of objective animal observations. Investigations intending to discover parallels between human speech and howling have until recently neglected other fascinating and complex aspects of wolf communication to which I have alluded in early chapters. Since we communicate verbally, our predilection for attempting to uncover the seeds of wolf language in howling may have obscured the importance of communication by scent and by other means.

Thus our assumptions about perception and thought present an initial barrier to understanding wolf communication. For instance, when St. Francis talks to the wolf of Gubbio, he engages in ordinary human speech as speaking is a readily apprehensible metaphor for communication even if it is between species. But most human communication is a nonverbal means of preserving relationships similar to wolf signs and involves body language, gesture, facial expression, and voice pitch. Since human communication is so oral and auditorially oriented, communication through elaborate scent messages seems foreign to us.

The Language of Scent

The cooperative effort needed to hunt relatively large game puts a premium on communication in wolf groups. Roger Peters has suggested that preadaptation to smell means wolves have developed a kind of language of scent.

I mentioned much earlier in this discussion the ability of wolves to create and use cognitive territorial maps to allow insightful travel through a large territory. Our human ancestors used visual cues to perform the same function. Wolves mark territorial boundaries, areas of previous kills, trails, and junctions. Raised leg urinations (RLUs) are performed only by dominant wolves and are used to locate significant places and convey important information to fellow wolves.

Subordinate wolves, while they may learn from the scent markings of dominant wolves, squat when they urinate. Thus, only dominant wolves convey through RLUs information crucial for the well-being of other animals. To date, scientific olfactory techniques are insufficient for uncovering the exact information conveyed to wolves through scent marking. Apparently, scent marking is a highly sophisticated means of communication that may reveal a number of significant cues to pack members.

Through experience wolves are able to take short cuts and perform route alternations, meaning they must have some form of mental representation of their specific territory and that they can combine old information in new ways to solve problems in their search for game.

Scent also allows individuals to recognize one another and determine emotional status, whether submissive, aggressive, or in solidarity with the pack. Natural selection predisposed hominids to perform the same functions through vocalization. Wolves produce distinctive odor, which social sniffing allows reduction of internecine strife among pack members by quickly establishing dominance and providing reassurance. Short-chain fatty acids account for wolf anogenital odor, which probably has pheromonal properties. Pheromones might also have provided distinctive clues to hominids about similar information useful to our distant ancestors.

In addition wolves may communicate important shared representations when they investigate smells applied to their bodies through rubbing. Not only do such odors account for the object the wolf has rubbed against, but, as Peters suggests, wolves may communicate crucial information about the place where the odor is to be found.

Early humans may have used sound in a similar way. By creat-

ing a string of significant sounds a series of these signals could have
provided the basis for the origin and development of spoken language. Since olfaction is not linear, in that many variations of
scent may be present at one time, olfactory communication would
not predispose wolves to developing linear language as we know it.
Might not our predisposition to linear perception and logical dis-
course hide from us a possible "wolf language," as sophisticated in
many ways as our own but nonlinear in nature?

A very sophisticated knowledge seems to be passed from wolf
generation to wolf generation allowing optimal group size in relation to available food. If food becomes scarce, like human hunting
groups, wolf packs break up and become nomadic until the availability of game allows them to become more sedentary. Cooperation, maintaining populations well below the environmental carrying capacity, the ability to plan and strategize, and nonaggression
help wolf packs maintain balance in relation to the ecosystem.

If the analogies between wolves and our ancient ancestors have
proven rich ground for discovering insights into our own nature,
wolves in and of themselves are deeply intriguing creatures. The
basis of human fascination with this animal may lie deep within
our own past. This ancient affinity between wolves and humans
has left its traces in our emotional makeup. It is an old love, this
feeling for wolves.

That Mexican wolves were eliminated before we have had a
chance to know them is a deep and abiding tragedy, and reason
enough that they should be returned to their natural home. If the
study of wolves in general has shown us our apparent affinity with
these animals, what new knowledge still eludes us because we have
been unable to observe Mexican wolves in their habitat? We may
never know about the everyday world of the Mexican wolf and
how she differs from her northern cousins.

But we do not, in truth, need to seek human-centered justification for returning the Mexican wolf to her homelands. It is a
deeply felt knowledge today surfacing within us, which says that all
creatures have a right to live undisturbed. Like the rejection of
slavery and racism, a new moral consciousness is being born that
says animals have inalienable rights to pursue their own lives without interference from humans.

We have in our power the ability to undo to some small extent
and reverse the cruel conscious elimination of the wolf from the wild

due to our own misapprehension and fear. A plea for the Mexican wolf is really a plea for all of what we have come to know as nature.

Without her and her creatures we are like shipwrecked sailors adrift and drowning, moving our arms to save ourselves. If such a movement is in favor of preserving our culture, it must be made in recognition of the deep and mysterious culture of wolves. This acknowledgment floats to the surface of our attention, an echo of our own hidden and ancient past.

CHAPTER NINE

When Wolves Run Free

*Empty this vast wilderness called
America. . . . Let us begin all over
again. Let us make new cathedrals,
let us sing again in unison, let us
make poems, not of death but of life!
Moving like a wave, shoulder to
shoulder, doing only what is
necessary and vital, building only
what will last, creating only for joy.*
—Henry Miller
Nexus

The road twisting up Clear Creek Canyon west of Denver, Colorado, passes from shade to sunlight and then back to shade once more. Like the wings of a great hawk light and dark alternate. Up the steep defile I wend my way until I pass the old mining towns of Central City and Black Hawk and then up onto the broad rolling spruce plateau that breaks suddenly into the tundra-clad mountains and escarpments of the Indian Peaks.

I am on my way to the Endangered Species Foundation, a private nonprofit wolf reserve established by Janet and Ron McFarland, two renegade wolf enthusiasts. I had met them the summer before when they were accompanied by their male timber wolf at an Albuquerque Coalition rally in support of Mexican wolf reintroductions.

McFarland, a lanky, 6'8" biologist and self-styled outlaw had engaged me in conversation during the wolf rally while I contemplated Wolf, the large dominant male McFarland had on a choke collar and leash. McFarland characterized himself as part redneck and part rebel. He refused to think like other people and preferred following his own path.

"Here," said McFarland, "hold him for a minute." He walked off while I took charge of the wolf. Holding a timber wolf is nothing like restraining a dog. The wolf goes where he will and he drags you along with him.

At first I attempted to keep him confined to a narrow periphery around the display table where wolf T-shirts and other lupine paraphernalia were for sale. Wolf sought some shade by a cottonwood and pulled me over to his desired locale.

Wolf and master were in many ways reflections of one another; each knew what he wanted and pursued his ends whether conventional or not.

A tan stocky woman in a cowboy hat offered to take Wolf's leash. She introduced herself as Janet McFarland, Ron's wife, lit a cigarette and settled back in her camp chair. The animal was persistently pulling me toward some better shade on the opposite side of his tree. I began discussing wolf beliefs with Janet McFarland as I reluctantly found myself being hauled around by Wolf.

"You don't have to put up with that, you know," she said, offering to relieve me of leash duty. We spoke for awhile about the need for wolf education.

She explained how much of her free time was engaged in taking the McFarland wolves to various schools in order to reeducate children and create a more positive view of wolves. When I told her I was writing a book about Mexican wolves, she invited me to stay with them at the foundation and study the two Mexican wolves they had acquired.

A Self-styled Outlaw

Several months following the rally I called McFarland, who gave me a set of arcane and complicated directions to their place. Now, this chill November morning I was driving Biscuit, my recalcitrant 1979 Honda hatchback, slowly up the highway to Golden Gate Park where McFarland had explained I would find the intricate system of backroads leading to the Endangered Species Foundation.

After negotiating several tricky dirt roads, I made my way down a steep hill, around a hairpin turn to the head of a small valley. In the distance the Indian Peaks lowered as clouds grazed their imposing summits. Here, nestled in this tiny vale were a small log cabin, several outbuildings, and a fenced enclosure that held two light tan timber wolves.

I recognized immediately that neither of these wolves was the male I had met several months before at the rally. The animals' stance informed me that these beasts were somehow different from the male that had accompanied the couple to the rally the summer before. It was hard for me to put my finger on that difference, and yet, in the way those two wolves stood, I could discriminate some subtle variance from the wolf I had seen the previous season.

As I drove up to the front of the house, a swirl of dogs emerged from behind the house. Two black labs barked and ran up to the car while a golden retriever wagged his tale in greeting.

"I see you survived the dogs," McFarland said as he emerged from his house onto the porch and I got out of the car. He filled the doorframe and ducked as he came out, tossing the remainders of a cup of coffee over the railing and onto the ground. Distracted, the dogs investigated the discarded coffee, having momentarily lost interest in me. At his casual invitation to enter I followed McFarland into his house, which gave in its particulars an impression of incompletion and work unfinished or in process. Raw sheetrock covered the kitchen ceiling. Dishes, tools, and coffee cups occupied the counters. Boxes were stacked everywhere, papers littering desk and table tops in chaotic profusion.

Stanley, one of the labs, quickly sneaked his way inside followed by two rangy cats.

McFarland motioned for me to sit on an old overstuffed couch across from his desk. One of his cats nimbly jumped on the old upright piano next to the sofa. McFarland grabbed a plant sprayer and aimed a neat stream of water at the feline, who scooted off into the dark interior of the living room.

McFarland and I began to engage in wolf chatter. He explained that he had wanted to breed his Mexican she-wolf with the animals in the Captive Breeding Program. He had completed an exhaustive genetic study of the female which he sent to the Albuquerque Fish and Wildlife Service office for approval, but his request had just been denied by Russell Earnest, then acting director of the Fish and Wildlife regional office. McFarland's DNA workup and his M.A. degree in molecular biology apparently were not enough to satisfy the service that the animal was all Mexican wolf. Fish and Wildlife rejected his offer. He handed me the letter from Earnest.

"I think they just want the Mexican wolf to quietly disappear by simply not letting the animals they now have breed," McFarland said. "You know, they have complete control." Our conversation drifted to a discussion of the antagonism between ranchers and wolf supporters. McFarland described himself as a rancher. He runs about sixty head of cattle on his Colorado holdings.

We began talking about environmental politics. He expressed the view that grazing on public lands had done little to harm western and southwestern arid lands. In this view he supported ranchers who deny that cattle grazing has been responsible for erosion and desertification on public lands. Iconoclast that he was, he said there should be no human presence above 9,000 feet. Even hikers, in McFarland's view, should be prohibited from intruding on the delicate country above timberline.

He attacked both environmentalists and ranchers for their wolf views. Environmentalists he chided for misleading and betraying ranchers and playing politics with our precious lands. Ranchers he excoriated for their ignorance and narrow mindedness about the wolf. He expressed his undying hatred of bureaucrats and public meddlers who attempt to restrict individual liberty.

No one was spared McFarland's acid assessment. It was refreshing to hear this outlaw soundly thrash everything and everyone held sacred or meaningful, no matter which side of the environmental or political fence they wandered on. Here was a man who was the archetypal Western individualist, afraid of no one's opinion, bitterly contentious, unerringly true to himself, even if his views seemed cockeyed and ardently crazy to others.

McFarland's Wolves

McFarland invited me outside to visit his wolves. We walked up a short hill in back of his house to an enclosure containing five wolves, including the large male that McFarland had brought to Albuquerque. I immediately spotted the three Mexicans, who were smaller than the large male timber wolf and possessed mottled dun coats. The three exhibited an active curiosity as we approached the pen. Up the hill a cautious black timber wolf observed our movements.

McFarland explained that I should avert my eyes when we entered the area. The wolves were extremely alert to any opportunity for escape. McFarland said we had to go in quickly and close the gate as rapidly as possible to avoid a wolf exodus.

I did as McFarland requested and we were instantly in the wolf enclosure. Wolf came up to us immediately and McFarland responded by scratching his back. Wolf was aloof, but friendly, allowing me to pet him. McFarland continued to attend to Wolf while I took out my camera and walked to the center of the pen.

The three Mexican wolves jumped up on my chest, pulled my clothes and nipped at my camera while they seemed to grin in pleasure at my efforts to protect myself and my clothing from their probing attention. I tried to keep my gaze from them, but all this apparently humorous prodding and investigation required me to regard them unless I was to lose my balance. Amid tail wagging, nipping, tugging, and pushing, I observed how mobile their facial expressions were. They seemed to be testing me in a jovial sort of way that I found very appealing. They continued jumping on me and tearing at any loose clothing, my camera, my legs, and shoes. They showed a preference for poking and exploring my groin with their noses. I found this kind of attention rather embarrassing.

Sunshine, the Mexican female jumped up and began licking my face just as I was focusing my camera. Without thinking, I stepped gently on her hind right paw as I would to make a rambunctious dog get down.

"Bad move," said McFarland who was still scratching Wolf.

"Me, or the wolf?" I asked.

"You," he replied. "They take any sign of possible aggression as a signal to attack. You were lucky."

"Oh," I said. It seemed as if all this nipping, pushing, and pulling were just good-natured fun. Later I was to learn how close I had been to a potentially terrifying and dangerous incident.

McFarland had stopped attending to Wolf and had walked slowly over to some boulders where he sat down. The male Mexican wolf was approaching the huge male timber wolf with a slow stiff-legged gait, head down, body slightly crouched, tail flickering back and forth.

Wolf began to growl. I had never heard a sound like the slow ominous thunder that emanated from deep within his chest, seeming to shake the earth. Immediately the Mexican wolf, as if knocked over by the growl, collapsed on his side, tail twitching frantically between his legs.

Wolf approached the supine form, sniffed between his legs a couple of times, and with a dismissive snort, turned around and stalked to the corner where he flopped down, head erect, almond eyes surveying his domain. The Mexican scampered over to McFarland, jumped on his chest, and licked his face vigorously.

After I had snapped the remainder of my film roll, we quit the enclosure and ambled back to the porch. McFarland's he-goat wandered over and began to butt and prod me as we continued our conversation.

McFarland explained he had to return to his work raising investment funds, which he does using a fax machine and the telephone in his living room office. He said it had been difficult for him and his wife Janet to keep the nonprofit Endangered Species Foundation going on contributions and what little money he could spare from his income. But demand for guest wolf appearances in local schools and public forums continued to be brisk. About three times a week he and Janet visited the schools to educate the kids about wolves, their habitat, and what kind of animals these predators really are.

I told McFarland I had to get back to town and thanked him for allowing me to shoot pictures of his wolves. He bade me goodbye as the wolves crowded up to the enclosure fence to see me off. I headed back up the first hairpin turn back to Denver and I thought about my encounter with the wolves and McFarland's response to my ill-timed gesture. What had he meant, I wondered, by telling me that I had been lucky? The wolves had seemed playful enough, like strong unruly dogs, I thought.

A Complex Array

I had no idea then that my behavior might have provoked a full-scale group attack. When a human goes into an area where wolves are kept, he must realize that he is entering into the wolves' world and that he will be subject to wolf society rules. For instance, when McFarland told me to avert my gaze from the wolves, he was invoking a key wolf greeting rule. To gaze directly into the face of another may be perceived as a sign of challenge and subsequent attack. Though they share common behavioral traits with domesticated dogs, wolves are the "adult" members of the canine community exhibiting mature canine behavior.

People have socialized dogs to display many juvenile traits that keep them locked into a kind of canine infancy, allowing them to be subject to discipline and ready dominance at human hands. Recent research using wolves in zoos and other captive situations has revealed a complex array of lupine behavior to which humans must adapt if they are to understand and successfully communicate and deal with the wolf world.

Since many wolves are threatened or endangered, like many creatures in our time, several zoos have captive breeding programs designed to increase wolf populations for possible reintroduction to the wild some day. Two theories currently dominate the thinking of researchers who are now attempting to raise and keep wolves in zoos. One theory holds that wolves in zoos should not be exposed to human contact. The other theory is that the wolves should be socialized to people. Kent Newton, chairman of the Mexican Wolf Captive Breeding Program at the Rio Grande Zoo in Albuquerque, recently detailed for me one theory that supports raising wolves with as little human contact as possible. Newton explained that if traditional avoidance of humans is encouraged and supported, Mexican wolves who may one day be reintroduced into the wilds, will respond by fleeing people. Flight from humans will protect the wolves and enhance their chances of survival in the wilderness, as humans are about the wolf's only natural enemy.

The Mexican wolf enclosure at the Rio Grande Zoo is designed with this philosophy in mind. Provided with only two viewing portals, the wolf area allows the animals as much isolation from humans as possible. When Newton and I visited the enclosure, he looked out the viewing window. The dominant male wolf immediately spied Newton. In extreme nervousness, he ran up to the enclosure wall, bared his teeth, and snapped and bit at Newton, who moved away from the portal.

"He doesn't like me," Newton said. "I had to give the pups medical treatments with the vet and he recognizes me." Zoos now integrate medical treatments for wolves with consideration for the rules of wolf society. All wolves in a pack are often treated at the same time. If only the dominant or alpha animal received treatment and displayed just some slight sign of weakness as a result, the other animals might immediately test and subsequently attack the alpha. The same holds true in the case of subordinate animals. Hence, all animals are either treated at the same time or given simultaneous placebo treatments to avoid confrontation. This practice is called "embedding."

If a wolf must be removed from the enclosure for an extended period, upon return it will be greeted by the others who will probe for any sign of weakness or vulnerability. If the wolf that reenters the enclosure, due to medical treatment, has been bandaged or has a wound or cut, the others will nip, bite, and worry the affected area until the animal is either severely hurt and must be removed, or until he is actually killed by his fellows.

Newton said he had removed the dominant Mexican wolf male from the enclosure for a few hours. On returning, the male scent-investigated each pack member to make sure they were all in good condition. Newton removed the Mexican wolf alpha male several years ago for a few months to prevent mating. When he came back to the enclosure he asserted dominance on each pack member in turn and then engaged in scent marking his territory. If any animal is reintroduced or if a new animal is placed in the pack, greeting rituals always take place. Wolves that are socialized to people adapt greeting to humans. I had experienced this salutation bestowed on me by the two Mexican wolves at McFarland's Endangered Species Foundation.

The greeting ritual allows a newcomer to be tested and explored to see what order he or she will assume in pack hierarchy. When I entered McFarland's wolf compound I immediately became subject to the greeting ritual. Wolves that are socialized to humans jump up on the newcomer human's chest and assess where he is in "pack order." The apparently playful nips and incessant proddings were actually means of testing my wolf worthiness. If, during such an encounter, a human makes a move interpreted as aggression, this will be taken as a sign calling for all-out attack, perhaps engaged in by the entire pack. I was indeed lucky, as McFarland had noted.

Studying wolves in the wild is a long distance affair. Knowledge of wolf society has in large measure been gleaned during intensive wolf observations conducted with captive populations. It is true that captive animals may behave differently from their wild counterparts because they are in much smaller enclosed areas, they do not have to hunt for food, and they are subjected to many strange sights, sounds, and smells not present in their native environment. Nonetheless, as far as scientific examination has determined, much of wolf social behavior seems to be the same whether in a zoo or in the wilderness.

❂ ❂ ❂

A Lupine Ritual

This observation brings me to the second theory about wolf captive management—that captive wolves become socialized to humans. Not only are people able to learn about wolf behavior from such a zoo situation, but wolves are more easily treated and moved about if they are used to human presence. Such animals most probably would not be good subjects for reintroduction into the wilds. A chance encounter with a stranger might induce an approach response, in which case the animal could be injured or killed or might test and possibly attack the person encountered.

Newton noted that perhaps as little as 2 percent and as much as 15 percent of Mexican wolf behavior involves aggression. Agonistic behavior, as aggression is termed, is handled symbolically by wolves through displays and postures signalling emotional cues to fellow wolves. The articulate and intricate interplay between pack members establishes who will assume dominance and under what conditions dominance will be asserted. This wolf symbology rarely ends in open battle between pack members, although fights with intruders and outsiders protect pack integrity.

A dominant male and female and their offspring comprise the pack. Male offspring may challenge the alpha male and be driven from a pack. Such a lone wolf may wander through wolf territories until he finds and mates with a receptive female, thus creating another pack.

Biologists have spent more time observing and recording dominance and aggression within the pack than any other behaviors. Human interest in these behaviors rather than others such as play, for instance, shows how fascinated we are by our own violent predatory tendencies.

A study of ten to twelve wolves over a four-year period conducted at a Nova Scotia wildlife park showed that emotional behavior in a wolf pack is highly fluid. A wolf may initiate aggression against a fellow pack member and have the recipient turn around and suddenly become the aggressor. Such behavior is as complex and quixotic as aggression and assertion among people—although wolves rarely wantonly destroy one another.

Aggression against another is marked by circling, raising the hackles, biting, snapping, growling, lunging, retracting the lips vertically, snarling, and raising the tail. The recipient of aggressive wolf moves may hunch or arch his back in response, wheel and face his antagonist, gape at the other, roll on his back, place his shoulder on the ground, tuck his tail between his legs and flee, or reciprocate with his own aggression.

Behaviors may show a mixture of aggression and uncertainty. Harmonic vocalizations such as whining, whimpering, and yelping occur in nonaggressive situations. Growling, snarling, woofing, or barking comprise the nonharmonic noises which signal aggression. Whines, moans, or growls accompany ambivalent aggressive displays. Fighting is ritualized in packs and follows a set order of behaviors—baring the teeth and then growling, for example.

Ritual fighting among wolves does not fit the stereotypical picture of aggressive animal behavior in which each combatant expresses a relatively consistent, limited repertoire of fixed behaviors. Rather, fights in a wolf pack are more akin to a ritualized dance. The participants carefully observe the same relative interbody spacing, move parallel to one another while circling, twisting and turning, hip thrusting or following one another, and readily respond to signals that an opponent is giving up his or her claim.

Biologists think submissive behavior is based on the actions of young wolf pups during food solicitation and other interactions between pups and mother. Dominance may be linear or pyramidal in form, showing the loose fluid structure I've noted.

In addition to the dominance display, one animal may pass under the head of another in a semicrouch from a lateral position barely touching his nose to the chin of the other. Mounting with or without pelvic thrust also establishes dominance, as does biting the neck of the submissive animal. Placing the paws on the head or back of the other and genital licking or sniffing are dominance behaviors typically observed among wolves. In large packs dominance is displayed by relative low and high postures. Such posture displays are more frequent among high-ranking animals of the same sex. Larger packs may be too much for one alpha animal to control. In this instance a group of subdominant males may be delegated the responsibility of assuring control on behalf of the alpha male.

In terms of male and female interactions, wolves have preferred partners with whom they engage in dominant-submissive interactions. Females will present themselves to males to have their coats licked and males will respond. At the height of breeding season, threats and assaults and side-rubbing crescendo, showing that both aggression and affection are at their peak. Some researchers speculate that threat and assault may be more situational than dominance oriented. A subordinate animal can dominate in a threat-assault encounter but still maintain his subordinate status in the pack.

Sexual and pack affiliation behavior seems to be carefully distinguished from dominance behavior. Both males and females, depending on ability, may be involved with hunting. Our human assumption about sex roles should not influence observations of wolf society. A subordinate male may be the most proficient hunter in the pack and a female may be the dominant alpha. Usually males dominate most female wolves. Dominant and submissive males tend to engage in more behavior that confirms dominance. Between males and females, there is more acknowledgment of subordinance on the part of females. In one long-term study of a captive pack, however, not only did a female achieve high rank, but her rank exceeded the alpha male's. Her dominance focus seemed concentrated on other females. She bit and intimidated the other she-wolves so they would have no opportunity to mate (alpha males also usually prevent their fellow males from mating). Her relationship with males tended to confirm her dominance. Other females acknowledged their subordinate status. Thus, in this pack, the alpha female was treated like a dominant male.

There may be subtle interchanges of wolf behavior that humans may never understand. In the bond between submissive animals and dominant animals, subordinate wolves could have a kind of power over their supposedly dominant counterparts. It is, after all, humans who attribute and characterize the wolf behavior they observe. What we describe as the interplay between dominance and aggression may be more sophisticated than we are able to perceive.

In the human realm, as psychologists have observed, often people who are apparently submissive exert a kind of control over those who are apparently dominant. Could this not also be the case in wolf society? Evidence for such complex emotional patterns among wolves may exist in behaviors involving complicated mixed emotions.

A relationship between two wolves might be described as the interplay between a dominant-submissive wolf and his submissive-dominant partner, for example. Many combinations of dominance and submission might be in play during pack interactions. Thus, an animal may approach its fellow displaying apparent dominance, but its tail position may be held down with a slight crook in the end, showing both threat and defense. A wolf who has been submissive for some time may also reverse roles and strive to assert its dominance over its once ascendant partner.

Wolves also exhibit extraordinary affection, especially as mating season approaches. They may press, rub, or wrap their bodies around one another, stand together, walk in accompaniment, or bound about together, wrapping their forelegs around the neck of the other while moving the feet rapidly in place, tossing the head, and gazing at the partner. One wolf, while staring intently at his partner, may approach stiff-legged with ears cocked forward and then suddenly turn away. The alpha male does not always couple with the alpha female. Beta males may mate with the alpha female too. And if the alpha male mates with a subordinate female, her pack status does not alter as a result. Whether or not the alpha male fathers her pups, after birth, the dominant male inevitably acts as her consort.

The sudden transformations from submission and dominance may indicate that these relationships are far more complex than our current understanding allows us to perceive. We may never be able to penetrate the hidden emotional lives in which wolves engage. Given the articulate behavior patterns wolves exhibit, however, it is not difficult to imagine these sophisticated behaviors emerging in wolf interactions.

The Pariah Wolf

It is more difficult, perhaps, to understand the phenomenon of the outcast wolf—an animal who exists on the fringes of wolf society, at the very bottom of the pack order. Such a wolf is harried and worried, excluded and threatened constantly by the others who drive him or her away from food, and persecute this beast in a number of apparently cruel ways. The pariah wolf may inspire pity or compassion, or challenge us to ask how wolves can exhibit such cruelty. There are, however, sufficient examples of our own injustice, exclusionary behavior, and persecution of our fellow humans to warrant reflection on our own actions, and the ways they influence our perception of the wolf behavior.

The pariah wolf may for a time accept its role and then suddenly start to challenge others in the group and assert position to rise again within the pack. On other occasions, a pariah may acquiesce to his fate. Old wounds may be opened again and again by pack members who may persecute a pariah until death occurs.

A distinction must be made between the highly subordinate pariah and a wolf who challenges the alpha's position and is subsequently driven from the pack by the rest of the members, who gang up against him. The lone wolf, as I have stated previously, may form a new pack under his own alpha leadership. While a pariah may reassert his position, often he remains on the fringes of wolf society, due to weakness the other pack members perceive.

Thus the pariah is an outcast because of vulnerability and lack of strength determined through pack testing. The challenger who becomes a lone wolf is driven from wolf society for the exact opposite reason—his strength and dominance pose a challenge to pack social order that can only be met through ritual challenge or battle, or by the lone wolf's exclusion from the pack. A challenger may usurp an alpha wolf by mounting a successful bid for alpha status. If he wins the challenge, the previous alpha assumes a subordinate role in pack hierarchy, and the challenger assumes his place at the head of the pack.

An Aside on the Mexican Wolf

I asked Kent Newton if he knew of any differences between Mexican wolf behavior and society and that of other wolves, since he has spent considerable time observing his own Mexican wolves. As has been noted previously, Mexican wolf prey is smaller than that of the northern timber wolf. Together we speculated that such a relationship to prey may mean that Mexican wolf society is less organized, since it requires less group effort to hunt smaller animals such as antelope, white tail deer, peccary, and so forth. We do know Mexican wolf packs are smaller, just as the Mexican wolf himself is smaller than his northern cousin. Judging from samples collected during extermination efforts, the Mexican wolf's skull is actually larger than the timber wolf's, but we don't know why.

Canis lupus baileyi, the classic Mexican wolf, roamed from the Sierra Madre range in Mexico north to southern New Mexico, southeastern Arizona and west Texas. *Canis lupus mogollonensis* and *Canis lupus monstrabilis* roamed parts of Texas and Arizona. Researchers Michael Bogan and Patricia Melhop suggested that both *Monstrabilis* and *Mogollonensis* be considered Mexican wolves. This argument may be of mere academic interest, since both subspecies are extinct and were replaced by the opportunistic *C.L. baileyi* in the Texas Pecos area and other ranges where its close relatives once roved.

Many ranchers reported that there were wolves everywhere in the far southwest range of the Mexican wolf. But analysis of data collected during the height of the wolf-killing craze indicates that population levels were always low. A few wolves were probably seen many times, and these observations were a factor of the Mexican wolf's broad range. Mexican wolves may still range north from Mexico. James Bednarz conducted an assessment of the White Sands Range, estimating a population of from 480 to 1,030 Mexican wolves roaming 92,000 square kilometers of New Mexico montane and subalpine regions during historic wolf days.

The Wolf Hybrid Question

Wolf hybrid breeder and owner Michael Belshaw, who lives near El Rito, New Mexico, thinks wolves have changed their habits to avoid detection and that they are still present and active in New Mexico. They have learned that being in packs threatens their welfare, Belshaw surmises, and they pursue solitary, elusive lives now to avoid human detection.

Belshaw wrote a book entitled *All the Loving Wolves: Living and Learning with Wolf Hybrids,* which details how to raise, own, and breed wolf hybrids. He estimates that there are about 130,000 wolf hybrid owners in the United States. He makes no distinction between his hybrids and full-blooded wolves. Indeed, these animals exhibit many of the traits more typical of wolves than dogs.

Why would so many people want to own and breed such animals? Belshaw thinks that because we are now in danger of experiencing the disappearance of wildness, in order to sustain a connection to the wild and untouched, people yearn to possess such creatures. Wolf hybrid ownership brings up a number of interesting practical and moral questions.

Some naturalists and biologists shudder at the thought of people owning a wolf hybrid, due to potential unpredictability of these animals, who are neither wild wolves nor domesticated dogs. A noted biologist of my acquaintance asked what might occur if a child provoked a hybrid and the animal responded by issuing a dominance challenge and subsequently attacking the child.

The same individual expressed outrage and anger because a wolf hybrid who escaped into the wilds might affect the potential success of wolf reintroduction programs, because there could be no assurance that an escaped hybrid might not breed with full-blooded wolves. A possible threat-defense attack by such a creature could negatively affect wolf reintroductions.

Belshaw examines the pack behavior of these animals and, from his account, hybrids seem more wolf in many ways than dog. Ownership of hybrids seems to be a wealthy person's game. They must be located in rural areas and they require a lot of specialized handling, care, and knowledge—and they are expensive.

I wondered about McFarland's pure wolves in the same context. There are many examples of wild animal trainers who have had their charges suddenly become unpredictable. Such incidents are perhaps subject to becoming overblown, and the popular press loves to feed on the danger and violence of an apparently tame animal that suddenly runs amok and turns on its owner or an innocent bystander. Two years ago a bear trainer was attacked in this manner and news of the attack ran for several nights on local TV news. An animal trainer whom I met swore that the trainer had beaten and mishandled his bear and that these incidents never occur if animals are treated well.

Belshaw shows how loving, mysterious, and intelligent his "wolves" are and he goes into considerable detail explaining just what is required to own a hybrid. Many hybrid owners are committed to seeing the wolf returned to the wilds. They profess a love for wilderness that is both sincere and convincing.

The very concept of personal ownership of a wild or semiwild creature brings up deeper questions. Can one ever truly possess that which is wild? In the very act of possession, is not the wild thing itself altered and destroyed by the human desire to own, control, and manipulate that which is in its essence mysterious and Other? Is not some perverse economy at work here, a kind of mutation and enslavement of Otherness in service of personal fulfillment?

And there remains the question of hybridization itself. Researchers have even created a poodle-wolf cross which they call the "Puwo." They have created such an incongruity in order to explore and compare wolf and hybrid friendliness to man. Aside from the humorous implications of the weird poodle-wolf hybrid, is not breeding, selling, and owning wolf hybrids for personal gain or pleasure a perversion of an animal's right to live wild and free and a repetition of all the perversions of the past that have led to the decimation of so many of our wild fauna and flora?

Belshaw expresses many fine insights into his hybrids, but something in the idea of wolf or wolf hybrid ownership sticks in my craw. Wolves do not exist merely for the satisfaction and pleasure of people. Ownership of such an animal enslaves that creature to serving human needs.

Wolves for and in themselves deserve and have a right to an existence free and independent of human needs. It seems like wolf ownership is just one more extension of the human desire to exploit, control, and dominate nature for our own ends. During the last century the slavery question suddenly made people aware of the moral dimension of owning another human being for one's own use and profit.

Owning wolves or other wild creatures is like trying to own the thunder and lightning which precedes a turbulent rain storm. The evanescence, the very perishability of wilderness, its instantaneous quality, are what makes the wild and free valuable for and in itself. Wilderness and wild things truly exist only in their freedom, independent of human pleasure. This freedom, this independence is the essence of living immitigable nature. Let the wolves run free, for in their freedom and the beauty and strangeness of their ways lies their value—mysterious, immutable, and beyond human comprehension.

CHAPTER TEN

The Green Fire
Dying in her Eyes

Just your pity,
just your hate
invincible, limitless,
hatred will never let you face
the beast in man.
And one day when you face this
beast alone, your courage intact,
your eyes kind,
out of your smile
will bloom a flower
And those who love you
will behold you
across 10,000 worlds of birth and dying.
—Thich Nhat Hanh
Being Peace

In February 1990, six environmental groups gave sixty-day notice to the U.S. Army and U.S. Fish and Wildlife Service that they intended to file suit in order to force Mexican wolf reintroductions under the powerful Endangered Species Act. The legal action not only denoted the onset of a landmark case, but marked the clash of two different and opposing philosophies as well.

The Wolf Action Group (WAG), Mexican Wolf Coalition, Audubon Society, Environmental Defense Fund, Sierra Club, and the Wilderness Society named Interior Secretary Manuel Lujan and Defense Secretary Dick Cheney as defendants. The plaintiffs claimed the Fish and Wildlife Service (FWS) had been dragging its feet during the three-phase captive breeding, site selection, and wolf reintroduction program. They noted the breeding program had successfully produced thirty-nine Mexican wolves located in zoos and other facilities throughout the country.

A 1988 FWS Biological Suitability Study, called the Bednarz Report, had concluded that White Sands Missile Range (WSMR) was an excellent location to conduct experimental wolf recovery, but the army rejected reintroductions, claiming wolves on the range would jeopardize security at the installation. The Fish and Wildlife Service had done little to identify other suitable wolf habitats, the plaintiffs said, and the Service had also been remiss in moving forward on vital public wolf education efforts.

The timing of the suit caused a rift in the Wolf Coalition, the primary New Mexico group advocating wolf recovery. More conservative members, aligned with mainstream environmental organizations, thought the suit to be premature and that other negotiation measures needed to be taken before engaging in legal action.

Twenty-eight-year-old Dan Moore, an American Studies graduate student at the University of New Mexico and a suit proponent, thought that the coalition had lost momentum. The legal action offered a perfect opportunity to move forward in the fight to return wolves to the Southwest, Moore surmised.

Members of the Wolf Action Group who supported the suit subsequently met with Grove T. Burnett, a Glorieta, New Mexico, environmental attorney, and his partner Steve Sugarman to discuss the possibility of starting legal action to promote wolf recovery. Burnett had gained a reputation for pursuing and winning a number of precedent-setting cases.

In Colorado, he successfully won out over the U.S. Forest Service to stop environmentally destructive tree-cutting practices. After a ten-year battle against Arizona Public Service Company, Burnett forced the company to install sulfur dioxide pollution control equipment at the Four Corners Power Plant near the intersection of the Arizona, Colorado, Utah, and New Mexico borders. Under the Clean Water Act, Burnett successfully acted to halt fifteen years of pollution of the Red River near Questa, New Mexico, by a molybdenum mill owned and operated by Molycorp.

Deep Ecology and New Environmentalism

For eighteen years, Burnett was involved in representing mainstream environmental groups. He was a fighter committed to the battle against environmental degradation and those who wreaked havoc on the environment. Then, in his late thirties, sudden illness forced him to examine what he called his warrior role in the environmental struggle.

"I basically crashed and burned," Burnett said of this period of disorientation and introspection. He had to redefine his relationship to the struggle in which he was engaged. Burnett discovered that he couldn't fight effectively against what he termed ecological violence while he was seized with a deep rage against those whom he considered adversaries.

"It consumed me. It nearly did me in," Burnett said. He began to question his anger and his burning desire to vanquish his foes. He discovered and began to practice Buddhist meditation. At the same time, Burnett began to join Buddhist ideas about detachment from results, compassion, and respect for those one must oppose with his own discoveries in so-called deep ecology.

In December 1989, he wrote about his view of deep ecology in an article entitled "Thinking Like a Mountain" which appeared in the *New Mexico Young Lawyer's Newsletter*. He pointed out the contrast between conventional environmental causes and a new philosophy that is now posing a challenge to the idea of man as the center of the universe and the crown of creation.

Burnett cited Aldo Leopold's concept of human beings as occupying but one position among many composing the biotic community. In contrasting them with the assumptions of Western humanism, Burnett likened the traditions of native peoples, Buddhism, and other Eastern beliefs to deep ecology, which challenges the notion that man is given by God dominion over nature to exploit natural resources in the causes of progress and development.

"This man-over-nature assumption is the fundamental delusion of our time and culture," Burnett wrote. "This new philosophy of deep ecology is a spiritual view of nature which honors, in a religious sense, all species, all things."

He also began to sense that the real environmental and political movements surfacing in the West were not coming from formal and established social leadership, but from informal grassroots opposition predicated on deep intuition, a kind of felt sense about the direction for effective change. This emotive awareness which issues from a kind of body knowing, Burnett feels, will be the ground for profound change in the 1990s. This physical, intuitive awareness, a kind of political and environmental gnosis, stands in sharp contrast to the view of natural resources and human stewardship that has guided and controlled evolution and change in American society since its inception.

When Burnett heard members of the wolf group request his legal expertise and describe the plight of the wolf, he perceived the importance of this lawsuit in light of his own profound convictions. In working for the reversal of centuries of persecution against the wolf, brought to this country from Europe with the Pilgrims, Burnett saw an opportunity to enact a fundamental change in the way we relate to nature. The case to recover the Mexican wolf was not just another environmental suit to Grove Burnett, but an opportunity to touch deep mythological roots of ancient prejudicial beliefs and to challenge the dark history of our relationship with the wolf, our own deep-seated intolerance and hatred of the natural world.

A Return to Controversy

Burnett accepted the challenge and on Monday, April 23, the suit to compel the government to implement its 1982 wolf recovery plan was filed in federal court.

The history of the wolf recovery program, plaintiffs contend, indicates the Fish and Wildlife Service failed to act in accord with Section 7 of the Endangered Species Act to restore the wolf to its natural habitat. The army, by not allowing wolves on its White Sands Range, in effect acted to abort the reintroduction program.

New Mexico ranchers, who have fought long and hard to eliminate the wolf, have been deeply embittered by attempts to reintroduce the predator. Their relationship with White Sands and the Department of Defense has been troubled since the end of World War II.

In 1942, ranchers in the White Sands area gave up their lands after the federal government and the army issued orders to vacate 2.2 million acres, which was subsequently devoted to military testing. Most sacrificed their land as a patriotic duty to win the war effort against Japan and because the army promised to return their property after the war.

The army never fulfilled its promises, leaving ranchers bitter and distrustful. In the early 1950s, after the Feds decided they still needed the lands, they offered ranchers limited lease compensation, but ranchers argued payments were insufficient. Then in 1976, the government permanently condemned and confiscated the lands in question.

Betrayed and alienated, in October 1982, eighty-one-year-old rancher Dave McDonald, toting a .30-.30, slipped into his old ranch under cover of darkness accompanied by his daughter and a news photographer from the *Albuquerque Journal*. After a three-and-a-half-day confrontation, McDonald agreed to quit the premises following promises by New Mexico's congressional delegation to win a settlement for the ranchers.

The following year Rep. Joe Skeen, himself a sheep rancher, proposed a bill to pay ranchers $40 million, but the legislation was withdrawn after the senate sent the case to the U.S. Court of Claims. Years of inaction and delays followed until the court finally turned down the ranchers' demands for compensation.

In October 1989, Skeen introduced another bill to pay $17.5 million to ranchers, but the legislation has to date simply languished.

In early spring 1990, after I had written an article about the controversy surrounding Mexican wolf recovery for *New Mexico Magazine*, I received a phone call from a federal government source in Washington who told me he had inside information that the army had rejected wolf recovery at White Sands as it did not want to stir up disgruntled ranchers whose prior claims to the White Sands country had consistently been denied.

Denny Gentry, former executive director of the New Mexico Cattle Growers' Association, had already confirmed the truth of these allegations in an interview conducted with him the previous year before his resignation. Powerful New Mexico ranchers would take wolf reintroductions as additional salt in their wounds, given the fact that their own claims have been brushed aside for forty years.

Vic Culberson, the association's new chief, said that when ranchers found out about the suit they were deeply concerned. He compared returning wolves to the wild to opening up prisons in order to set the most dangerous criminals free.

"The wolf's a destroyer," Culberson said. "People forget that. They want to see some kind of ultimate balance. They want their food on the table and they want to see predators back. There's simply no constructive use for the wolf. I'm like everybody. I hate to see anything lost, but we have to be practical."

Culberson said that ranchers had succeeded in making a good living from public lands. He advocated the multiple use concept and ranchers utilizing public land resources to the full so that the range does not deteriorate.

"We're doing a good job of land management," Culberson said. "Once people realize what we've accomplished, I think they'll be impressed. The range is in the best shape it's ever been in." According to Culberson, the association doesn't condone overgrazing. He termed soil erosion, desertification of the Southwest, and loss of plant diversification due to overgrazing "sensationalist claims."

"Sure people can manage the lands," Culberson said. "There are the little tricks of Mother Nature, but we can do a good job of land management. We've proven that."

The White Sands land claims and the fact that ranchers comprised the primary lobbying group for wolf extirpation have put a great deal of political pressure on the wolf reintroduction program since its inception. The Wolf Action Suit contends that the federal bureaucracy, in direct contradiction to the spirit and intent of the Endangered Species Act, stalled and delayed wolf recovery in the Southwest to avoid dealing with these political realities.

A Dismal Chronology

Since early 1979, when the first Mexican Wolf Workshop was hosted by the Arizona Sonora Desert Museum to discuss recovery, introducing the wolf to the wilds has been a subject of considerable political sensitivity.

Workshop minutes clearly stated the position that the only reason for the Fish and Wildlife Service to be involved in captive breeding efforts was so that wolves could be introduced into their historic habitat and reestablished in the wild. Harold Olson, head of the New Mexico Department of Game and Fish, detailed the importance of federal and state cooperation, which he viewed as essential for recovery success.

By late September 1979, the Mexican Wolf Recovery Team had been appointed to advise FWS and had met in order to develop a workable recovery plan. The team was composed of biologists, administrators, and experts from the service, state wildlife agencies, zoos where the animals would be held, and a representative from Mexico. Norma Ames, assistant director of public affairs for the New Mexico Department of Game and Fish, was to serve as team leader. Team members were already expressing concerns about becoming enmeshed in the complex emotional politics surrounding wolf recovery.

During its second meeting held early in June 1980, the Wolf Recovery Team stated its optimism about future success of the recovery program. Such a statement seemed to be a trial balloon to begin what would amount to a ten-year testing of the Fish and Wildlife's willingness to engage seriously in the business of wolf recovery.

FWS staff biologist Curtis Carley noted during the same meeting that his recommendations for the Mexican wolf program had not been adopted because of the administrative and political concerns affecting the program. Carley asked for a less visible and active role due to potential impact on his "professional reputation." It appeared the service was acting under its own marching orders, orders that apparently left the Wolf Recovery Team out of the communication loop.

Another political sensitivity the team faced involved ownership of the breeding animals that had been captured in Mexico. José "Pepe" Trevino, project leader for Mexico's Dirección General de Flora y Fauna Silvestre, represented Mexican interests on the recovery team.

Suddenly and without explanation, the Fish and Wildlife Service moved one of the breeding female wolves from the Arizona Sonora Desert Museum near Tucson to the Wild Canid Research and Survival Center in St. Louis. The service failed to inform the team and especially the Mexican representative about the move.

On July 16, 1980, team member Dennis Merritt, assistant director of the Lincoln Park Zoological Gardens, in Chicago, wrote to team leader Norma Ames about the move:

Regardless, it is clear the USFWS knew what it was to do with the female, chose not to contact Pepe, and only sought Team recommendation, after the fact, as it were. I feel somewhat disappointed and somewhat distressed at the choice of method . . . . I believe there was an alternative method available and a better one for accomplishing the objectives. I am not questioning the decision, only the way it was handled. I feel let down, perhaps taken advantage of, and will carry these feelings into future discussions with the FWS in this Recovery Effort. While I (and we) are not privy to internal FWS decision making, it is unique to say the least.

By December 1980, Bob Stevens, assistant director of the FWS Regional Office, expressed concern about the captive wolves' genetic viability during the third team meeting. By the following spring the genetics question had still not been resolved. Jack Woody, Endangered Species coordinator for Fish and Wildlife, wrote Stevens suggesting that if a location for wolf release could not be found, then the questions of genetic viability as well as continued FWS participation in the captive breeding program were moot. Woody urged release site selection go forward within the next five years if it was "biologically and politically" reasonable.

"If this cannot be assured," Woody wrote, "then FWS should get out of the Mexican wolf program and turn it over to the AAZPA [American Association of Zoological Parks and Aquariums] or a similar non-federal government body."

Political Problems and a Lack of Clarity

Gary Nunley, staff biologist for the Animal Damage Control Division and author of a history of wolves in New Mexico, told the next team meeting in May 1981 that unless FWS and Fauna Silvestre (the Mexican agency supervising mammalian government programs) specified a release site, there was really no need for a captive breeding program. The team estimated there were fewer than thirty wolves remaining in Mexico.

Concerned about the genetic status of the captive wolves and continuing decline in the wolf populations in Mexico, team leader Norma Ames wrote Woody, recommending an increased survey and capture program during the next fiscal year to benefit the recovery program.

In November, she again sent a letter to Woody citing "political problems" that continued to hinder the team in its work. She noted that agency review required that problems either be confronted face-on or that the plan be clarified to postpone resolution. Ames mentioned that wolves in the program were considered Mexican property and that a priority for the program was recovery in that country.

"Another matter that relates to this problem," she wrote, "is your office's present detectable ambivalence about pushing the breeding program to produce as many wolves as soon as possible. . . . I am concerned, however, about the premature setting of a trend toward the holding of a small, token population of captive Mexican wolves, held in check by drugs."

In January 1982, the fifth meeting of the recovery team still was debating the lack of clarity in recovery policy directions. Mexico as yet had not given permission for use of captive wolves in U.S. releases. Roy McBride, the hunter who had captured the original animals in Mexico, had been unable to obtain additional animals and had expressed his dissatisfaction with facilities availability and his dealings with the FWS.

Merritt, who already felt distrust of Fish and Wildlife, complained about lack of consistent procedures as well as goals that had not been established by FWS between breeding facilities. Representatives from the Wild Canid Survival Center and the Arizona Sonora Desert Museum voiced concern about lack of information from FWS regarding short-term plans for the recovery program.

Jack Woody, as acting assistant director of the service's regional office, corresponded with José Rodriguez, subdirector of Mexico's Fauna Silvestre in May 1982. If Mexico was not prepared to reintroduce wolves or transfer ownership of captive-born wolves for U.S. recovery efforts, Woody told Rodriguez that breeding activities would have to be curtailed until Mexico was prepared to reintroduce animals. If Fauna Silvestre could transfer ownership to FWS, Woody concluded, then selection of release sites in the southwestern United States could proceed.

At the same time Woody was writing to Mexico, Norma Ames was informing team members that Nina, one of the breeding female wolves, was approaching the end of her fertile life.

No Hope for Restoration

By late summer of the following year, Ames informed team members that FWS was responsible in 1979 for establishing the policy that the wolves taken south of the border were Mexican property. Now the recovery program was locked into those early promises. Propagation in captivity remained the sole hope for introductions, since little hope remained that additional wolves could be obtained beyond the eighteen already under FWS care. Ames urged the service to consult with Mexico in order to get more animals.

Wolf recovery did not seem to be much on the minds of Fish and Wildlife administration, though. On September 2, 1983, the assistant regional director denied the Wild Canid Center's request for an additional wolf enclosure at the center, citing that the agency had not even determined a direction for the program and that wolf recovery was simply not a high priority item for the region.

"As I understand it," Norma Ames wrote team members during the same month, "limited FWS funds had to be committed to other projects because FWS sees no hope for restoration of the Mexican wolves anywhere in the wild."

Ames went on to say that in going ahead with a recovery program, FWS had already made a commitment to the effort as well. She emphasized that the contributions and the time invested by recovery team members "far surpass[ed] FWS's own contributions to the particular project. . . ."

"That obligation," Ames continued, "is to refrain from actions that could sabotage the particular recovery effort. Regardless of whether or not its actions are intentional or even conscious, FWS can sink the Mexican wolf recovery effort by repeatedly stating that the effort is futile. The chapter, 'A Dire Prognosis,' in Brown's book is already such a statement, despite its disclaimer that it does not represent the views of FWS or the team."

Ames referred to David Brown's book, *The Wolf in the Southwest*, which concluded the wolf was "doomed to extinction." Brown said in his concluding chapter that lack of public support, administrative commitment, and complex legal ramifications were barriers too great for wolf recovery to overcome. The disclaimer referred to by Ames stated that Brown's book was not "necessarily" a reflection of FWS policy. The close cooperation and support Brown received from the agency, Ames seems to feel, made the work tantamount to an expression of Fish and Wildlife Service policy.

Doomed to Extinction?

Ames expressed concern that those who might support wolf reintroductions might never even know of the program before it had totally faded away. She urged that the issues surrounding recovery be aired before the public prior to halting efforts to return wolves to the wild.

In the October team meeting, Ames expressed her concern that recovery seemed to be doomed "if a few key FWS authorities abandoned the idea. . . ." Some team participants felt that the reintroduction hot potato should be laid aside until the issue cooled and that full efforts be devoted to reproduction in captivity. But FWS continued to push for curtailment of reproduction efforts.

In addition, FWS administration had already stated that it would support captive breeding only in the event recovery site location could move forward. The agency had already expressed its lack of support for reintroduction by denying the Wild Canid Center's funding request. Team members wondered why the regional office pushed for reintroduction to go forward when the political climate seemed so unfavorable. Public wolf education had not even begun, yet the agency was pressing for recovery to move forward without even minimum groundwork and preparation that could have rallied public support for wolves in the wild.

In February 1984, Jim Johnson, chief of Endangered Species for FWS, during an interview with the *Albuquerque Journal*, suggested that the agency had determined that there were enough wolves for recovery to move ahead. Ames wrote Johnson asking official notification for authorization to proceed. Why had the agency notified the press of the decision to go forward? The team had recommended the previous fall that discreet site selection should be made following the go-ahead from the regional director. Only later was public notification to occur.

Dead or Alive

The next month, Ames wrote Johnson and the New Mexico Department of Game and Fish, distressed about reports that FWS and Animal Damage Control personnel had been instructed to bring in any wolves "dead or alive" that happened to be sighted in the vast Gray Ranch area in the boot-heel of New Mexico on the border with Mexico. Ames underscored the importance of state and federal commitment to preserving wolves and providing new animals for captive breeding efforts. Additional rumors were circulating that ranchers were trapping and killing wolves in this area and hiding these illegal efforts from government officials.

At the team meeting, members voiced concerns that not maintaining viable specimens could be "programming the subspecies to extinction." Relations with Mexico concerning the wolves had deteriorated and communications had apparently become difficult. José "Pepe" Trevino had been moved in a reorganization of the Dirección General de Flora y Fauna Silvestre (DGFS). Others were now in charge of wolf work in Mexico and the two-nation cooperation program appeared to be in limbo. In December, the American Association of Zoological Parks and Aquariums indefinitely tabled FWS's application for creation of a Species Survival Plan for the Mexican wolf. The team recommended the FWS immediately establish a Wolf Breeding Committee to carry out the captive management plan and begin public education efforts.

By February 1985, site-selection criteria had been developed by the team. In a handwritten attachment to an internal FWS memorandum delivered to Jack Woody, FWS biologists said agency administrators were pushing for recovery site identification or abandonment of the program. A detailed timetable was being circulated within FWS that suggested wolves would be released in spring 1988 and delisted by 1990. But in March 1986, Jack Woody, FWS Endangered Species biologist, once again reported that because so few animals existed in Mexico the species could already be considered biologically extinct. There were thirteen males and fifteen females in the captive breeding program. Woody noted that the goal of establishment was to save the species only if wolves did not have any impact on people. He further commented that public education to correct the public perception of wolves was crucial for program success.

Advise and Consent?

In mid-March 1986, Michael Spear, regional director of FWS, wrote to game and wildlife officials in Texas, Arizona, and New Mexico to initiate the search for reintroduction sites in the various states. By summer, Spear requested state wildlife officials attend a reintroduction meeting to determine the scope of problems confronting state and federal agencies in wolf recovery.

The day of the meeting, Spear wrote to the congressional delegations in the concerned states. Strangely, Spear cited the success of the captive breeding program in saying that the agency was now ready to go forward with site location and release. Sensitive to the political ramifications of the service's decision, Spear suggested the service had neither identified nor gone forward with the site selection process.

By July, Spear sent lists of potential sites to the various state wildlife agencies. He backed away from prioritizing the sites, but said that the selection process would be one of elimination. Clearly, Spear had already determined that the states would have a large role in the selection and implementation procedure.

By late July, New Mexico game officials responded that the only suitable location for nomination was White Sands Missile Range. Arizona cited the difficulty of picking a site because of cattle-predator interactions. Texas responded in August that the Big Bend and Guadalupe Mountains were suitable. Texas already had a law that made wolf introductions illegal.

As 1987 opened, Spear contacted General Joe Owens, telling him the site selection process was still in the early phases of consideration. Later in January, he informed the general that all introductions would be experimental under the Endangered Species Act. He told Owens this would mean that any wolves wandering from the missile range could be killed legally.

In March, Harold Olson, head of the New Mexico Fish and Game Department, wrote members of the state game commission telling them that the FWS had misrepresented the site selection process. The next stage in the process involved site study, not selection.

By April, the army gave permission for the Bednarz study to go forward. Late in September, Spear wrote Owens telling him that FWS had established a policy that affected states and land managers would have the right to refuse authorization of the reintroduction efforts in their jurisdictions. Owens responded that he had decided not to allow recovery to take place on the range because the program was "not in the best interests of the Range. . . ." Spear abruptly terminated wolf reintroductions for the range. Two days later, Albuquerque Tribune reporter Mark Taylor wrote that the wolf recovery program seemed to have evaporated.

The Program Is Now Terminated

"We have no sites," Spear commented. "The wolf reintroduction program, as of now, is now terminated." Spear underscored his early decision to allow states and land managers to have veto authority over recovery on their lands, but White Sands spokesman Ed Williams said the army was being made a scapegoat. The army, according to Williams, had informed FWS of its decision during an acrimonious meeting held with Fish and Wildlife officials on February 26. Range officials had at that time expressed their negative perception of wolf reintroductions. The army's objections centered on the presence of biologists on the range and the fact that the introductions would occur in an impact area of the range.

In addition to the political problems already existing with local ranchers, the army may not have understood the experimental population provisions of the Endangered Species Act when it rejected wolves. Army officials may have believed that if wolf experiments proved successful, the wolves on the range would then fall under the protection of Section 7 of the Act and the army would then be constrained by the act's requirements. The experimental populations provision establishes a limited exception to the substantive protection made under Section 7. Thus, wolves that stray from the range would be subject to being taken by ranchers or others affected by their actions.

Members of the Captive Management Committee and Wolf Recovery Team were caught by surprise when FWS terminated the program. Kent Newton, mammal curator at the Rio Grande Zoo and chair of the committee, said he had not even been informed of Spear's decision. On October 1, Newton delivered a letter to Jim Johnson, chief of the FWS Endangered Species Program, expressing distress that the Fish and Wildlife Service might be pulling out of the program and declaring the Mexican wolf extinct.

"It seems real strange to me," said Newton of the FWS decision during his interview with Taylor. Norma Ames expressed concern that public education efforts had not been undertaken by the service and necessary groundwork was not prepared by FWS to allow recovery to take place.

Carol Cochran, with the Arizona Sonora Desert Museum, responded that she and Dave Henderson of the Audubon Society had met with Spear in late August to offer assistance in informing members of the public about the wolf recovery program, but that Spear had asked them to delay making any statements until mid-October. Cochran suggested that Fish and Wildlife was using the Owens letter as an excuse to back away from the controversial program. Spear, who had been scheduled to appear in November in front of the New Mexico Game Commission to lobby for the wolf program, said he had made other plans for that day.

Early in November, the Defenders of Wildlife requested that

the Secretary of the Interior and the Secretary of the Army reconsider the decision to terminate wolf introductions.

In March of the following year, Spear once again requested the army reconsider its decision. The army rejected Spear's request.

Will Wolves Howl Again?

In January 1990, Secretary of Interior Manuel Lujan was briefed on the status of the Mexican Wolf Recovery Program. The briefing noted that Fish and Wildlife had received over 350 inquiries regarding the Mexican wolf. Ninety-seven percent of the respondents favored introductions. The briefing also cited the 1988 survey conducted by the New Mexico Department of Game and Fish that showed a majority of those polled favored wolf recovery. Yet the briefing concluded that the department concurred with the FWS position that state and federal land managers must give consent before introductions take place.

Section 7 of the Endangered Species Act, passed in 1973 and amended in 1978, requires close cooperation among Federal and state agencies in order to recover threatened or endangered species. The scope of the act and the importance of recovering such species is highlighted by the broad powers granted through this legislation to prevent the endangerment and extinction of plant and animal species. In June 1978, the Supreme Court blocked completion of Tellico Dam in Tennessee when it concluded the project would jeopardize the small, obscure perch called the snail darter.

Following amendment of the act during the same year, Congress established a high-level Endangered Species Committee to determine the importance of saving a species against the need for federal action. The so-called "God Committee" composed of the Secretaries of Interior, Army, Agriculture, and other key federal and state authorities, is empowered to grant exemptions to the protective provisions of Section 7. Fish and Wildlife is directly charged with initiating and carrying out recovery efforts as well as seeking the cooperation of other state and federal agencies in these crucial efforts. In 1976, New Mexico signed a cooperative agreement with FWS to promote endangered species recovery. Texas and Arizona have no such agreements.

In 1979, when the Mexican wolf program was just beginning, the Comptroller General reported to Congress that enforcement of the act under the Department of Interior needed to be strengthened and clarified. The Government Accounting Office warned that unless key management improvements were made by the Secretary of the Interior some endangered or threatened species could be subject to selective extinction.

The dismal chronology presented in this chapter shows that except for recovery efforts conducted through the captive breeding program, the Mexican wolf most surely faces extinction. The program has consistently faced bureaucratic problems. Members of the Wolf Recovery Team themselves have said that FWS administration not only failed to communicate with them, but seemed to act in direct contradiction to Recovery Team purposes.

The current Secretary of the Interior, former New Mexico Congressman Manuel Lujan, appears to have little understanding of the origin, purpose, and intent of the legislation he is sworn to enforce. In May 1990, Lujan stirred up a storm of controversy by commenting that he thought Congress should amend the act by weakening species and habitat provisions so the law would not interfere with economic activities. Lujan's long-term support for the $580 million Animas–La Plata dam project in southwestern Colorado was jeopardized because the Colorado squaw fish is endangered in the San Juan River.

Lujan was also wrestling with the spotted owl controversy. Designation of the owl as an endangered species in the old timber stands of the Northwest, opponents say, threatens as many as 50,000 jobs. Lujan also commented that no one had ever told him the difference between a red squirrel and any other squirrel. He was referring to a controversy surrounding the endangered red squirrel on Mount Graham in Arizona that halted construction of a National Science Foundation telescope installation. The Secretary has gone on record characterizing public lands as "places where cows graze." After the Exxon Valdez ran aground, blackening Alaska's beaches with oil, Lujan suggested the disaster would promote a tourism boom.

I have spoken much about meanings the wolf holds for various cultures. The suit to force FWS to comply with the Endangered Species Act shows that, in the West, new meanings regarding the wolf in particular and our place in nature are now confronting the old habits of mind that we have developed about our place in the natural world.

These meanings, as I have indicated, are evidence of a new awareness surfacing in the "body politic": a physical, emotive awareness based on intuitive discovery and change.

In its most enlightened form this new awareness challenges human dominance over nature. It still strives to preserve respect and compassion for those who hold other views while continuing to seek to establish environmental and political holism. This detachment from attaining results and the view of natural and human systems as interconnected link these new views to Native American and Eastern thought.

If there is any hope for us in this time of environmental degradation it lies in our ability to restore to its place the wolf, this most powerful predator whom we loathe and fear. In accepting the role of caretaker for animals and plants that are threatened with extinction, we may come to have a new relationship with our world. Perhaps wolves have more to teach us than we might ever dream. Restoring the wolf to its range means much more than simply returning another threatened animal to the wilderness. In reintroducing the wolf, we are engaging in a vision of our own future and overcoming the dark history of prejudice against wildness and Otherness.

This present age has come to prefer the sign to the thing signified, the copy to the original, image to substance, appearance to essence. The illusion only is sacred and truth itself has become profane. Indeed, the preciousness of illusion is enhanced to the proportion that truth decreases so that the greatest illusion becomes tantamount to the greatest truth. The vision of preserving species that by our own actions are threatened with eternal death, the foresight to save the Mexican wolf from a twilight existence in zoos—seeing ourselves as responsible members of the natural community—these are profound indicators that the light of truth has begun to break through the web of symbols with which we have blurred our sight.

CHAPTER ELEVEN

Eco Rage:
Howling at the Empty Moon

> *Careful:*   *my knife drills your soul*
> *listen, whatever-your-name-is*
> *One of the wolf people*
> *listen*   *I'll grind your saliva into the earth*
> *listen*   *I'll cover your bones with black flint . . .*
> *Because you're going where it's empty*
> *Black coffin out on the hill*
> *listen*   *the black earth will hide you, will*
> *find you a black hut*
> *Out where it's dark, in that country*
> *listen*   *I'm bringing a box for your bones*
> *A black box*
> *A grave with black pebbles*
> *listen*   *your soul's spilling out*
> *listen*   *it's blue*
> —Cherokee, Jerome Rothenberg
> Technicians of the Sacred

It was a chill spring morning when I met Brad Lagorio at E.J.'s Cafe in Albuquerque's University district. My editor in Dallas with Reuters News was anxious that I complete my assignment about the Mexican wolf controversy as soon as possible.

I had been referred to Lagorio by a source who told me that the environmental activist would prove a knowledgeable contact, in touch with the latest efforts to save the Mexican wolf. I had been briefed that Lagorio belonged to Earth First!, an amorphous group of environmental radicals who were prepared to use a range of tactics, including ecological sabotage or "ecotage," to fulfill their goals. Critics have dubbed them "environmental terrorists."

When I arrived at the restaurant, I quickly identified Lagorio, a thin intense guy accompanied by a blond outdoorsy looking woman from southern New Mexico whom I'll call Jean. Jean wanted to remain anonymous, she said, because she was currently involved in activities that some people might consider illegal.

In preparation for the interview, Lagorio had quickly put together a folder of information he thought might be of use to me in
writing my story. I hastily looked through the information as we ordered coffee, and I asked a few brief questions. There were a number of things that looked as if they might be of use in completing
the article, so I requested Lagorio furnish me a copy of some of the
documents in his folder.

One of the papers that intrigued me was a copy of a letter from
Gerald Maestas, chair of the New Mexico Game Commission. His
well-known opposition to wolf introductions and his comment
that wolves were "not smart enough to survive" in the wild had intrigued me about the wolf story in the first place. But this letter addressed to state public land users was of an entirely different flavor.

It articulated the wolf's role as necessary predator and supported wolf education measures in favor of aiding wolf reintroduction efforts in New Mexico. I thought the missive an odd statement from a man who had openly claimed his opposition to
dealing with wolf recovery. I asked Lagorio if he thought Maestas
had changed his position and if this might be significant in view of
the attempts to reintroduce the lobo.

"I don't know," he replied. I set aside the information I thought
of interest and asked Lagorio if I might have some of the documents.
He wanted to keep the originals, but I asked if I could retain copies?

"No problem," he said. "I'll go get these run off right now."
Lagorio took the folder and left to get the copies while Jean and I
sipped our coffee and chatted.

"What is your organization about?" I asked her.

Jean told me Earth First! was not really an organization but a
diverse group of individuals who were committed to stopping environmental destruction—the group's motto is "No compromise in
defense of Mother Earth!" The group admired the tactics used in
Edward Abbey's classic novel, *The Monkey Wrench Gang*, and believed in using a kind of freewheeling pranksterism, or monkey-
wrenching, as a challenge to industry and government environmental politicking and compromise.

Lagorio returned and handed me the copies. He quickly outlined what he thought was going on with wolf recovery in New
Mexico. He drew my attention to some additional papers he had
copied that he thought might explicate important points.

The discussion turned eventually to tactics used by environmental radicals who attempted to save old timber stands from logging activity by driving spikes into trees in order to jam up logging company band saws. What if some logger with a wife and kids were to get hurt or killed when a saw ripped into a spike, I wanted to know.

Lagorio said that when Earth First!ers spiked trees, they always informed the lumber company beforehand, to avoid possible injury. The goal was to infuriate and enrage those engaged in environmental destruction and gum up the works so it would prove extremely costly to go forward with environmental exploitation through clear-cutting old timber stands.

Lagorio had to go to work, Jean was leaving in an hour or so to get back to southern New Mexico, and I had some interviews to do, so we soon parted.

Two days later, I received a call from my friend Ray with whom I had taken that memorable walk at the Rio Grande Nature Center, during which I had discovered the *Albuquerque Tribune* story describing the Gerald Maestas "not smart enough to survive" wolf quote. Ray invited me to dinner that evening. He explained that the other guest was Brad Lagorio, whom he had met and gotten to know at nuclear test site demonstrations in Nevada.

I gladly accepted his invitation. I was interested in hearing more about Earth First! and finding out why the group and its activities appealed to Lagorio.

Clandestine Support from Responsible Officials

That evening we sat around drinking wine and conversing. Lagorio explained that he had been a committed nonviolent activist in the peace and environmental movements for some time, but now he had changed his position. He outlined the severity of global environmental destruction, decimation of rain forests, and massive despeciation. The catastrophic proportion of these problems and the fact that society, government, and business were unwilling to change had further radicalized him. Stronger and more forceful action was necessary and justified in order to reverse ecological devastation.

He cited the group's positive results in stopping lumber companies from clear-cutting old timber stands, achieving listing for endangered species, and getting the programs of more moderate environmental groups accepted by application of more radical tactics.

Officials in the Audubon Society and other conservation organizations had told me privately they thought that environmental radicals had been most effective in promoting positive change. A biologist professionally involved in Mexican wolf recovery confessed off the record that he felt extremely frustrated because all that seemed to matter to officials charged with saving the wolf was power politics. So little thought and care were being devoted to the seriousness of species depletion that he had felt overcome by a sense of despair and helplessness.

He had confessed to me, "Earth First! has been crucial in putting pressure on the government to commit resources and effort in enforcing the Endangered Species Act." He likened the government to an old mule that had to be slapped between the eyes with a two by four just to get its attention.

Lagorio was amused and interested when I told him of this clandestine support from responsible officials. His sense of humor and his obvious commitment I found winning without being overbearing and dogmatic. It takes courage to stand in front of a bulldozer and delay a logging road from being completed, or sit in a tree for weeks to prevent loggers from cutting it while angry lumberjacks threaten you.

Yet, I felt uneasy about embracing violent or destructive tactics no matter how important the goal. There was something perhaps too sanguine, too clear cut in his embrace of any means to save wilderness.

A Curious Affair

Several days passed as I continued work on my story. I began to discover that sources involved in the Wolf Coalition that I had come to rely upon were either directly linked to Earth First! or at least sympathetic to the group's goals and philosophy of environmental activism. It became apparent to me that many of those directly responsible for promoting wolf recovery were inclined to support environmental radicalism as a key to promoting wolf action.

As I was nearing the completion of my research I kept thinking about Maestas's letter. I thought his change of view might make a good riposte for my article, showing that there was hope for wolf recovery if a man whose point of view seemed so hardened could reverse his position and come out for public wolf education.

I had already interviewed Maestas, but I decided to get his comments on the letter and the apparent inconsistency between his original ideas and his current stance. After several tries, I finally spoke to him at home around 11 P.M. after he had returned from a Game Commission meeting. I asked him about the letter. A long pause followed.

"I didn't write that," he said. "It's a fake."

"A forgery?" I asked.

"Yeah," he responded. "And I'll tell you who did it—those nuts from Earth First!"

"Any names?" I wanted to know.

"I don't know who specifically, but I'd watch out if you're dealing with those crazies."

Maestas said forging the letter was one reason why the commission would never hear the wolf issue, as long as he served as chair at any rate.

The next morning I called Mark Watson, a biology student at the University of New Mexico who had provided me with consistently good information on several occasions. I asked if he knew what the story was with the Maestas letter. Despite his own sympathies with Earth First!, Watson had helped me contact ranchers dead-set against wolf recovery and he had provided me good technical information and verifiable tips a few times. Rumor had it that Watson had lost a job with the Forest Service because of his Earth First! connections.

He readily admitted that some Earth First!er had indeed forged the letter. Watson didn't know if Lagorio was aware the document was false and suggested I contact him to verify this. I also called Dave Henderson, Audubon spokesman in Santa Fe and Wolf Coalition member, who said he too thought the forged letter had originated with someone in Earth First!

I was saddened and disappointed by this incident. I felt I had been set up. Under deadline pressure, had I gone ahead and written the piece using the letter, I would have sacrificed my integrity and possibly my already tenuous position as a freelance journalist.

I held the piece back while I attempted to contact Lagorio to get his comment, but he was out of town attending an Earth First! rendezvous. Three days later I finally reached him. I asked him if he knew the source of the Maestas letter. He professed ignorance. Did he know the letter was a fake? Was he aware that Maestas had named Earth First! as the source of the letter? Lagorio said he knew nothing about it. I told him that even if he was without blame, I would not be able to use his information for any story I was writing. This was the last conversation I had with Lagorio.

There appeared to be no point to this forgery. It had not helped the wolf and it destroyed whatever developing confidence existed between Lagorio and me. It seemed a frivolous piece of trickery that served no purpose except perhaps to enrage Maestas. According to Mexican wolf lawsuit principal and Earth First! member Dan Moore, the Maestas forgery was drafted at a time when not much was happening on behalf of the wolf. The intention of the letter, which Moore characterized as a "childish prank," was to "stir the pot." He assured me that Lagorio was not the source of the forgery.

Not until shortly after the Wolf Action Group filed suit in federal court did I hear about Lagorio again, when he was named as a spokesman for the group in a release issued to announce the legal action. Seeing Brad's name made me think of our strange encounter.

The incident underscored the strengths and weaknesses of Earth First!'s support of wolf recovery. On the one hand, I had formed reliable contacts who supported or belonged to the group. On the other hand, the reliance of certain members on coyote-like tricksterism and the group's internal leaderless individualism posed hazards for a journalist intent on covering the story.

Wolf Politics Revisited

The Mexican Wolf Recovery Team, mandated by the Endangered Species Act and appointed by the Fish and Wildlife Regional Director in 1979 to oversee wolf recovery, was another element in the Mexican wolf puzzle. As I've reviewed in the previous chapter, the team became enmeshed in the politics of wolf recovery.

Norma Ames, chair of the team and public information officer for the New Mexico Department of Game and Fish, had proved quite outspoken in her frustration at apparent delays, inefficiency, and inaction on the part of Fish and Wildlife. Ames had also given voice to concern that the public might never know about wolf recovery until the program faded from sight.

José C. Trevino, appointed to represent Mexico's Fauna Silvestre, akin to the Fish and Wildlife Service, was transferred by Mexican authorities late in the program's life, perhaps due to mounting stress with the United States because of the legal complexities surrounding ownership of the wolves captured in Mexico but raised and bred in the United States.

Fish and Wildlife biologist Gary Nunley was the author of an article, "Wolves in New Mexico," which was included in David Brown's pessimistic assessment of wolf recovery entitled *The Wolf in the Southwest*. Nunley's appointment to the team typified Fish and Wildlife's possible bias and its fear of getting embroiled in opposition to wolf recovery.

Ames herself criticized Brown's prediction that the Mexican wolf would never be reintroduced because of the politics surrounding recovery. Other team members such as Dennis Merritt, assistant director of Chicago's Lincoln Park Zoo and chairman of the Wildlife Conservation and Management Committee of the American Association of Zoological Parks and Aquariums, represented the strong technical and professional expertise of the team.

The association became involved in controversy over whether Mexican wolves were to be permanently retained in zoos (an idea the association rejected) or whether captive management mandated under the Wolf Recovery Plan would prove effective given the complex political considerations of wolf reintroduction.

Under the Wolf Recovery Plan, several facilities had signed agreements with the Fish and Wildlife Service to conduct captive Mexican wolf breeding. Cynthia Pitsinger of the Wild Canid Survival and Research Center (WCSRC) near St. Louis and Dr. Ingeborg Poglayen of the Arizona Sonora Desert Museum near Tucson represented captive breeding program interests on the team.

Kent Newton, mammal curator for the Rio Grande Zoo in Albuquerque, serves as chair for the captive breeding program. Newton also had expressed frustration at FWS management of recovery efforts. FWS biologist Curtis Carley, despite his association with the agency, proved an outspoken critic of the service and was quietly removed from wolf recovery efforts by Fish and Wildlife.

Tom Smylie, assistant regional director for the service said that the last meeting of the Recovery Team occurred in December 1986, just when public sentiment for wolf recovery was gathering steam. Smylie's statement amounts to a tacit recognition that the program was willfully terminated by FWS, an admission supported by correspondence issued by regional director Michael Spear.

The more I delved into wolf recovery politics the more I discovered environmental radicalism at the roots of Mexican wolf activism. Indeed, the Wolf Action Group suit may prove a singularly effective strategy for forcing governmental action on Mexican wolf reintroduction.

The suit was conceived and executed by "radical" elements within WAG who pushed for legal action at a time when more conservative voices spoke for continued negotiations with the Department of Fish and Wildlife and the U.S. Army. Even some activists in WAG had balked at the timing of the action, fearing that a premature wolf suit might force an untimely test of the Endangered Species Act that could weaken the powerful legislation.

The suit issued by WAG underscores the importance of so-called radical environmentalism to wolf recovery efforts in the Southwest, because without the pressure exerted by those who pushed for the suit, wolf recovery would probably have stayed on hold, according to suit proponents.

On May 15, following Secretary of Interior Manuel Lujan's challenge to the sweeping powers of the Endangered Species Act, wolf suit attorney Grove Burnett received an unsigned "deep throat" communique. Members of the Wolf Coalition speculated that the typed note originated from a well-placed source in the government who had inside knowledge of the decision-making process conducted by FWS.

The Suit a Joke?

"Fish and Wildlife thinks wolf lawsuit is joke," the communique said, according to Burnett. The letter said that Fish and Wildlife intended to settle the suit and "then goof off." It went on to refer to regional director Michael Spear as a "holdover from the [James] Watt administration," who "tells [his] staff he hates wolves." The communique then went on to list witnesses to depose and previously unknown documents to subpoena detailing relations between Mexico and the United States and the ongoing dispute over ownership of Mexican wolves captured south of the border for the captive breeding program.

On July 31, Burnett released this information to the press in preparation for a "howl-in" conducted by wolf advocates on the courthouse steps that day. The action was a protest against the government's motion to dismiss the lawsuit as a "moot" procedure. The motion for dismissal cited FWS actions in favor of wolf recovery.

FWS assistant regional director Tom Smylie termed the communique "erroneous and false." He detailed FWS moves to push wolf recovery and negotiations with the army conducted by Michael Spear.

Smylie expressed dismay at the time and energy the suit was taking away from actually saving the wolf. He said wolf proponents' time would be better spent attempting to educate ranchers about the wolf rather than engaging in legal maneuvering.

He suggested they make use of a recently produced wolf education slide show sponsored by FWS. A year before the slide show had been produced, however, Smylie had admitted to me that perhaps the Fish and Wildlife Service had been remiss in not taking enough initiative to educate the public about Mexican wolves.

When questioned about the suit, Smylie dismissed contentions that FWS had been dragging its feet on wolf introductions, saying that the regional director had moved to obtain wolves from Mexico in the first place and had contacted states to receive their feedback on possible wolf introductions in their respective locales.

Television reporter Dan Sterling of Channel 7 News in Albuquerque did a story featuring the communique. Smylie said Sterling had not verified the source for the communication independently and had not gotten FWS comment before running the story. An unnamed source said Smylie was furious about the story and he conveyed his anger to Sterling who was subsequently scolded by the station's management.

Subsequently Smylie visited the station to complain about the handling of the story. Smylie denied that FWS administrators were turning the agency upside down to discover who had leaked the information. While he said he did not know the source of the communique, and he hinted the letter might be a forgery perpetrated by wolf suit litigants, Smylie referred to a "disgruntled employee" who may have been the letter writer.

The "howl-in" on the courthouse steps was only the most recent display of rage by wolf proponents at apparent FWS recalcitrance to move forward with Mexican wolf recovery. It should be noted that only following the filing of the suit did the army and FWS move forward on wolf recovery.

☉ ☉ ☉

A Spectacle of Rage

The "howl-in" and previous wolf demonstrations received lots of media attention. Through television, print media journalism, and other means, contemporary society mirrors itself through spectacle. The spectacle of rage is not only visually moving and appealing, but it reflects our fascination with display for its own sake without confronting the meaning of display. Confrontation and rage produces fear and anxiety in those who behold spectacle. The generation of excitement is a goal for the culture of reason that has separated itself from emotive meanings.

For those who call themselves "deep ecologists" and profess an interest in radical ecology, the wolf and returning the wolf to the wild holds special meaning because of the symbolic association of wolves and wilderness already discussed in this book. It is the recognition by radical ecologists of the wolf's importance that is interesting because the wolf herself not only faces extinction, but as the most wild creature, stands for the disappearance of wildness from our world.

The psychological associations between radical ecopolitics and deep anger at human-centered destruction of nature unmask ancient associations with wolves. Rage is a word often heard in discussions revolving around radical ecopolitics. Christopher Manes, associate editor of the journal *Earth First!*, has written an articulate, revealing, and thoughtful book about the group, entitled *Green Rage: Radical Environmentalism and the Unmaking of Civilization*, which explores the history and evolution of Earth First!

Rage is a wolf emotion. The use of the word *rage* has deep and ancient associations with wolves extending back to the very origins of language. The word comes from the Latin *rabere*, meaning "to rave" and is associated with lupine rabies. The word is probably from the Sanskrit *rabhas*, "violence or force." Manes quotes Earth First! hero Edward Abbey, who compared the response to the ecological devastation happening today with the response produced by a brigand who forces his way into a person's home. An individual to whom this had happened would respond, not from logic or reason, but in "rage." Similarly, business, government, and other social forces and institutions have invaded nature which is our home. Abbey favored striking back with emotion.

Radical environmentalist and Earth First! cofounder Dave Foreman often refers to Aldo Leopold's encounter with the she-wolf in New Mexico as a crucial event in the development of radical ecology. He ends his presentations with a soul-stirring wolf howl.

Rage is grounds for ecopolitical action—rage at the numbness and indifference of society to the crisis we face as a result of our own actions in massive despeciation; rage at incessant profiteering which displaces decision-making that takes into consideration the greater good, not only of humans, but of all of nature; and rage at the violence being perpetrated by humans on other life forms.

Species devastation is one of the most important crises of our time. Not since dinosaurs disappeared have so many creatures faded from existence. Even when the great reptiles died off, plant diversity maintained. Today plants are being wiped out with unprecedented rapidity. Destruction of flora and fauna means the earth is being depleted of genetic richness and diversity that has taken millions of years to create. Some experts estimate that within ten years, from twenty to twenty-five percent of animal and plant life will be decimated through human action. This is a terrifying prospect produced by our own predation.

Wolf as Sign, Wolf as Symbol

The threatened disappearance of the Mexican wolf is a sign that if we lose the wolf, we lose the diversity and vitality of nature herself. Once gone, the Mexican wolf will have vanished forever, and with her our own genetic vitality may vanish as well, because what we do to nature we will sooner or later do to ourselves.

In view of the magnitude of our destruction brought on by greed and carelessness, rage is perhaps an appropriate reaction. I have detailed our kinship with wolves and how we share a common predatory past that casts an ancient shadow across our consciousness. In rejecting our own predator nature and ascribing these attributes to wolves, we have refused to take responsibility for our own present actions and our destiny. Man is the ultimate predator and is efficiently, if unconsciously, destroying the natural world within which he must survive. Deep ecology, in rejecting human-centered politics and philosophy and recognizing the importance of the destruction of nature, is now pushing society to recognize and respond to the great crisis destroying nature as it is now unfolding. Deep ecologists are questioning the very foundation of our social system that is reliant on profiteering and exploitation.

In a culture addicted to drama and conflict, environmental radicals realize they must seek dramatic means to demonstrate their concerns. The analysis that spawned radical ecology is based on a profound feeling that technological culture is destroying nature and that development, mining, logging, and grazing not only have to be halted, but that society itself must be altered or even destroyed.

Deep ecologists correctly perceive that the argument of God-given dominion served and still serves as the rationale for this ongoing destruction of the land, animals, environment, and the ancient cultures that have always existed, embedded within nature. Environmental radicals have, however, as a reflection of the society in which they operate, taken their cue from their own culture, in order to destroy the instruments of destruction themselves and halt the perpetrators of destruction.

E.J. Hobsbawm, in his book *Primitive Rebels*, explores several archaic social movements in preindustrial society. These movements were somatic in the sense that they issued forth not from a carefully reasoned examination of social ills, but from a felt sense of social problems. Robin Hood bandits, sects of illiterate laborers, and millenarians who desired the apocalyptic end of society acted from irrational and inchoate sources and not from rational investigation of society and its problems. These were body awarenesses. I propose that body awarenesses emerge in the felt sense of our ancient predator past and affinity with wolves.

In England, around 1779, a supposedly feeble-minded worker named Ned Ludd smashed two textile frames of his Leicestershire employer. From 1811 to 1816, English workers called Luddites destroyed the new labor-saving mill machinery as a protest against lowered wages and unemployment that they attributed to these devices.

It was not through Marxist or other theoretical social perspectives that the Luddites acted. Rather, it was a purely physical emotional response to conditions which drove them to take action. Earth First! cofounder Dave Foreman named his publications Ned Ludd Books in honor of the English mill worker. Foreman's volumes tell the reader how to decommission bulldozers, pull out survey stakes, and in other ways disrupt industrial resource exploitation.

✿ ✿ ✿

Primitive Rebels

Christopher Manes describes radical environmentalism as a sensibility, not an attempt to create a new philosophy in order to replace old ideologies. The root of the word is *sentir*, "to feel or perceive." Thus, radical ecologists' beliefs issue directly from body awareness and not rational analytic thought processes.

In fact, systematic philosophy is seen by many deep ecologists as part of the problem, which has resulted in species extermination and the elimination of wilderness.

Radical environmentalism embodies a kinesthetic knowing producing movement, abiding in action, and not a monolithic system of static ideas developed through reason and thought. It is related to the emotions, the root of the word coming probably from the French, *emovere*, meaning "to move."

Christopher Manes, writing of environmental activism, links this body knowing directly to Aldo Leopold's awareness evoked by his encounter with the she-wolf in the New Mexico wilderness. As an embodiment of wildness, not only is this an expression of wolf nature, but it is an expression of the most important change in human awareness to occur since the Renaissance split reason from emotion and accentuated the already-growing chasm between rational awareness (reality) and the chaos of denied feelings (wildness).

Manes himself calls this emerging awareness a kind of second Copernican revolution. Actually, I think this supposedly new awareness is a rediscovery of our ancient predator past linking us to wolves. Environmental radicalism is an attempt to absolve terror and fear, and bridge the ever-widening gap that has opened in human awareness between reason and body awareness.

This kinesthetic and kinetic revolution recognizes first and foremost that man is not the center of the universe, but that nature and wildness is the real world. Hence, other species have as much right to exist as have humans. This shift of awareness abides in wildness and emotive perceptions of rage and anger at the destruction of the real world of nature by industrial, technocratic civilization.

Timeless Bios

In this sense, deep ecology attempts to rescue the self from chaos and fear because the self is given a new expanded definition through this awareness. The self defined through environmental radicalism includes the entire biota of nature.

The whole biotic community merely includes humans who have equal membership in it. The natural world is timeless, universal, and true. To melt and disappear into nature is the desire of this form of awareness. Contemporary society's reliance on the primacy of human utilization of "resources" cuts off meanings which allow rich, poetic, and wild associations to grow unfettered.

The claim of absolute value (God's law) for meanings which in truth just support the ascendancy of the rich and powerful seeking only to exploit nature is a deeply perverse tendency of modernity. Equally perverse is the rigid and brutal assertion that allows for no compromise, no other meanings, no dialogue in defense of the greater goal of nature's absolute salvation through the actions of the elect environmental crusaders.

Consciousness of our old affinity with wolves and our ancient past as predators and as hunter-gatherers can create a deeper understanding of what we are as creatures and our own biological roots, which have previously been hidden from our awareness. The word consciousness derives from the Latin *conscius,* meaning "awareness of sensation, or feelings or things." Consciousness is a knowing and a discovery of deep meaning through sensation and emotion. Consciousness is the foundation of respect and compassion for all being which is at the root of primitive or primal cultures and is conveyed through myth and legend so that mindfulness is constantly preserved throughout successive generations.

Primal hunting cultures may serve as the basis for rethinking our world and our relationship to nature once the old order has been destroyed. But that relationship, as defined by primal cultures, is rooted in respect for all things living and nonliving. This respect is seen in the intimate and beautiful relationship of the hunter who speaks with the prey to ask her forgiveness for her own death.

That love is seen in the haunting and touching belief that animals willingly give their lives to the hunter so that he may live. That relationship of honor and compassion is embodied in story, legend, and myth, which act as constant reminders drawing people toward right relationship with the world. Primal societies exist in a kind of web or net of beliefs, traditions, and practices inculcating mindfulness.

Each day plant and animal species pass from our world in silence. Their death whispers to us in our blood and speaks to us in a chaotic language that thrums, buzzes, and roars in our ears, summoning us to face our sorrow. Like the nineteenth-century buffalo hunter who wept after he destroyed a herd of bison, we stand in the midst of the carnage we are creating, aghast at this dying world that we are killing through our own predatory nature.

CHAPTER TWELVE

The Moon Howls
and the Wolves are Silent

*Man is no longer at the center of life. He is
no longer that flower of the whole world,
which has slowly set itself to form and
mature him. He is mingled with all things,
he is on the same plane as all things, he is a
particle of the infinite, neither more nor less
important than the other particles of the
infinite. The earth passes into the trees, the
trees into the fruits, the fruits into man or
the animal, man and the animal into the
earth; the circulation of life sweeps along
and propagates a confused universe wherein
forms arise for a second, only to be engulfed
and then to reappear, overlapping one
another, palpitating, penetrating one
another as they surge like the waves.*

—Elie Faure
History of Art

1.

In a secret recess of my being a wolf had been born. She nurtured herself there in my body's den until she had grown into her fullness and vitality. She spoke to me of her wolf secrets—the power that causes her fellows to avert their gaze from her eyes.

To speak with her, I turned my eyes from her face and heard her utter words within me as if her voice was one with my own. She spoke to me of a time before time when humans and wolves talked to one another—when the world was green, numinous, unripe, and unformed.

This she-wolf told me how people long ago had discovered a way up through into the world above where time had hardened, and wolves and humans no longer understood one another, the birds and deer possessed their own tongues.

I had struggled up from below and things were ready, things were prepared, she told me. This journey had occurred a long time in the past and I remembered nothing of my travels, but she would tell me in her own way, in a way that I might hear this tale and learn her secrets.

"Now you are strong, because I have given you strength," she said. "Have courage, look into my eyes." I did as she demanded and gazed directly into her green and glowing eyes.

Reflected in each of her pupils I saw a small image of my own face lined with fear. Slowly her black lips pulled back and she sneered, revealing her long sharp teeth. Her broad forehead wrinkled and a deep growl rumbled in her chest, shaking the earth.

I saw how completely separate she was from me as if she had risen up out of me. Now she stood utterly apart and wild in her ferocity.

With a sudden leap she attacked me, tore at my clothing with her teeth, knocked me down. Her strength overwhelmed me and she stood over me, her eyes afire, her head erect, her ears forward. I looked around and I saw standing about me various other predators. The raptors looked down on me and the mountain lions and the coyotes fixed me with their gaze. They were all there, the predators.

"Get up now," commanded this she-wolf. "We are your friends. We love you." As I stood she embraced me, pulling me to her with her paws. I sensed she was part human, this wolf, and I was part wolf. Then she gave me tools to survive, weapons so that I might hunt as a predator hunts and roam as a predator roams. As she embraced me, she melted into me and disappeared inside where for awhile I heard her voice, so much like my own voice that it too faded from my awareness.

As time passed I forgot her. I forgot that part of me which was wolf. In place of my memory of this she-wolf, a terror filled my heart, fear of the mirroring power of her gaze. I saw my separateness and I was alone. In my loneliness and fear I began to build a world of discrete objects, a world in which reason and logic alone were king, where I could hide and mask my fear in a thin gauze of order and proportion.

I invented a story about myself—how God had given me

dominion over all the creatures of the air, earth, and sea, how God had told me I was to use every being for my own benefit and pleasure. To absolve my terror I used the things of the earth, air, and water. To destroy was my greatest pleasure. I wasted the creatures of the air, of the earth, and of the waters. From the death of others I gained life . . .

2.

Midway through life's journey, while wandering through a deep wilderness, I encountered a she-wolf. With my weapons and my power I attacked this savage beast, with loathing I set upon her and killed her. I turned to run away, but she rose up, grinning at me, this she-wolf. Again I tore the life from her and again she rose. Three times more I slew her and each time she rose up again, this evil beast who would not die. At last she laughed and spoke to me.

"Take a look around," she said. "How barren the earth is, how poisoned the water, lined with the corpses of animals you have slain. The birds have stopped singing and have fallen from the trees. Deserts spread where once forests flourished. The world which was given you, you have destroyed and now you must make your way from here. You must emerge into a new world or you will die, because there is nothing here for you to eat." Then I sat down and wept and my eyes were clear as if they were the eyes of one who had but recently awakened from a long and deep sleep.

3.

Extraordinary experiences occur when we least expect them. These incidents pierce our lives like bones projected by a sorcerer, entering the victim's skin, causing sickness, madness, or death.

So the faces of wolves appeared to me in odd moments when, unguarded, I happened to catch from the corner of my eye a flash of wolf menacing my perception. These faces seemed almost to enter my body and to cause some hidden transformation, some terrible sorrow to shake in my bones.

In the midst of traffic, from the corner of a darkened room, in alleyways, and from around buildings, these hauntings occurred with greater frequency and filled me with terror, woe, a deep sadness.

I grew to dread these times, though gradually I came to see that in this parade of lupine visages, each different, yet each filled with a like sorrow, were the faces of all the wolves slaughtered through human aversion and loathing. They began to speak to me, these wolf voices; they howled to me of their desolation, and they conveyed to me a new knowledge, a wolf knowing coloring everything I saw and felt with a deep and abiding sadness. It was not only in mourning that they talked to me of their passing from the earth, but of a new emergence from this world into the next.

Then, one night, as suddenly as they had begun, these wolf images vanished and in their place remained only silence and the cold howling light of the moon . . .

Toward a New History

The history of our relationship to the Mexican wolf is the story of powerful currents surfacing unbidden in the body, and shows that often we are driven by factors we can hardly perceive or understand, let alone control. It is this kind of subterranean history that the story of the Mexican wolf reveals.

In discussing historical trends and developments as a rational, progressive movement of events, a plausible fiction called the past, we have failed perhaps to grapple with the underlying impulses that find expression through the unfolding pageant of happenings and images we call history. Historically, symbolic images like the wolf assume a kind of logical inevitability when a culture such as ours rejects its own irrationality and believes that reason sanctioned by God gives such imagery divine imprimatur.

Denial of human animality, violence, and wildness, and the ascription of these traits to the wolf and to the world of nature has resulted not only in the eradication of wolves, but in the decimation of the natural world as well under the label of economic imperative.

Destruction of nature and exploitation of resources seem to be hallmarks of our time. Like wildfire, this seemingly inexhaustible process burns with inferno-like persistence, ravaging all in its path.

The Mexican wolf has fallen prey to this process which marks Western culture. The ghosts of all those wolves who have been killed call out to us. Their voices have entered my being and filled my heart with vague dread. The extermination of wolves perhaps marks a special case in the history of our brutality against the natural world. Because of our ancient long-buried likeness to this creature and because wolves have remained embedded in the natural world, their extirpation stands for all the havoc our culture has wreaked on nature.

Saving the Mexican wolf, the most endangered among wolves, is especially meaningful in that we bear such commonality and estrangement from the wolf. Returning the Mexican wolf to the wilderness would be a small sign that we have recognized our cruelty and the error of our ways and we are ready to atone for our misdeeds against the natural world. A token gesture, perhaps, but a gesture nonetheless of our increased understanding, not only of ourselves, but of those others whom we have destroyed in our heedlessness. Certainly we have other examples of how to look at the world.

A Myth for Our Time

People have not always chosen negative meanings for the wolf and wilderness. I have cited examples from Native American belief showing how humans are viewed as citizens of the natural world. Nor is violence against nature purely a Christian propensity. Christianity has within it influences which have mitigated against rationales justifying expansionism and commercial exploitation. I have discussed how St. Francis talked with animals, plants, and inanimate objects, though the urge to seek unity with nature is a subterranean theme in Western history.

These ideas seem ludicrous when placed in the context of modern industrial society. In our day we seem to be approaching the end of the cancer economy with its high technology and dependence on resource exploitation. Deep ecology, as a reaction against rampant materialism, has evolved from an awareness that our world has about run its course and rampant exploitation is approaching its natural limits. Those who are discussing so-called paradigm shifts are giving expression to the feeling that a great and powerful change is at hand, a change as profound as the developments of the Renaissance or the Copernican revolution.

If our industrial world is really now facing a serious crisis and we are confronted with the problem of making peace with nature before we ourselves are consumed by our own foolhardy exploitation, it seems imperative to turn to those cultures we have previously ignored or destroyed, in order to learn how we might make peace with our planet, its plants and creatures as well as other peoples. Let us hope for forgiveness and for more understanding than we have shown other peoples and our fellow creatures in the past.

In Chapter Two, I discussed the Tewa and other Pueblo tribal myths of emergence. To me the emergence myths so prevalent among American tribal peoples have great meaning for our time because we ourselves are going through a kind of emergence into a new and radically different world. These myths tell us that people have gone through several radical transformations brought about by the inability of people to understand and react to the demands of their world and time.

We can call this radical transformation a paradigm shift, an emotive physical transformation, or the surfacing of a new body awareness. In any case, the myth of emergence tells us that humans have been forced to confront such transformations before, not once, but repeatedly in the past. Emergence, indeed, may record the evolutionary journey of homo sapiens developing into the current state.

Shadows on the Sands of Time

Pueblo myths portray emergence into the current world from beneath a lake. The shadows of our ancient prehuman evolution from sea to land may have traced their lineaments across these myths. Parturition itself is the individual repetition, not only of the birth experience, but of the evolution of our species repeated in the evolution of a people and the journey of each individual life.

In the version of Tewa emergence recorded in this book, the wolf stood at the entrance of the new world to instruct humans about the sacred knowledge of hunting, a key to survival. As I have detailed, the proper attitude toward prey—respect and honor—were the traces of wisdom brought into this world from the time before time, when animals and humans communicated freely as brothers and sisters.

Radical ecopolitics, as an emotive body awareness, is an absolute rejection of contemporary cultural conditions and an attempt to restore humans to living within the natural world. It reflects a howling wolf knowing and a felt sense that yearns for the restoration of wildness and a deep desire to sink back into the wondrous panoply of living natural forms comprising the biosphere. Thus, it embraces human cultures that see no difference between themselves and nature, and reside within the natural world.

Emergence in the modern context must have new meaning. I would like to suggest a departure from the views espoused by those who believe in violent confrontation as an extension of ideology, even if it be a felt ideology. Body knowing itself has presented horrible challenges through human history, as witnessed by historical phenomena ranging from the persecution of suspected werewolves, witches, and all suspected "others" in the Middle Ages, to the eradication of wolves in the last century.

Ascription of negative attributes has been exactly the process that has resulted in extirpation of the Mexican wolf, as well as persecution of peoples whose ways are seen as foreign, different, and therefore savage. We have used the same approach to justify the destruction of the land and its resources in the name of progress. These are predatory human behaviors disguised by elaborate rationales that cover the fact that these attributes are our own.

Allowing the Mexican wolf to once more roam free means coming to terms with our predator nature and healing the damage we have so carelessly wrought on our world. We must look deeply at things as they truly are to see our own animal nature and to be animal. In our society we are imprisoned in our small selves, thinking only of our immediate comforts while we blindly destroy our larger self that we call nature. If we can be the other, if we can be like wolves, we can understand what it means to live as wolves live and we can seek then reconciliation with and not victory over nature.

This book has been an impassioned plea, a journey, a watch, and a vision. In the name of ideologies and doctrines people have killed one another and they have eradicated the wolf. No ideology is the truth. Peace with ourselves can only be attained when we are no longer attached to the slavery of conceptual viewpoints and the passionate adherence to ideas. We must renounce fanaticism and narrowness, awaken to suffering, anger, hatred, and delusion—awaken to the wolf within us. These are the secrets the wolf has given over to us, the wolf who stands guard at the edge of the new world into which we will either emerge or perish in the attempt of crossing.

Postscript

Not until early spring 1990 did the Mexican Wolf Coalition of Texas finally form. On February 18, the Board of Directors met at Glen Rose to begin campaigning for reintroduction of the Mexican wolf in Texas. The board, headed by president Elizabeth Sizemore, viewed wolf education as essential for successful wolf recovery in the state.

The coalition sought to establish a rancher compensation fund for any losses that might occur due to wolf predations in the event the wolf was eventually introduced. Efforts focused on Big Bend National Park and Guadalupe Mountain National Park. Big Bend's status as a U.N.E.S.C.O. Biosphere Reserve seemed to favor the area. Biosphere Reserve status is granted by the United Nations to areas representative of major world ecosystems. The Chihuahuan desert ecology of the park, coalition members contended, would be incomplete without the presence of the Mexican wolf.

The coalition had waited until 1990 to organize because supporters believed Texas politics favor ranchers who were expected to mount strong opposition to wolf recovery.

Biologist Rick Lo Bello, director of the Big Bend National Park's Natural History Association, became the editor of the coalition's newsletter. In 1988, Lo Bello had written the Texas Parks and Wildlife Department about possible wolf recovery in Texas. In June, he received a reply from executive director Charles Travis explaining several objections to Texas recovery efforts.

Travis said the department had met with Fish and Wildlife officials, but review had shown there was no area in the state big enough to consider effective introductions. Travis cited state law 63.102, which forbade wolf introductions in the state. He stated that while the law was not a current consideration, the existence of the statute could pose future legal problems for wolf recovery.

Section 68.019 of the state's wildlife conservation code, however, stated that all endangered subspecies would be excluded from other Texas provisions. The Mexican wolf's status under the federal Endangered Species Act thus exempted the Mexican wolf from consideration under the previously cited law.

In January 1990, *Texas Monthly* published a blistering condemnation of the department, claiming Parks and Wildlife was dominated by influence peddling and political gamesmanship in managing the state's wilderness resources. The article faulted the nine-member Parks and Wildlife Commission, composed of wealthy businessmen and political contributors, for mismanagement and corruption. The Texas Department of Parks and Wildlife had earlier vetoed U.S. Fish and Wildlife consideration of the Big Bend area as a possible Mexican wolf reintroduction site. The coalition decided to hold its first public meeting in conjunction with Earth Day on April 22, 1990.

Early in May, announcement of a 2.5 million acre joint U.S.-Mexico megapark that would join Big Bend and portions of Coahuila and Chihuahua states gave new hope that the wolf might be introduced in the area. The prize feature of the new park would be the Sierra del Carmen and Maderas del Carmen mountain ranges.

Here, subject to moist, warm breezes from the Gulf of Mexico, the Maderas nurtures a luxuriant forest of Douglas and Coahuila fir, Ponderosa pine, aspen, cypress, and oak, somewhat similar to the New Mexican highlands that were once ideal range for the Mexican wolf. In mid-May, Michael Spear, regional director of the Fish and Wildlife Service, accompanied by U.S. and Mexican officials, took a three-day raft trip through Boquillas Canyon in the area. One of the objectives of the trip was to consider possible reintroduction of endangered species in the area. Tom Smylie, assistant regional director of FWS, has said that White Sands remains the area preferred by the service for wolf location. He disclaimed any knowledge that the new megapark might be under consideration as a possible wolf site.

The legal status of the Mexican wolves used for captive breeding had long been an issue between this country and Mexico. The new international park holds promise that this vast, wild area may one day be the home of Mexican wolves.

Wolf Readings

Chapter One: First Encounter

Information for Chapter One was drawn from two generally available sources, which are both highly recommended for those who wish to gain a basic familiarity with wolf behavior and biology as well as wolf-human interactions. L. David Mech has established a well-deserved reputation as one of the foremost wolf biologists. His thorough and detailed examination of wolf behavior and interactions with humans is entitled *The Wolf: The Ecology and Behavior of an Endangered Species* (Natural History Press, Garden City, New York, 1970). In a more popular vein, Barry Holstun Lopez has written a classic wolf book, *Of Wolves and Men* (Charles Scribner's Sons, New York, 1978). This work covers a great deal of ground by discussing cultural and mythological ideas of the wolf as well as wolf behavior and general biology. For European and general American Indian wolf beliefs this book is an excellent resource as it conveys the author's love of and respect for the mystery of his subject. There are many topics only touched upon which others may wish to expand. The Lopez book is invaluable for anyone wishing to approach his or her first wolf reading. For wolf aficionados the work is equally interesting.

Background information on New Mexico ecology and wolf introductions was derived from *The Mexican Wolf: Biology, History and Prospects for Reestablishment in New Mexico* and *An Evaluation of the Ecological Potential of White Sands Missile Range to Support a Reintroduced Population of Mexican Wolves,* two reports prepared for the U.S. Fish and Wildlife Service (P.O. No. 20181-87-00570) by biologist James C. Bednarz. Both of these reports, available from Fish and Wildlife, provide essential history and background of Mexican wolf behavior and biology as well as a thorough discussion of the ecology of the state and the White Sands area.

Chapter Two: Brother Wolf

Roger Peters' *The Dance of the Wolves* (McGraw-Hill, New York, 1985) provides the basis for Naked Wolf and human-wolf map-making comparisons. Peters tells of his three years spent researching wolf populations. His account is a well written and beautiful exposition of his personal relationship with wolves told without romance. For those who are more scientifically inclined, Peters's *Mental Maps in Wolf Territoriality* presents his study of wolf cognitive map making and territorial migrations. This paper is included in *The Behavior and Ecology of Wolves* (Erich Klinghammer, editor, Garland STPM Press, New York, 1979). There is a lot of other material in this book which will prove of interest to students of wolf behavior. Wolf conservation and population studies, wolf ethology (behavioral studies), and some fascinating work on howling and wolf syntactics.

Unfortunately, *The Dance of the Wolves* remains Peters's only available work to date written for a general audience. We would be well served by an author of his gifts writing his observations in accessible formats. Recent discussions with the author reveal that Peters has continued his research into comparing human and mammal cognitive comparisons, but he has not continued his wolf research.

R.D. Lawrence's *In Praise of Wolves* (Henry Holt, New York, 1986) is a popular account of the author's wolf relationships spanning several years. The book is a good general source and contains small snippets of wolf behavioral details that found their way into this chapter. Those interested in exploring the work of Carveth Read may find *Man and his Superstitions* (1925) and *The Origin of Man* of use in determining Read's outlooks. Both books were published by the University Press, Cambridge, England and may be available in larger libraries or through interlibrary loan. *Conversations with Claude Levi-Strauss* (G. Carbonnier, ed., Grossman Cape Editions, London, England, 1969) is the fulcrum on which is based discussion of hot and cold cultures and the take-off point for primitive wolf cultures versus industrial orders.

John Collier's *On the Gleaming Way* (Sage Books, Denver, 1962) is a fascinating and beautifully written exposition comparing Pueblo and Navajo traditions with white cultures. Collier provided the authority for the comparison between Buddhist and Pueblo world views. The reader interested in Pueblo ideas about time and an intriguing perspective on native cultures of the Southwest will discover many delights in this unusually insightful and artfully written small volume. Sage Books no longer publishes, but most libraries will be able to get this little book.

Information on Pueblo languages was gleaned from *The Pueblo Indian World*, by Edgar L. Hewett and Bertha P. Dutton, a monograph published in Albuquerque, New Mexico, by the University of New

Mexico Press in 1945, which details investigations into language and culture of Pueblo peoples. Another monograph, *The Wolf Ritual of the Northwest Coast*, by Alice H. Ernst (University of Oregon Press, Eugene, 1952), is the basis for information about Northwest tribal wolf beliefs. This study goes into much more detail about specific traditions and ceremonies than this chapter allows for and will be of great interest for those who want to explore this subject more deeply. When taken in contrast to Lopez's discussion of Northwest coastal and Alaskan Indian beliefs, this monograph proves particularly interesting.

A delightful book that is an inclusive source for Indian beliefs, traditions, and outlooks is *The Sacred: Ways of Knowledge, Sources of Life*, edited by Peggy V. Beck and A.L. Walters (Navajo Community College Press, Tsaile, Arizona, 1977). I have drawn on this work to provide insight into hunter traditions and other general beliefs. Those interested in research about Indian ideas and ways of life will find this book a genuine aid to understanding.

There are certain books to which one refers again and again during one's life. Such a book is *Memories, Dreams and Reflections*, C.G. Jung's autobiography (Vintage Books, New York, 1965). The cover to my volume disintegrated long ago, but somehow this book has always proved a fascinating source of inspiration on all sorts of topics. The story of Jung's visit to Taos Pueblo seemed of particular moment for this chapter.

Chapter Three: Great Beast God of the East

Elsie Clews Parsons's two-volume study, *Pueblo Indian Religion* (University of Chicago Press, Chicago, 1939), provided the starting point for my examination of Pueblo wolf beliefs. Long out of print, this involved study of Pueblo beliefs is based on the odd premise that Pueblo "religious" ideas are a kind of misapplied science. Parsons believes Pueblos, in attempting to influence natural events through ceremony, are engaging in a sort of scientific method gone astray, if I read her introduction correctly. Despite this prejudice of her age, the books are an invaluable source of information, though her style is sometimes less than lucid. These books were, I discovered, difficult to locate and are now considered collector's items.

Pueblo Animals and Myths, by Hamilton Tyler (University of Oklahoma Press, Norman, 1975), presented me with information about

Wolf as Beast God and companion of Mountain Lion. This book is generally available and is a popular study. Tyler's research sometimes forms connections between villages and Pueblo peoples that can prove confusing, or so it seemed to me. Highly recommended is the fascinating *The Tewa World, Space, Time, Being and Becoming in a Pueblo Society*, Alfonso Ortiz's lucid and penetrating examination of Tewa moieties, from which was drawn most of the emergence story that is a take-off point for the discussion of predators and wolves in Pueblo traditions. Anyone who wishes to gain insight into Tewa views will be intrigued by this book, published by University of Chicago Press, Chicago, 1972.

The Pueblo Indians of North America, by Edward P. Dozier (Holt, Rinehart and Winston, New York, 1970), also provided additional readings and confirmation of information gathered on emergence mythology, Pueblo traditions, and the place of wolves in Pueblo society. Hamilton Tyler's *Pueblo Gods and Myths* (University of Oklahoma Press, Norman, 1972) also provided similar backup material and elaborations on views of Pueblo deities and animals.

Anthropologist Ruth Underhill presented fascinating information on southwestern communal hunting and ritual medicine in her *Ceremonial Patterns in the Greater Southwest* (Monographs of the American Ethnological Society, No. 13, University of Washington Press, Seattle, Washington, 1966). Parsons again came into play in furnishing the tale of Yellow Wolf. Ruth Benedict, in Volume II of her intriguing two-volume work, *Zuñi Mythology* (Columbia University Press, New York, 1935), related the Tale of the Ahaiyute and Beast Gods, one of the few wolf tales recounted in full to be found in literary accounts. L.A. White's *The Pueblo of Santa Ana* (Memoirs of the American Anthropological Association, No. 60, Menasha, Wisconsin, 1942) and M.C. Stevenson's *The Zuñi Indians* (23rd Annual Report of the Bureau of American Ethnology, Washington, D.C., 1904) gave additional information on hunter societies and beliefs. While White reports a "rich hunter mythology," very little has been recorded due to the prevailing secrecy of Pueblo beliefs.

There were many additional sources I used to attempt to determine the overall pattern of Pueblo wolf beliefs. I felt in researching this chapter that the truth could only be learned by placing a number of works together in context. It can never be assured with certainty exactly what these traditions and beliefs are, or were, due to the wish to keep outsiders from knowing with exactitude ceremonial and ritual tradition. Anthropologist Nathaniel Tarn, in conversations about this research, frankly admitted he had been studying one Guatemalan village for some twenty years and he still was not sure what the villagers believed. Since so much anthropological data relies on personal report, I can only hope this discussion of wolf tradition and belief has retained a degree of accuracy and interest for the reader.

Chapter Four:
Wolf Way, Skinwalkers, and Shape Changers

The fictional account detailing Navajo Wolf Way hunting traditions is based on W.W. Hill's thorough study entitled *The Agricultural and Hunting Methods of the Navaho Indians* (Yale University Publications in Anthropology, No. 18, New Haven, Connecticut, 1938). Hill studied these traditions at about the last possible time they were actively being followed by sizeable hunting parties. His recording of Wolf Way is the most thorough made of all the hunting rituals he observed. Information on Navajo origins, language, and early lifestyles was gleaned from several sources.

Of most interest on general Navajo ways was *The Book of the Navajo,* by Raymond Friday Locke (Mankind Publishing, Los Angeles, 1976). *The Navajo,* by James F. Downs (Waveland Press, Prospect Heights, Illinois, 1984), gave some good details on agriculture, shepherding, and witchcraft. Karl Luckert's *The Navajo Hunter Tradition* (University of Arizona Press, Tucson, 1975) provided the philosophical meat and backbone for this chapter. An intriguing book, the work is strangely structured, giving mythological and personal accounts of hunting traditions before providing context through the author's interpretive essays buried in the back of the book. Read the essays on prehuman flux and interpretation before embarking into the material gathered from original sources if you want to understand what you are reading.

A number of works by Clyde Kluckhohn are of interest to the investigator delving into Navajo witchcraft. I found *Navaho Witchcraft* (Papers of the Peabody Museum of American Archaeology and Ethnology, Vol. XXII, No. 2, Harvard University, Cambridge, Massachusetts, 1944) to give a pretty good basic account of skinwalking practices and beliefs. This account was verified by much secondary research. The amount of information on Navajo traditions and beliefs exceeds Pueblo research by tenfold, but solid research on hunter traditions and witchcraft is much rarer. It would be pointless to cite the dozens of works I perused in search of wolf material.

One gem I discovered that proved useful in my witchcraft readings was *Navajo Children's Narratives: Symbolic Forms in a Changing Culture*, Margaret Brady's Ph.D. dissertation presented to the University of Texas, Austin, Texas, in 1978. This source proved extraordinarily rich in summarizing traditional witch practice and belief. The author totally neglects wolf's place in witchcraft in favor of more popular trickster interpretations of Coyote as the chief witch patron. While Coyote does play an important role in witchcraft, wolves are the animals almost invariably associated with Navajo skinwalking. The scholarly and popular emphasis on Coyote as arch trickster has perhaps obscured the role of fluid identity in imbuing all beings with trickster attributes.

Chapter Five: Lobo Misterioso

Marc Simmons has written the only detailed account of southwestern witchcraft, entitled *Witchcraft in the Southwest* (Northland Press, Flagstaff, Arizona, 1974). The book details accounts from contemporary records gathered during the Southwest Inquisition. Simmons argues that historians should pay attention to witchcraft and other topics usually ignored by professional scholars, as these subjects shed light on the development of consciousness. Information about Paleolithic cultural traditions was derived from anthropologist Clyde Kluckhohn, whose insights into Navajo witchcraft proved of interest in previous chapters of my own work. Simmons mentions werewolves only tangentially in his work.

Myths to Live By, by Joseph Campbell (Bantam Books, New York, 1978), provided me with a few details on the evolution of scientific thinking that proved of use in writing this chapter. Reading Campbell allowed a certain flavor to permeate my research and gave me strength in delving more deeply into the subterranean subjects covered in this section. Colin Wilson's *Witches* (Crescent Books, New York, 1988) introduced me to several werewolf accounts, including the Gandillon episode. Francis X. King's *Witchcraft and Demonology* (Exeter Books, New York, 1987) also provided some werewolf background. *Women's Encyclopedia of Myths and Secrets*, by Barbara G. Walker (Harper and

Row, San Francisco, 1983), provided insight into classical and pre-classical sources of wolf myth and lore.

C.G. Jung's work permeates my treatment of medieval tradition. Two works in particular provided substantial revelations for this chapter. *Man and his Symbol* (Dell, New York, 1968) gave much of the overview of Jung's beliefs about the origin and development of the unconscious. Jung's landmark *Psychology and Alchemy* (Princeton University Press, New York, 1968) is a fascinating study of dreams compared to medieval alchemy. The birth and evolution of the unconscious is detailed with startling clarity by Jung, who shows how unconscious imagery appears in the dream life of modern subjects little changed from medieval alchemical symbols.

The stories of Pernette Gandillon and Pierre Bourgot are told in Michael Jenkinson's *Beasts Beyond the Fire* (E.P. Dutton, New York, 1980). Jenkinson, a New Mexico author, provides evidence for New Mexico wolf and werewolf lore in this fascinating study of man's relationship with wild beasts.

One of the most interesting books I encountered in my researches for this chapter was *Man into Wolf*, by Robert Eisler. The book presents material given in a lecture Eisler delivered at a meeting of the British Royal Society of Medicine. Eisler then details in notes his sources for the talk and goes to considerable length filling out the topics delivered in his presentation. This is one of those rare finds—this book opened whole new realms of research that were invaluable for the work at hand. Eisler, who was a Holocaust survivor, was a brilliant Jungian scholar. After the war, he became intrigued with the roots and causes of human violence and began amassing information about sadism, masochism, and lycanthropy. This fascinating and obscure monograph is the result of his investigation. Much of the material on Classic beliefs and the sources for such beliefs were drawn from Eisler's study.

I owe a great debt in writing this chapter to Morris Berman, author of *Coming to our Senses* (Simon and Schuster, New York, 1989). His treatment of our relationship to animals and his penetrating insight into our estrangement from ourselves I found absolutely absorbing. Anyone interested in the history of consciousness will find Berman indispensable. Any misinterpretation of his ideas are entirely my own.

Simone de Beauvoir's lucid work, *The Second Sex* (Bantam Books, New York, 1952), is well known to feminists and provided me with a few apt details I found crucial for this chapter. I used *Chaucer's Poetry*, selected and edited by E.T. Donaldson (Ronald Press, New York, 1958), for evidence of medieval remnants of classical belief.

The Oxford Annotated Bible (New York, 1962) was my Biblical source for this chapter, though I also referred to my boyhood King James version. Another childhood book I perused for this chapter was *Aesop's Fables*, edited and illustrated by Boris Artzybasheff. This delightful collection allowed me to compare the ancient versions with New Mexico folktales about the wolf.

In writing this chapter I had occasion to talk to many friends about their recollections of Hispanic wolf tales and lore. These discussions were fascinating and invaluable. I also researched over a thousand tales in the *Folklore and Mythology Studies* series, Vol. 31, compiled from the *R.D. Jameson Collection* (University of California Press, Berkeley, 1980).

Chapter Six: And God Gave Man Dominion

Early chapters of David R. Williams's book *Wilderness Lost* (Associated University Press, Cranbery, New Jersey) provided me the starting point for this chapter. Williams does a creditable job of outlining early Puritan beliefs, especially on typology. *New Mexico: An Interpretive History*, by Marc Simmons (University of New Mexico Press, 1988), provided focus on early Moorish Spain and also offered a clear and insightful picture of ranching in the Southwest during the late 1800s.

The work I'm most indebted to for this chapter is Frederick Turner's *Beyond Geography: The Western Spirit Against the Wilderness* (Viking Press, New York, 1980). Turner attacks the theme of estrangement from the land and traces with great eloquence the story of western exploration, dominance, and settlement. I recommend this solid and brilliantly written book as a thorough, though arduous, journey through difficult thematic country. Turner relates with clarity the sorrowful tale of conquest and domination with which we as a people have yet to come to terms. There are some books one is grateful for in the same way that one is happy family members inform our lives with their words and their particular ways of speaking. Turner's words have that kind of intimate way of penetrating deep into one's being.

The Gnostic Gospels, Elaine Pagels's excellent treatise (Vintage Books, New York, 1981), gave salient ideas about Gnosticism that I touched upon in this chapter. Quotes from Puritan figures were drawn from Roderick Nash, *Wilderness and the American Mind* (Yale University Press, New Haven, 1982). Etymologies for wilderness terminology and Teutonic myth were also drawn from this book, which originally appeared in the 1960s.

Viktor Frankl's *Psychotherapy and Existentialism* (Washington Square Press, New York, 1967) gave me details on American psychology and industrialization. Frankl's life-long examination of individual psychology and personal meaning is a wonderful and inspiring tonic for our world. Details concerning de Tocqueville are again drawn from Nash's work. Information and basics on "Manifest Destiny," as well as Frederick Jackson Turner, Henry Adams, and western ranching were drawn from *The American Republic,* by Hofstadter, Miller, and Aaron (Prentice-Hall, Englewood Cliffs, New Jersey, 1959). This two-volume exposition of American history has remained in my library for years and I have continually referred to it for basic research. Additional information on Turner was gleaned from *Turner, Bolton and Webb,* by Jacobs, Caughey, and Frantz (University of Washington Press, Seattle, 1965), a monograph comparing these three historians. Somewhere along the line, I acquired a small copy of Francis Parkman's *Oregon Trail* (Macmillan, New York, 1921). I read this book with a mixture of horror and fascination. Anyone interested in the nineteenth-century American mind will find Parkman's little book an enlightening glimpse into narrow thinking and a total conviction in the absolute rightness of exploitation. Alice Miller's *For Your Own Good* (Farrar, Straus and Giroux, New York, 1984) details the horrifying practices of hidden cruelty involved in standard child rearing. She explores Hitler's story and touches on wolfish preoccupations secretly fostering social violence and dishonesty. Philip Ashton Rollins's book, *The Cowboy* (University of New Mexico Press, Albuquerque, 1922), gives the reader contemporary glimpses into the fascinating world of ranching as it occurred in New Mexico during the end of the last century and the beginning of our own period.

Chapter Seven: Too Stupid to Survive

David E. Brown edited *The Wolf in the Southwest* (University of Arizona Press, Tucson, 1983), a collection that documents the destruction of the Mexican wolf and other lobo relatives in the Southwest. It is an odd book in its way—thorough, complete, and scientific, though lacking self-examination and attempts to interpret what extinction of the wolf means. Brown's long-time career as a specialist in game management and wildlife conservation in Arizona lends a curiously flat tone to the work, reflecting perhaps the circumstances under which it was written. The U.S. Fish and Wildlife Service, successor of the Biological Service, provided partial funding for manuscript preparation.

The Mexican Gray Wolf in New Mexico, by Gary Lee Nunley, provided valuable information concerning the language and methodology of wolf slaughter in New Mexico. Commissioned by the Animal Damage Control Division (ADC), Nunley's monograph details Biological Survey annual reports and summarizes the methods and ideas of wolfers from the early days of the service. Written in 1977, it was perhaps of more use in some ways than Brown's book, since the information is from contemporary sources and is presented in a fashion I found extremely useful.

The ADC has inherited the unfortunate responsibility of eliminating "problem animals" from the United States. Though I broke the ADC story a year and a half ago for Reuters International News, it was not until spring 1990 that CBS became interested in mountain lion extermination by the agency in Arizona. ADC has accounted for millions of animal exterminations and has attracted the attention of animal rights activists because of its work. Several years ago, the agency was moved from the Fish and Wildlife Service to the Department of Agriculture. Animal rights proponents await filing of the agency's Environmental Impact Statement, which will detail exactly which species have been decimated by the agency. Annual reports for the agency are not completed except by region. In order to trace the extent of the agency's work, I compiled statistics from annual reports in each region going back over five years.

Another book helped furnish a different tack on wolf destruction in New Mexico. *In the Cause of Progress: A History of the New Mexico Cattle Grower's Association,* by Robert K. Mortensen, was a private, limited-edition history funded by the association. While merely summarizing minutes of the association's meetings, the book provides a rare look at the thought processes of ranchers who lobbied long and hard for wolf extermination. One can sense the great difficulties of raising cattle as the range goes through ecosystem depletion, which coincides with extermination of species the ranchers thought were competing for resources they felt rightly belonged to the cattle industry.

Most of the information in this chapter regarding Stoke Ligon was drawn from "The Story of J. Stokley Ligon," by David G. Jackson, which appeared in *New Mexico Wildlife*, May-June 1961. Ligon was a man of contradictions. His love of wilderness, and his dedication to preserving wildfowl seem to stand in sharp contrast to his determined work in eliminating wolves. Ligon was a creature of his age, dedicated to wildlife management techniques. Generations to come will no doubt find our own era full of contradictions. It is only now that the wolf has been destroyed that it has gained ardent advocates. Quotations detailing Ligon's philosophy of wildlife management were provided by the *New Mexico Conservationist*, September 1927.

Sharman Russell, in her article "Aldo Leopold, Father of Wildlife Management in America" (*New Mexico Wildlife*, November-December 1984), insists that Leopold's writing originated from a strictly rationalistic and scientific mind. This proved somewhat puzzling. Anyone who has had the pleasure of reading Leopold may sense the scientist and the poet blended together, hence the powerful appeal of his work.

Free-lance editor and nature writer Alan Pistorius has written a well-styled and beautiful account of Aldo Leopold's career that appeared in the November-December issue of *Arizona Highways*. "When the Green Fire Died" provides deep insight into the man, his life, and his work. It is always of interest to me to view people who have over the period of a lifetime come to great discoveries. To me these people always seem braver and more interesting than those who are simply born to their talents and who never seem to grow into greater vision. Leopold is especially interesting in this regard because of the level and depth of his insight which then predicts the great awakening that was to happen when Americans became aware that wilderness and wildness were disappearing. We still are coming to terms with the insights that Leopold came to in his life. That a man would start as a wolf killer and come to regret his fervor is a sign of vulnerability and courage.

One spring afternoon I happened to be visiting a small New Mexico public library with a friend who was taking me to see some petroglyphs. I happened to be browsing in the used book bin and found a copy of Leopold's *A Sand County Almanac* (Ballantine Books, New York, 1966) on sale for fifty cents, the exact amount of money I had in my pocket. It was one of the discoveries of a lifetime. I had wanted to read Leopold for a long time and the book was put into my hands at just the time when I needed his voice whispering in my ear. For those who have not had the blessing and opportunity of reading

Leopold, this book will serve as a reminder of what it means to be alive to our world.

I also drew on Roderick Nash's *Wilderness and the American Mind* (Yale University Press, New Haven, 1982) for background regarding Leopold. Once again I drew on Alice Miller's *For Your Own Good* for details regarding degradation, shame, and cruelty in child-rearing practices (see notes to previous chapter).

Chapter Eight: Beloved Wolf

Ernest Thompson Seton's *Wild Animals I Have Known* (Scribners, New York, 1907) provided me a starting point for this chapter. The book has been recently reissued in softcover. Seton served as naturalist for the Manitoba government and wrote several books, including *Biography of a Grizzly*, which proved very popular around the turn of the century. He tends to anthropomorphize his animal characters, which perhaps accounts for the strong following he developed among the general public. His observations and his animal drawings provided the first glimpse many north Americans had of the wilderness.

David Brown's book, *The Wolf in the Southwest* (University of Arizona Press, Tucson, 1983), provided valuable information on wolf outlaws for this chapter.

Wolf and Man: Evolution in Parallel, edited by Roberta L. Hall and Henry S. Sharp (Academic Press, New York, 1978), presents a fascinating summary of current research linking the lifestyles of early humans to wolves. I've summarized much of this research in my chapter. The layperson should be aware that many of the papers presented involve pretty arcane research. One wonders at scientific procedures that seem to limit speculation. Section introductions written by the editors are more intriguing, as they seem to take more risks than many of the papers presented as chapter material. I can't tell if this is merely my personal inclination at work or if this is a problem with the book. I find it surprising that such a book has not made a larger impression. Unfortunately, technical research often does not reach the reading public. For those generalists who are interested in extending their wolf knowledge, however, this book is highly recommended.

On the one hand, the insistence in some scientific and research communities upon narrow research and the refusal to admit speculation has done nothing to further applicability of research. On the other hand, the layman's inability to understand scientific concerns has been problematic for researchers who want to reach wider audiences. Perhaps more could be done for wolves if so-called ordinary people understood how fascinating these animals are and in how many ways they resemble our ancestors. I'm not pushing for human-centered interest in the wolf, merely noting that when people see commonality between creatures and humans they usually respond with greater understanding.

I've mentioned Roger Peters's research on wolf communication and cognition. Peters's technical book, *Mammalian Communication: A Behavioral Analysis of Meaning* (Brooks/Cole, Monterey, California, 1980), is of interest to anyone who wishes to investigate the behavior of mammals. It is, to this generalist, the most detailed examination of animal behavior in one volume I've seen, and the chapters are concise and usually well written.

Peters is a gifted writer as well as an important researcher and his work, even if technical, is written *for* the reader, not to exclude the reader. He delves into the meaning of animal behavior by attempting to establish a clear, independent system of analysis to apply to animals expressing widely different habits. Peters's work is especially thorough in regard to wolves, as they have been one of his major topics of research. Peters's research on Raised Leg Urinations (RLUs) is also included in the aforementioned work.

One can't go very far in learning about wolves without encountering the name L. David Mech. Howling information is gleaned from Mech's compendious book *The Wolf* (The Natural History Press, Garden City, New York, 1970).

R.D. Lawrence's *In Praise of Wolves* (Holt and Company, New York, 1986) is an eloquent account of the author's relationship to wolves. His is an intuitive exploration of the wolf's world and an attempt to provide clues to understanding wolf behavior in terms of human meanings. It is Lawrence's interaction with wolves that provides the focus of the book. I have also drawn on his work in regard to howling.

Chapter Nine: When Wolves Run Free

An interesting book written for those directly involved with captive breeding, *Wolf and Man: Advances, Issues and Problems in Captive Wolf Research*, edited by Henry Frank (D.W. Junk, Boston, 1987), is constrained to a limited readership due to its highly technical nature. The value of some research—a study of wolf-poodle (Puwo) hybrids, for instance, which tries to determine if wolf and Puwos approach or flee humans—is debatable. Other chapters discuss wolves living in captivity that are socialized to humans and those that are not. This book provides the essential information base for discussing captive wolf research and lifestyles. If the reader is patient, the various technical chapters provide interesting information.

The Mexican Wolf Recovery Plan developed by the U.S. Fish and Wildlife Service in 1982 provided the basis of Mexican wolf information in this chapter. In 1980, Patricia Melhop and Michael Bogan published their monograph entitled *The Systematic Relationship of Gray Wolves in Southwestern North America*, sponsored by the National Fish and Wildlife Laboratories in Washington and the University of New Mexico. Information on Mexican wolf taxonomy is derived from this study.

A study by Dr. William Shields and Dr. Alan Templeton for the New Mexico Department of Game and Fish, *Genetic Assessment of the Current Captive Breeding Program for the Mexican Wolf*, provided some information on Mexican wolf genetic viability. Information regarding Mexican wolf habitat and lifestyles was drawn from the two-part report by James Bednarz on Mexican wolf recovery potential in the White Sands area, commissioned by the Fish and Wildlife Service in 1988.

All the Loving Wolves: Living and Learning with Wolf Hybrids, by Michael Belshaw (Red Crane Books, Santa Fe, New Mexico, 1990) provided the basis for information on wolf hybrids. The author draws on his personal experience raising wolf hybrids. Several biologists have commented to me that they think Belshaw's profit motive makes him short-sighted in his sanguine views of wolf hybrid behavior. They have remarked on the unpredictability of such animals and have questioned the ethics of wolf hybrid breeding, selling, and ownership. The book is a guide to the pleasures and problems of wolf hybrid ownership and is written with the wolf hybrid owner in mind. Belshaw has also commented on the genetic diversity of such creatures, and advocates the formation of a wolf hybrid owner's association.

✪ ✪ ✪

Chapter Ten: The Green Fire Dying in Her Eyes

Information for this chapter was assembled from daily press accounts, detailed personal interviews, and internal memos and correspondence of agencies involved in Mexican wolf recovery efforts.

Chapter Eleven:
Eco Rage—Howling at the Empty Moon

Most of the information in this chapter was gleaned from personal experience and interviews. Ideas about the relationship between physical-emotive awareness and body politics were formulated after reviewing Christopher Manes's book, entitled *Green Rage: Radical Environmentalism and the Unmaking of Civilization* (Little, Brown and Company, Boston, 1990).

Since Manes's book was written, Dave Foreman has quit Earth First! He is currently under felony indictment for his supposed connection to a 1986 sabotage attempt allegedly directed at destroying power lines from the Palo Verde nuclear plant in Arizona. Foreman withdrew because new Earth First! membership has taken the organization too far to the left, in his estimation. Some new liberal members of the group claim Foreman is rigid in his control of Earth First! and planted his cronies to lead the group. Prominent new Earth First!er Mike Rosell calls Foreman supporters "Foremanistas." It should be noted that both California and Oregon Earth First! groups have renounced tree spiking.

Manes's book is a passionate apology for early founders of Earth First! and an attempt to explicate radical environmental views. The book is a well-written, unabashed, and enthusiastic defense of Earth First! and an enlightening examination of the people and politics behind the organization. Whether or not one sympathizes with the positions expressed in this work, the book will tell the reader about the origins, evolution, and growth of this intriguing segment of environmental politics.

Primitive Rebels, by E.J. Hobsbawm (Norton, New York, 1965), provided some connective tissue to draw together ideas about radical politics as an expression of physical body knowing. My own ideas herein expressed owe much to concepts developed by Morris Berman and cited in notes for earlier chapters.

Chapter Twelve:
The Moon Howls and the Wolves are Silent

A source of inspiration for this chapter was *Teachings from the American Earth: Indian Religion and Philosophy*, edited by Dennis and Barbara Tedlock (Liveright, New York, 1975). This book presents a concise, beautiful, and coherent philosophy derived from various Native American perspectives. Especially valuable for the chapter at hand were Tedlock's introduction and the summary of Tewa emergence mythology by Alfonso Ortiz. Also of use for this chapter was Raymond Friday Locke's *Book of the Navajo* (Mankind Publishing, Los Angeles, 1979). I must say in reference to emergence mythology that the interpretations developed in this book are entirely my own and should not be interpreted as representing any tribe or people. I'm sure I approach such material with my own perceptual and interpretational screens.

Global Mind Change, by Willis Harman (Knowledge Systems, 1988), provided some background on paradigm shifts.

Information about Big Bend and the potential megapark was provided from current press accounts and research information provided by Rick Lo Bello.

Index

Abbey, Edward, 162, 170
Acoma, 26, 28
activism, environmental, 164
adaptation, 115-18
affection, 122, 139
Ahaiyute, War Patron, 35, 49
Alameda Park Zoo, breeding program
    at, 9
Albuquerque Journal, 148, 154
Albuquerque Tribune, 154, 163
*All the Loving Wolves: Living and Learning
    with Wolf Hybrids* (Belshaw), 141
alpha wolf, 118-19, 122, 134-36; behav-
    ior of, 137-40
American Association of Zoological Parks
    and Aquariums (AAZPA), 151, 155
Ames, Norma, 149-155, 157; concerns
    of, 166
ancient humans, wolves and, 116-18
Animal Damage Control Agency, 104,
    154
animality, 20, 58, 59, 75, 179. *See also*
    predatory nature; wolfishness
animal rights activism, awareness of, 2
animals: changing into, 52; dismember-
    ment of, 65; domestication of, 62-64;
    early observations on, 116; marriages
    to, 44; spirit, 33-34; talking to, 71-72,
    180-81
Animas-La Plata dam project, Lujan and,
    159
anogenital odor, 120, 125. *See also* scent
apex hunters, description of, 117
Apollo Lykeios (Wolf Apollo), 60
Arizona, reintroduction in, 5, 158
Arizona Public Service Company, 145
Arizona Sonora Desert Museum, 9, 149,
    150, 152
Artemis, 60, 61
Artemis Lykaiæ (Wolf Artemis), 60
Athapascan languages, 43
attacks, wolf, 7-8
Audubon Society: recovery and, 164; suit
    by, 144
Aztecs, St. Francis and, 74

Bailey, Vernon, 101
balance, 20-21, 49, 52; restoring, 50, 53,
    58

Barker, Bob, 2
barking, 50, 121-22; description of, 10
Basic Fault, description of, 62
Beast Gods, 26, 35-36
Beasts Beyond the Fire (Jenkinson), 66
Bednarz, James, 141
Bednarz Report, 144-45, 156
behavior, 6-7, 16, 61, 112, 133-34, 136-
    39, 142; dominance, 138; fixed, 137;
    Mexican wolf, 132, 136, 140-41; sex-
    ual, 138; submissive, 138; understand-
    ing, 182
Being Peace (Thich Nhat Hanh), 144
Belshaw, Michael, 142-43; writing of, 141
Benedict, Ruth, 35, 37
Beowulf, 78-79
Berman, Morris: writing of, 61-62
berserk, 87; etymology of, 78
Biano, Ochwiay, 23
Big Bend National Park, 183-84
Big Trotter (ma'iitsoh), 41, 46-48
Biological Suitability Study (FWS). *See*
    Bednarz Report
biotic community, fighting for, 146, 173-
    74
biotic history, nature of, 110
bison, slaughter of, 86, 88
Black God, 41-42, 45
Blanca (wolf), story about, 111-14
Blessingway, 42
Blue Corn Woman, 30
Bogan, Michael, 140
Bosque Redondo Reservation, 87
bounties, establishing, 98, 101
bounty hunters. *See* wolfers
Bourgot, Pierre, story of, 55-56
bravery, 35-36, 44
Bring Back the Lobo Week, 3
Brother Wolf, 74-75
Brown, David L., writing of, 106, 153, 167
Brut, wilderness in, 80
Burnett, Grove T., 145-47, 168

Calkins, Hugh, 99
calls, 24; examining, 121-24
cancer economy, 88; description of, 83-
    84; end to, 180
Canis lupus baileyi, 100, 140
Canis lupus mogollonensis, 140

Canis lupus monstrabilis, 140
Canis lupus youngi, 100
cannibalism, 51-52
captive breeding programs, 5, 8-9, 130,
    134, 151, 159; legal status of, 184;
    Mexico and, 168; support for, 154-55
Captive Management Committee, 157
Carleton, James, 87
Carley, Curtis, 150, 167
Carruthers, Garrey, 2
Carson, Kit, 87
Catharists, influence of, 73
Cattle Grower's Advisory Board, work
    of, 99
Causey, George, 86
Causey, John, 86
cave paintings, animals in, 116
ceremony, 22-23, 118; greeting, 120;
    group, 120. *See also* ritual
Changing Woman, 49
chaos, 51, 52, 79
Chaucer, 61
Cheney, Dick: suit against, 144
Che-to'kh (war club), 22
children, subduing, 85
Chisum, John, 87
Christianity: dominance of, 76; gold
    and, 77; nature and, 180; wolves and,
    80-81
Chuang Tzu, 1
Clean Water Act, 145
Cochran, Carol, 157
Cody, Buffalo Bill, 86
Collier, John: writing of, 18-19
Colorado squaw fish, 159
color associations, 27
Coming to Our Senses (Berman), 61
communication, wolf, 16-17, 124-26. *See
    also* information, exchanging; vocal-
    izations
conquistadors, 76, 77
conservation, 11, 102, 108, 154
conversation of death, description of, 21
Copernicus, 54
corn mothers, 30-31
Coronado, Francisco Vasquez de: expedi-
    tion of, 76-77
Cowboy, The (Rollins), 88
Coyote: reputation of, 47, 49; witchcraft
    and, 48, 52
coyotes, 33, 36, 46; encounters with, 87;
    proliferation of, 8, 47, 97

Crisler, Lois: work of, 123-24
Crow, 45
cruelty, 105-6, 113, 180
Culberson, Vic, 148-49

dances: ritual, 33; wolf, 19
Darwin, Charles, 113
De Beauvoir, Simone, 61; writing of, 59
De Benevente, Toribio: writing of, 74
deep ecology, 145-47, 170-73, 180
deer, 42; Coues white-tailed, 97, 117;
    magic, 33; Pueblo Indians and, 33-34
Defenders of Wildlife, 157
Demeter, 60
demonstrations, 168-70
denning, 104; description of, 99
Department of Interior, reintroduction
    and, 158
Descartes, René, 57
Desert Land Act, 88
De Tocqueville, Alexis, 83
Dineh, 47, 49, 51, 53; style of, 43-44
Dirección General de Flora y Fauna Sil-
    vestre (DGFS), 150, 151, 154, 166
disease, 49-50; causes of, 38
Dis Pater, 60
dogs, 133; evolution of, 116-17; relation-
    ship with, 47, 115-16
domestication, 47, 83-84
dominance, 84, 118-20, 122, 136; chal-
    lenging, 140; establishing, 125, 137-39;
    howling and, 123; urinating and, 125
dominant wolf. *See* alpha wolf
dreams, i, 12
Duchess of Malfy (Webster), 55

Earnest, Russell, 130
Earth Day, 184
Earth First! (journal), 170
Earth First!, 161-66, 172
economic determinism, 83
ecopolitics, 170-72, 181-82
ecotage, description of, 161-62
education, wolf, 129, 133, 154-55, 162,
    164, 169, 183
Eichler, Robert, 113
Eisler, Robert: writing of, 64
embedding, description of, 134
emergence, modern, 181-82
emergence myths, 181; hunting and, 32-
    33; Tewa, 31, 37, 181; wolves and, 29,
    49. *See also* mythology

Endangered Species Act, 3-4, 144, 149, 156, 157, 159, 164, 166, 168, 183; description of, 158; suit for, 147
Endangered Species Foundation, 128, 129, 133, 135
Environmental Defense Fund, suit by, 144
environmental movement, 68-69; suits by, 144-45; wolves and, 131
Environmental Protection Agency, 104
epideictic displays, 121
eradication, 24, 37, 47, 59, 66, 68, 86-87, 89, 97-99, 102-8, 113, 117, 141, 154, 160, 179-80, 182
Ernst, Alice, 19
Eskimos, wolves and, 7-8
evolution, 115-18, 181
exploitation, 83, 86, 88, 180, 181
Exxon Valdez disaster, 159

falta de cultura, 78
Father Wolf, 34
Fauna Silvestre. *See* Dirección General de Flora y Fauna Silvestre
Faure, Elie, 176
feminine imagery, wolves and, 59-61
Fenrir (Fenris), 79
Fentress, John, 7
Ferdinand and Isabella, 55
Feronia (Mother of Wolves), 60
Feronius, 60
Festival of Lupercalia, 60
fighting, 136; ritual, 137
Foreman, Dave, 170-72
Four Corners Power Plant, 145
Frankl, Viktor, 82
Frate Lupo, 74-75

Galileo, 54
Game Management (Leopold), 108
games, learning through, 120
Gandillon, Pernette: story of, 58-59, 61
Garden of Eden, lycanthropy and, 64
Genesis, 70, 71, 82
genetic diversity, content of, 119
Gentry, Denny, 148
Gila National Forest, wilderness designation for, 108
Glen Rose, 183
Gnosticism, 71
"God Committee," members of, 158
Goddess (Gaia), 59
Goodnight, Charles, 87

Goodnight Loving Trail, 87
Government Accounting Office, 159
Gray Ranch area, eradication in, 154
Great Goddess, 59-61, 64
Great God of the East, 40
Great Wolf, 48, 49
Greenpeace, 3
Green Rage: Radical Environmentalism and the Unmaking of Civilization (Manes), 170
growling, 121, 136-37. *See also* communication, wolf; information, exchanging; vocalizations
Guadalupe Mountain National Park, 183
Gubbio, wolf of, 73-75

Ha-Sass, 22; story of, 36
Hall, Roberta L.: writing of, 122
Harrington, Fred, 123
Henderson, Dave, 157, 165
Hill, W.W., 41, 46
Historia de los Indios de Nueva España (De Benevente), 74
History of Art (Faure), 176
Hitler, Adolf, 85
Hobsbawm, E.J.: writing of, 172
Homestead Act of 1862, 88
Hopi, 44
howl-in, description of, 168-70
howling, 121; group, 123; human speech and, 124; information from, 123; studying, 123-24. *See also* communication, wolf; information, exchanging; vocalizations
howling wilderness, 80-81
hunter-gatherers, 115, 117, 174
hunters, transformation of, 39-40, 43, 49
hunting, 21, 22, 108, 117, 181; deities, 41-42; myths of, 32, 45; rituals for, 34, 42, 44
hunt magic, receiving, 37
hybridization, questions about, 141-43

imbalance, 20-21, 35, 40, 52, 58
immensidad, 78
information, exchanging, 120-21, 123. *See also* communication, wolf; vocalizations
Inquisition, 54-56, 59, 61, 65
interbreeding, genetic diversity and, 119

Jean (Earth First!er), interview of, 161-62
Jenkinson, Michael, 67-68; writing of, 66

Jesus, 65, 71, 76
Johnson, Edward, 81
Johnson, Jim, 157; interview with, 154
Jung, C.G., 24, 54, 59, 77; writing of, 22-23

Kabbalah, 65
Kallisto, 60
Keeper of Game, 41
Keres, 33
Knight's Tale, 61

Lagorio, Brad, 161-66
lake of the dead, 30
Lawrence, R.D., 17
Layamon, 80
Leopold, Aldo, 97, 171, 173; biotic history and, 110, 146; transformation of, 101-2, 107-10; wolves and, 102-3, 107-9; writing of, 108-9
Leopold, Estelle, 108
Lesbians, 60
Lévi-Strauss, Claude, 17
licking, genital, 137
Ligon, J. Stokely: wolf eradication and, 100-104, 106-7
Little Trotter (*ma'ii*), 46-48
livestock, 47, 65-66; damage to, 46, 88, 98, 103, 106-7
Living Desert State Park, 9
Lo Bello, Rick, 183
Lobo, King of the Currumpaw: story about, 111-14
Loki, 79
lone wolves, 119; howling by, 122-3
Long Walk, 87
Lopez, Barry Holstun, 7-8, 17, 21
Loving, Oliver, 87
Luckert, Karl, 44
Luddites, 172
Lujan, Manuel, 168; suit against, 144; wolf recovery and, 158-59
Lupa Romana, 60
lupo manero (werewolf), 55-56
lycanphobia, 57-59, 65; roots of, 57
lycanthropy, 56-59, 61; Bible and, 64-65; Native Americans and, 65; roots of, 57
Lycaon, 60

McBride, Roy, 152
McDonald, Dave, 148

McFarland, Janet, 128, 129, 133
McFarland, Ron, 128-31, 142; wolves of, 131-33
Maenads, 60
Maestas, Gerald, 162-66; interview of, 2-4
Makahs, wolf dances of, 19
Mammalian Communication (Peters), 120
Manes, Christopher: environmental radicalism and, 173; writing of, 170
Manifest Destiny, idealism of, 84-85
Man into Wolf (Eisler), 64
Manwolf, 52, 53
map making, wolf, 15-16. *See also* scent
Mather, Cotton, 81
mating, 10, 139
meaninglessness, 82
Mech, L. David, 7-8, 10, 123
medicine man, 58. *See also* shamans
medicine society, initiations for, 38
medicine way, 50
Melhop, Patricia, 140
Memories, Dreams and Reflections (Jung), 22
menagerie concept, description of, 11
Merritt, Dennis, 150, 152, 167
Mescalero Apaches, subduing, 87
Mexican wolf, 2, 15, 66, 117, 129, 130, 171; eradication of, 24, 66, 89, 182; photographing, 131-33; relationship to, 179; saving, 126-27, 144, 147, 160, 180; search for, i. *See also* wolves
Mexican Wolf Coalition of Texas, formation of, 183
Mexican Wolf Recovery Program, Lujan and, 158
Mexican Wolf Recovery Team, 4, 149-50, 166-67
Mexican Wolf Workshop, 149
Miller, Alice, 85, 105
Miller, Henry, 128
missing link, preoccupation with, 115
Molycorp, 145
Monkey Wrench Gang, The (Abbey), 162
Moore, Dan, 145, 166
mortality, knowledge of, 31-32
Mother of Game Animals, 33
Mother Wolf, 34
Muhammed ben Isa, 65
Murie, Adolph, 7
mysteries, 21, 23

mythology, 22; culture and, 70; evolution of, 29; hunting, 32, 45; Pueblo Indian, 27-28, 70, 181; Roman, 60; Teutonic, 78-80; Tewa, 28-30; Zuñi, 35-36. *See also* emergence myths

naatl'eetsoh, wolf power and, 44-46
nagualism, Pueblo Indians and, 38-40
naked wolf, 15-16, 18, 23-24
National Public Radio, 4-5
National Wildlife Federation, 3
Native Americans, taming, 84, 86-87
nature: Christianity and, 180; domination of, 82-84, 98, 102; separateness from, 76
Navajo, wolves and, 41-48, 52-53, 61; subduing, 87
Navajo Stalking Way Song (Hill), 41
new environmentalism, 145-47
Newhouse traps: description of, 104; using, 99
New Mexico Cattle Grower's Association, formation of, 99
New Mexico Conservationist, 102
New Mexico Department of Game and Fish, 149, 154, 166; poll by, 3, 158; reintroduction and, 5-6
New Mexico Game Commission, 3, 157, 165
New Mexico Game Protective Association, organization of, 100
New Mexico Magazine, 148
New Mexico Wolf Coalition, 3, 4, 128, 145, 164-65, 168; suit by, 144
New Mexico Young Lawyer's Newsletter, 146
Newton, Kent, 3, 7-11; concerns of, 167; interview of, 5-6, 157; work of, 134-36
Nexus (Miller), 128
numbing club, using, 99
Nunley, Gary Lee, 151; report by, 104; writing of, 167

Odin, 79
Of Wolves and Men (Lopez), 7, 17
Oku Pin (Turtle Mountain), 13
Old One Toe (Old Aguila), tales about, 113
Olson, Harold, 149, 156
Onothlikia, 27
On the Gleaming Way (Collier), 18

'opa, 32
Ortiz, Alfonso: meeting, 25-28
oryx, 6, 11
Other, 60, 62-66
Otherness, 57-59, 61-63, 68, 77; destroying, 80; embracing, 69
Owens, Joe, 156

paradigm shifts, 68-69, 181
pariah wolves. *See* lone wolves
Parkman, Francis, 84
Parsons, Elsie Clews, 25, 27, 33, 37-39; studies of, 30
Peloncillo Mountains, 106
Persephone, 60
Peters, Roger, 17, 61, 125; work of, 15-16, 124; writing of, 120
Pitsinger, Cynthia, 167
Plains Indians, 17; color associations of, 27; wolves and, 26
Poglayen, Ingeborg, 167
poisoning, 87-89, 99; cruelty of, 104-6
Polybius, 60
Popé, 39
power, 21-22, 48; wolf, 22, 44-46, 55
Power Wolf, 48
prayer sticks, 34-35
predation, 46; compensation for, 183
Predator and Rodent Control program (PARC), 107, 112; description of, 103, 104
predators: identification with, 32, 38; legend about, 31, 33, 37; views about, 23, 110
Predator Wolf, 48
predatory nature: denial of, 58; human, 23-24, 171, 174-75, 182. *See also* animality; wolfishness
pre-emergence world, 44, 51-52; communicating in, 29; wolves and, 49
prey, relationship with, 31-32, 181
Primitive Rebels (Hobsbawm), 172
Propertius Romulus, 60
Psychology and Alchemy (Jung), 54
Pueblo Indian Religion (Parsons), 27
Pueblo Indians, 18-19, 44; color associations of, 27; deer and, 33-34; myths of, 27-28, 70, 181; nagualism and, 39-40; studying, 30; Wolf and, 40; wolves and, 22-23, 25, 26, 28, 36-37, 61
Pueblo Rebellion of 1680, 39, 65
Puritans, 80-82

quasi silvestres hommes, 73-74
Quillayutes, wolf dances of, 19

radicals, environmental, 162-63, 171-74.
    See also environmental movement
rage, origins of, 170-71
ranching industry: establishing, 86-89;
    reintroduction and, 4, 97, 131, 147,
    148
rationalism, 58, 113
Read, Carveth, 15
Reason, 82
Redford, Robert, 5
red squirrel, 159
regurgitation, description of, 10
reintroduction, 3-6, 134, 144-45, 149-53,
    155, 168, 184; FWS and, 169-70, 183;
    hybridization and, 142; opponents to,
    148, 156-57; suit for, 145-47; support
    for, 153-54; in Texas, 156, 183
Reuters International News Service, 2,
    161
Rio Grande Nature Center, 1, 163
Rio Grande Zoo, 5, 9, 11
ritual, 22-23; acceptance, 31; fighting,
    137; greetings, 133; hunting, 42; social
    cohesiveness and, 121; wolf, 19-20,
    42, 118, 136-39. *See also* ceremony
Rodriguez, Jose, 152
Rollins, Philip Ashton: writing of, 88
Romans, wolves and, 60
Romulus and Remus, 60, 78
Rothenberg, Jerome, 161

S.S., wolf imagery of, 85
St. Anne, Tarasque and, 75
St. Francis, 73, 124; inspiration by, 71-
    72; wolves and, 73-75, 80, 180
Sand County Almanac, A (Leopold), 97,
    109, 110
Sand Dunes National Monument, 30
Sandia Mountains, description of, 13
Sandy Place Lake (*Ohange pokwinge*), 30
Santa Ana, 31
Satan, 52, 55, 56, 80, 81, 83; attributes
    of, 59; portrayal of, 64, 66
scent, 15-16, 120; investigation of, 135;
    language of, 124-25
Scientific Revolution, 68
scratching, test by, 31
Scyld, 78
Second Sex, The (De Beauvoir), 59

self, 63; alienation from, 77; recognition
    of, 62
Seton, Ernest Thompson: writing of,
    111-14
sexuality, 59; taboos in, 51
shamans, i, 37-38, 46, 72. *See also*
    medicine man
Sharp, Henry S., writing of, 122
sheep, 46, 47, 65-66
Shepard, Thomass, 81
Shipap (*Shipapolima*), 38
Sierra Club, 3; suit by, 144
Simmons, Marc: writing of, 54
Sipofene, 30
Sizemore, Elizabeth, 183
Skeen, Joe, 148
skinwalkers, 49-51; description of, 48
Smylie, Tom, 167, 169, 184
snarling, 136-37
sniffing: genital, 137; social, 125
socializing, 135-36
social order, wolf, 17-18, 20, 118-21,
    133-35, 140-41
soft words, 33
Soranus, 60
Southwestern Game Fields (Leopold), 108
Spear, Michael, 155-58, 158, 167-69,
    184
Species Survival Plan, 155
spirits, 28; wolf, 19, 33-34
spotted owl, 159
squeaking, 121; description of, 122
stalking, 99
stereotypes, wolf, 17-18
Sterling, Dan: report by, 169
Stevens, Bob, 150
strychnine, 104; using, 87, 99
submission, 119-21, 125, 138-40
Sugarman, Steve, 145
Summer people, 32
Superior National Forest, 15
sweat lodges, 45, 49, 51
symbolism, sexual, 35; wolf, 75, 85, 136,
    171-72

Talking God, 42
tameness, 63, 75, 115
Taos Rats, 39
Tarasque, taming of, 74-75
Tasuvah, 44
Taylor, Mark, 156, 157
Technicians of the Sacred (Rothenberg), 161

Tellico Dam, blocking of, 158
terrorists, environmental, 161. *See also*
    environmental movement
Tewa, 18, 29-30, 32
Tewa Emergence Myth (Parsons), 25
*Tewa World: Space, Time, and Becoming
    in a Pueblo Society, The* (Ortiz), 28
Texas, wolf reintroduction in, 5, 156,
    158, 183
Texas Department of Parks and Wildlife,
    183, 184
Texas Monthly, 184
Texas Parks and Wildlife Commission,
    criticism of, 184
therioanthropy, wolves and, 63
Thich Nhat Hanh, 144
Tierra Madre (Mother Earth), respect for,
    66
Tlingit, 44; wolves and, 43
Towa é, 13
transformation, 39-40, 43, 49, 52, 57, 59,
    77, 78, 181; denial of, 85
trapping, 99, 154
Travis, Charles, 183
Trevino, José C. "Pepe," 150, 154, 166-
    67
Tsotsi, execution of, 39
Turner, Frederick Jackson, 80, 85-86
Tyler, Hamilton, 36-37
Tyndale, William, 80
Tyr, 79

U.N.E.S.C.O. Biosphere Reserve, 183
U.S. Army, 157-58; negotiation with,
    168; suit against, 144
U.S. Biological Survey, 99, 101
U.S. Fish and Wildlife Service (FWS), 4,
    5, 11, 101, 130, 145, 149, 150, 151,
    153, 154, 156-58, 184; criticism of,
    152, 159; reintroduction and, 155,
    167-70, 183; suit against, 144, 147
U.S. Forest Service, 101, 108, 145, 165
U.S. Supreme Court, 158
underworld, description of, 31
Union Pacific, 86
United Nations, 183
Universe Man, 32
urinations, 104; raised leg, 16, 125; squat,
    16

vermin, eradication of, 98, 102
vocalizations: examining, 121-24; infor-

mation from, 123. *See also* communi-
    cation, wolf; information, exchanging

Wainhouse, Austryn: writing of, 111
War Patron. *See* Ahaiyute, War Patron
Watson, Mark, 165
Watt, James, 2
Webster, John: writing of, 55
werewolves, 46-47, 57-59, 61, 64, 87,
    112, 182; description of, 48; execution
    of, 56; fear of, 55; Hispanic tales of,
    66-67; psychology of, 84; transforma-
    tion of, 77
whimpering, 121, 124
whining, 122, 137
White Bison myth, 36
White Corn Woman, 30
White Sands Missile Range (WSMR):
    assessment of, 141; reintroduction at,
    3-6, 144-45, 147-49, 156, 184
Wigglesworth, Jonathan, 80
wild, etymology of, 78
Wild Animal Bounty Fund, 98
Wild Animals I Have Known (Seton), 112
Wild Canid Center, 154
Wild Canid Research and Survival Cen-
    ter, 150
Wild Canid Survival Center, 152
Wild Canid Survival Research Center, 9
wildeor, 78-81, 84
wilderness: Bible and, 81; conquest of,
    83-84, 86, 98; etymology of, 78; wolves
    and, 79-80
Wilderness Society, suit by, 144
wildness, 115; embodiment of, 173; em-
    bracing, 69; hybrids and, 143; restora-
    tion of, 182; taming, 81-84; wolves
    and, 58, 62-63
Williams, Ed, 156
Winter people, 32
Witch Boy, 39
witchcraft, 39, 49, 50, 53, 61; Coyote
    and, 48, 52; suppression of, 59, 65;
    Wolf and, 52; wolves and, 48
Witchcraft in the Southwest (Simmons),
    54
Witchery Way, 49-50, 52
witches, 38, 57-59, 182; Navajo, 49;
    purges of, 55-56, 65; wolves and, 39-
    40, 48
Witch Way, 50
Wodan, 79

Wolf (McFarland's): description of, 128-29, 131-32

Wolf (mythological), 32, 35; arrival of, 33; Mountain Lion and, 36; power of, 37-38; Pueblo Indians and, 40; reputation of, 45, 47; witchcraft and, 52

Wolf (name), etymology of, 79

Wolf Action Group (WAG), 145, 166, 168; suit by, 144

Wolf Action Suit, 149

Wolf and Man: Evolution in Parallel (Hall and Sharp), 115, 122

Wolf Boys, 27, 34, 39

Wolf Breeding Committee, establishment of, 155

Wolf Dung, 39

wolfers, 112; pay for, 98-99; work of, 99, 104, 107

Wolf in the Southwest, The (Brown), 106, 153, 167

wolfishness: denial of, 85; human, 113. *See also* animality; predatory nature

wolfman, 43, 50, 56; Navajo, 52, 58; shooting, 50

wolf packs: break up of, 126; hunting by, 117; Mexican, 140; social order in, 16, 118-19, 135, 142; starting, 119; studying, 15-16

Wolf Recovery Plan, 167

Wolf Recovery Team, 150, 157, 159

Wolf Ritual stories, 35

wolf substrate, evolution of, 55-56, 68

wolf walking, 50

Wolf Way, 50, 52; belief in, 43-45; description of, 41-42; study of, 46-47

wolves: antagonism for, 50, 54-55, 117; encounters with, 87; fear of, 23-24, 55-57, 66-68; identifying with, 15, 32, 43, 45; learning from, 29; medical treatment for, 134-35; reputation of, 65-66; taming, 75-76. *See also* Mexican wolf

Wolves of North America, The (Young), 100

womb-worlds: color of, 31; communicating in, 29

Woody, Jack, 151-52, 155

Wotan, 79

Writers in Revolt (Wainhouse), 111

Wulf, etymology of, 79

Wycliffe, John, 80

xenophobia, 120

Yellow Corn Girl, 27

Yellow Wolf, 34

yenaldlooshi, 49-51, 53

Young, Stanley P.: writing of, 100

Zeedyk, Bill, 3

Zeus, 60

zoos, role of, 11, 167

Zuñi, 26, 28, 33; medicine society initiations of, 38; myths of, 35-36